Principles of
Transactional Memory

Synthesis Lectures on Distributed Computing

Editor
Nancy Lynch, *Massachusetts Intitute of Technology*

Synthesis Lectures on Distributed Computing Theory is edited by Nancy Lynch of the Massachusetts Institute of Technology. The series will publish 50- to 150 page publications on topics pertaining to distributed computing theory. The scope will largely follow the purview of premier information and computer science conferences, such as ACM PODC, DISC, SPAA, OPODIS, CONCUR, DialM-POMC, ICDCS, SODA, Sirocco, SSS, and related conferences. Potential topics include, but not are limited to: distributed algorithms and lower bounds, algorithm design methods, formal modeling and verification of distributed algorithms, and concurrent data structures.

Principles of Transactional Memory
Rachid Guerraoui and Michał Kapałka
2010

Fault-tolerant Agreement in Synchronous Message-passing Systems
Michel Raynal
2010

Communication and Agreement Abstractions for Fault-Tolerant Asynchronous Distributed Systems
Michel Raynal
2010

The Mobile Agent Rendezvous Problem in the Ring
Evangelos Kranakis, Danny Krizanc, Euripides Markou
2010

Principles of Transactional Memory

Rachid Guerraoui and Michał Kapałka

ISBN:978-3-031-00874-0   paperback
ISBN:978-3-031-02002-5   ebook

DOI 10.1007/978-3-031-02002-5

A Publication in the Springer series
SYNTHESIS LECTURES ON DISTRIBUTED COMPUTING

Lecture #4
Series Editor: Nancy Lynch, *Massachusetts Intitute of Technology*
Series ISSN
Synthesis Lectures on Distributed Computing
Print 2155-1626   Electronic 2155-1634

Principles of
Transactional Memory

Rachid Guerraoui and Michał Kapałka
École Polytechnique Fédérale de Lausanne

SYNTHESIS LECTURES ON DISTRIBUTED COMPUTING #4

ABSTRACT

Transactional memory (TM) is an appealing paradigm for concurrent programming on shared memory architectures. With a TM, threads of an application communicate, and synchronize their actions, via in-memory *transactions*. Each transaction can perform any number of operations on shared data, and then either *commit* or *abort*. When the transaction commits, the effects of all its operations become immediately visible to other transactions; when it aborts, however, those effects are entirely discarded. Transactions are *atomic*: programmers get the illusion that every transaction executes all its operations instantaneously, at some single and unique point in time. Yet, a TM runs transactions concurrently to leverage the parallelism offered by modern processors.

The aim of this book is to provide theoretical foundations for transactional memory. This includes defining a model of a TM, as well as answering precisely when a TM implementation is correct, what kind of properties it can ensure, what are the power and limitations of a TM, and what inherent trade-offs are involved in designing a TM algorithm. While the focus of this book is on the fundamental principles, its goal is to capture the common intuition behind the semantics of TMs and the properties of existing TM implementations.

KEYWORDS

transactional memory, concurrent programming, shared memory, theory

To Anne.

To Agnieszka and Artur.

Contents

Acknowledgments

Many thanks to Hagit Attiya, Viktor Kuncak, Victor Luchangco, Nancy Lynch, Eric Ruppert, and Michael Scott for carefully reviewing this book. We are also very grateful to João Barreto, Aleksandar Dragojević, Faith Fich, Pascal Felber, Christof Fetzer, Seth Gilbert, Vincent Gramoli, Tim Harris, Thomas Henzinger, Maurice Herlihy, Eshcar Hillel, Petr Kouznetsov, Doug Lea, Maged Michael, Mark Moir, Leaf Petersen, Benjamin Pierce, Bastian Pochon, Michel Raynal, Nir Shavit, Vasu Singh, and Jan Vitek for their helpful comments on the topic of this book.

Rachid Guerraoui and Michał Kapałka
August 2010

CHAPTER 1

Introduction

Those are my principles.
If you don't like them I have others.

Groucho Marx

The clock rate of processors used to grow exponentially. Going from below 1 MHz to around 3 GHz took the computer industry less than 40 years. However, increasing the clock rate further has become infeasible. In fact, the ubiquity of portable computers, for which power consumption is a top concern, has forced the industry to keep the clock rate of many processors much below the achievable maximum.

The demand for computational power, however, has not ceased to increase. The result is a completely new trend, which is commonly referred to as a "multi-core revolution". Instead of increasing the clock speed of processors, more computing cores are put on a single chip. Multiprocessing, which used to be a feature of only high-end machines, has become commonplace in personal computers and laptops. It is possible that, in the near future, mobile phones, media players, and other small devices will become equipped with many processors.

This new trend has created a big challenge. Before, with each new processor, all existing applications would automatically get faster. Now, applications will need to get increasingly parallel in order to exploit the power of new processors. Therefore, parallel programming, which used to be the domain of a few high-performance computing experts, will now have to be mastered by common programmers.

1.1 PROBLEMS WITH EXPLICIT LOCKING

Creating threads is easy in any modern programming language. What is hard, however, is synchronizing their actions, especially if one wants to make those threads run truly in parallel. Consider, for example, an application in which threads operate on a big data structure. A simple way to ensure thread-safety is to protect the entire structure with a single lock (*coarse-grained* locking). Then, however, all accesses to the data structure are serialized, which can severely limit the scalability of the application. Moreover, lock contention may become a problem, especially if the number of threads becomes high.

Optimally, one would use many locks, each protecting a small part of the data structure (*fine-grained* locking). But this is an engineering challenge because one has to ensure that all components of the application follow the same locking policy. If even one method acquires locks in a wrong order, then a deadlock can occur. One missing lock acquisition can lead to race conditions, which are very difficult to debug. Indeed, concurrency-related programming errors often manifest themselves only in some, possibly rare, executions, and sometimes only when the application is run with all its debugging functions turned off. Those errors can result in effects ranging from program crashes, which are directly visible, up to very subtle data corruption, which may pass undetected for a long time.

The problem with following a complex locking policy in a big application is that this policy exists only in the documentation (e.g., comments in the code) or in the programmers' minds. Looking just at the code of a program, written in one of the mainstream programming languages such as Java or C++, one typically cannot tell which lock protects which objects, or in which order those locks should be acquired. Associating a monitor with each object, as in Java, does not really help in fine-grained locking when a single monitor or lock can protect a group of objects and, conversely, a single object can be protected by more than one lock. It thus takes a very disciplined team of programmers to do fine-grained locking right.

But even following a locking policy to the letter does not guarantee success in terms of performance on multi-core systems. Fine-grained locking involves many trade-offs. For instance, locks are not given for free, and acquiring them takes time. Hence, it might be hard to find the right balance between using too many locks, which can result in high locking overhead, and too few locks, which can lead to scalability problems. To give a concrete example, devising an efficient, scalable algorithm that implements a thread-safe queue, a data structure almost trivial in a single-thread program, is so hard that it deserved at least two papers in top computer science conferences [Herlihy et al., 2003b; Michael and Scott, 1996]. We cannot expect that ordinary programmers will spend so much effort in getting the last bit of parallelism from every part of their application, given how hard it is to do it right.

Obviously, modern programming languages offer libraries containing highly-optimized and thread-safe implementations of commonly used data structures. In many cases, it suffices to use those components to get a program that can make use of a few CPU cores. But here we face a problem with *composability*: a data structure composed of thread-safe objects is not necessarily itself thread-safe. For example, consider two thread-safe sets, and a problem of removing an element from one set and then adding it to the other. Often, one wants such a composite operation involving both sets to be *atomic*. That is, the intermediate step of this operation, in which an element is removed from one of the sets but still not added to the other, should not be observed by concurrent threads. But implementing such an operation requires either adding additional locks, which protect *both* sets, or extending the locking mechanisms used by the implementations of those sets. In the former case, one effectively devises a new locking policy for the two sets, which can introduce race conditions or scalability issues. In the latter case, one has to "open" the set implementations, understand their locking policies, and extend them, which not only is challenging, but also breaks object encapsulation.

Using locks explicitly to handle concurrency becomes even harder when threads operate on different priority levels, e.g., in a real-time system. If a high-priority thread wants to acquire a lock that is held by a low-priority thread, it has to wait until the lock is released. That is, the high-priority thread has to wait for the low-priority thread—a problem known as *priority inversion*. Synchronizing those threads using *nonblocking* mechanisms, i.e., without using any form of mutual exclusion, would solve the problem. However, designing those mechanisms is sometimes even harder than using fine-grained locking.

1.2   TRANSACTIONAL MEMORY

Given the above challenges posed by the explicit use of locks to manage concurrency, it is not surprising to see a large body of research aimed at making concurrent programming easier. One of the most appealing solutions is *transactional memory (TM)* [Herlihy and Moss, 1993; Shavit and Touitou, 1995]. The basic idea behind TM is to enable threads of an application to communicate by executing lightweight, in-memory *transactions*. A transaction is a sequence of operations that should be executed atomically. The purpose of a transaction is thus similar to that of a critical section. However, unlike critical sections, transactions can *abort*, in which case all their operations are rolled back and are never visible to other transactions. Also, transactions only *appear* as if they executed sequentially—a TM is free to run them concurrently, as long as the illusion of atomicity is preserved.

Using a TM is, in principle, very easy: the programmer simply converts those blocks of code that should be executed atomically into transactions. In some TMs, this can be as straightforward as annotating functions and methods with a special language keyword (usually: **atomic**), as illustrated in Figure 1.1. The TM implementation is then responsible for executing those transactions safely and efficiently. The TM might internally use fine-grained locking, or some nonblocking mechanism, but this is hidden from the programmer and the application. Thus, if the TM is implemented correctly, which can be done once by a group of experts, the programmer is less likely to introduce concurrency bugs in the code than if he or she had to handle locks explicitly. Indeed, a transaction is a very intuitive abstraction that has been used with success in databases for a long time.

A TM can be implemented in hardware, in software, or as a hardware-software hybrid. The TM API usually allows for (1) starting a transaction, (2) performing operations on shared data within a transaction, and (3) committing or aborting a transaction. Such an interface can be provided, e.g., by a software library. There are also experimental TM-aware compilers for languages such as Java and C++. Those compilers automatically convert blocks of code annotated with a special keyword (e.g., **atomic**) into transactions.

Even though a TM can internally use fine-grained locking, the paradigm is free of problems that explicit locking (i.e., locking used directly by the programmers) creates, and which we listed above. First, transactions are composable. For instance, consider the problem of moving an element between two sets. If both sets are implemented using transactions, then it suffices to create another transaction that will simply remove an element from one set and add it to the other set. Indeed, most TM implementations allow transactions to be *nested*. There exists also a technique, called *transactional boosting* [Herlihy and Koskinen, 2008], which allows transactions to use any thread-safe data structure, even one not implemented using transactions.

```
1 atomic
2   │  v ← x.getVal;
3   └  x.setVal(v + 1);
```

Figure 1.1: An illustration of a high-level interface of a TM. The programmer annotates the block of code that should be executed atomically with a special keyword (here: **atomic**). This block is then executed as a transaction. If the transaction aborts (e.g., due to a conflict with another transaction), an exception might be thrown or the block may be automatically restarted.

Second, even though transactions are not much more difficult to use than coarse-grained locking, they can execute in parallel, and so there is a hope that using a TM one can achieve performance close to that of explicit fine-grained locking. A TM also gives additional flexibility because the synchronization policy of a TM can be fine-tuned to a specific system, or even changed completely. For instance, the granularity of locks used internally by a TM can be adapted to the number of CPU cores, or the locking policy can be replaced with a nonblocking synchronization mechanism if priority inversion becomes an issue. All those changes are local to the TM implementation and the code of the application does not have to be updated. This also means that programs that use a TM for thread synchronization should be easier to maintain than ones that use explicit locking.

1.3   SCOPE OF THIS BOOK

The TM paradigm promises a lot, but it is not free of its own challenges. Some of those are: reducing the overhead of transactions (e.g., of logs that are used during transaction rollback), dealing with I/O and other irrevocable operations inside transactions, integrating transactions into programming languages, providing interoperability with legacy components whose source code is no longer available, and dealing with situations in which the same data can be accessed from within transactions and from non-transactional code. It is thus not surprising to see a large amount of research dedicated to addressing those problems and providing practical TM implementations (see Chapter 6 for an overview).

In order to be able to compare the various proposed TM algorithms and optimizations, we first need to know what a TM really is. That is, we need precise criteria according to which we can evaluate whether a given TM is correct and whether the TM gives guarantees on a par with other TMs from the same class. We thus need a theoretical framework that will allow for modeling a TM, defining its correctness condition, and expressing its properties.

Having a theory of TMs helps not only in fair comparison of various TM strategies but also in understanding the inherent power and limitations of the TM paradigm. For instance, we can seek to prove formally which properties of a TM are associated with which complexity of the TM implementation. That is, we can get a precise view of the different fundamental trade-offs involved in designing a TM.

Also, having a model of a TM and a formal definition of the correctness of a TM is the first, and necessary, step towards proving the correctness of TM algorithms, as well as verifying concrete TM implementations. Since a TM is meant to be a reusable component, relied upon by many applications, it is indeed crucial to be able to show that this critical component is implemented correctly.

1.4   CONTENTS

This book describes a theory of transactional memory. The questions that we try to answer here are, for example: How to model a TM? When is a TM correct? How to prove the correctness of a TM implementation? What properties can a TM ensure? What is the computational power of a TM? What are the inherent trade-offs in implementing a TM?

The theoretical framework we build here is deeply rooted in the theories describing database transactions and distributed systems. However, as we explain in this manuscript, TMs cannot be described precisely and comprehensively using only existing concepts, models, and properties from databases and shared memory systems. Indeed, even though a transaction is a very old abstraction, the set of requirements imposed on memory transactions is unique.

It is worth noting that the model we consider in this book is necessarily simplified. It provides an abstraction that allows us to focus on those aspects of a TM that are interesting from a theoretical perspective, without being too distracted by certain implementation issues. For instance, we do not model the interactions between transactions and non-transactional code, and we assume no nested transactions. We discuss, however, the recent work that has addressed some of those limitations.

This manuscript is split into three parts. In Part I, we give a model of a shared memory system (Chapter 2) and of a TM (Chapter 3). We also explain, in Chapter 4, the intuition behind a correctness condition for TMs, which we call *opacity*. Then, in Chapter 5, we show two example TM algorithms whose purpose is to illustrate the ideas and trade-offs behind a typical TM implementation.

In Part II, we first define opacity—our correctness condition for TMs (Chapter 7). Then, in Chapter 8, we show how one can prove that a given TM is correct, using as examples the two TM algorithms introduced in Chapter 5. Finally, in Chapter 9, we show that opacity is fundamentally different from classical serializability of database transactions: we prove a complexity lower bound that is inherent to opacity but can be overcome when a TM ensures only serializability.

In Part III, we focus on the progress semantics of TM implementations. We first give a general overview of the contents of this part (Chapter 11). Then, in Chapters 12 and 13, we discuss the progress properties of two main classes of TM implementations: lock-based TMs and obstruction-free TMs. We also determine the computational power of those TMs, and we prove various related results. In Chapter 14, we determine the boundary between the liveness properties that can be ensured by a TM, and those that cannot.

Each part ends with a chapter that highlights major references to the related work concerning that part. We try to list not only publications that first introduced some of the concepts and methods that we use in the manuscript and that influenced our TM theory, but also those that extend our work, give an alternative view, or provide additional information.

The content of this book is based on work that was originally published by Guerraoui and Kapałka [2008a,b, 2009a,b].

PART I

Basics

CHAPTER 2

Shared Memory Systems

A typical computer program, be it a word processor, a complex scientific application, or a video game, consists of one or more sequential *processes*.[1] Every process executes steps of its algorithm in a linear fashion, waiting for each instruction to finish before executing the next one. Actions of different processes, however, can be arbitrarily interleaved.

Even when processes are responsible for independent tasks, they usually have to communicate from time to time and synchronize their actions. We focus in this manuscript on systems in which this communication happens via *shared memory*—a memory fragment accessible to all processes of the application—be it provided in hardware or emulated in software.

In this chapter, we present the basic abstractions we consider to describe and reason about shared memory systems. First, in Section 2.1, we present a model of a shared memory system. Then, in Section 2.2, we summarize the notation introduced in this chapter.

2.1 BASIC ABSTRACTIONS

2.1.1 PROCESSES AND SHARED OBJECTS

A process is a sequential unit of computation. An application usually creates processes when necessary. However, it is easier to simply assume that all processes are created when the application starts and just wait until it is their turn to start executing their algorithms. We denote by $\Pi = \{p_1, ..., p_n\}$ the set of all processes that execute the application. Whenever we refer to symbol n in this manuscript, we mean the total number of processes—a parameter so important that it deserves its own reserved symbol.

Each process executes some *top-level* algorithm assigned to it by the application. We assume that processes are deterministic; however, they can interact with the environment, which can influence their actions. The environment contains everything that is external to the processes, for example, the user, the operating system, or the network.

Processes can perform local computations, as well as execute *operations* on *shared objects*. In order to execute an operation *op* on a shared object X, a process p_i issues an *invocation event* of *op* on X, which we denote by

$$inv_i(X.op),$$

[1]Or threads—the technical difference between threads and processes is not important for the theoretical aspects described in this manuscript.

and then receives a *response event* of *op*, which we denote by

$$ret_i(X \rightarrow v),$$

where v is the return value of operation *op*. When p_i invokes any operation on X, we say that p_i *accesses* X. A pair of an invocation event $inv_i(X.op)$ and the subsequent response event $ret_i(X \rightarrow v)$ is called an *operation execution*, and it is denoted by

$$X.op_i \rightarrow v.$$

An invocation event $inv_i(X.op)$ that is not followed by a response event $ret_i(X \rightarrow v)$ is called a *pending operation execution*. For simplicity, when there is no ambiguity, we often say *operation* instead of *(pending) operation execution*. We also omit elements of the notation that are clear from the context or can be arbitrary, e.g., writing $inv(X.op)$ instead of $inv_i(X.op)$, $ret(v)$ instead of $ret_i(X \rightarrow v)$, or $X.op$ instead of $X.op_i \rightarrow v$.

2.1.2   SHARED OBJECT IMPLEMENTATIONS

Every shared object has an *implementation*. An implementation I_X of a shared object X consists of n algorithms, $I_X(1), ..., I_X(n)$, one for each process. When a process p_i invokes an operation *op* on X, p_i follows algorithm $I_X(i)$ until p_i receives a response from *op*. We say then that p_i *executes* I_X. (Note that shared objects are *not* entities separate from processes, but they are simply abstractions that split the task performed by each process into a set of independent components.)

An implementation I_X of a shared object X may *use* any (finite or infinite) number of *base objects*, and other, lower-level shared objects. That is, a process p_i that executes I_X can execute operations on some base objects and invoke operations on some shared objects (whose implementations can use other base and shared objects, and so on). If Q is the set of base and shared objects used by implementation I_X of shared object X, we say that X is *implemented from* the objects in Q.

Base objects are the primitives that form the shared memory. Unlike shared objects, they are separate from processes, and processes do not see their implementations. Base objects can, e.g., be provided by hardware or a run-time environment. Every process has access to all base objects. Throughout this manuscript, whenever we say *object*, we mean *base or shared object*. We will talk more about base objects in Section 2.1.5.

Shared objects form a hierarchy, where implementations of shared objects at level 1 of the hierarchy use only base objects, and implementations of shared objects at a level $k > 1$ use only shared objects at level $k - 1$ as well as base objects (cf. Figure 2.1). This hierarchy is application-dependent, and so it can be different in different systems.

We assume that, intuitively, every shared object *encapsulates* its state. That is, every shared object, base object, or local variable, is used only by a single shared object implementation. Moreover, processes executing their top-level algorithms can access only those shared objects and local variables that are *not* used by any shared object implementation.

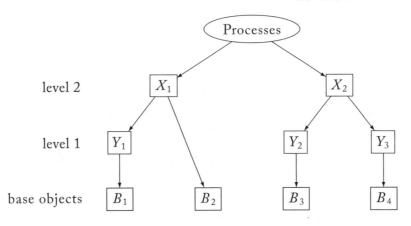

Figure 2.1: An example 2-level hierarchy of shared objects. The implementation of shared object X_1 uses shared object Y_1 and base object B_2, the implementation of X_2 uses Y_2 and Y_3, and the implementations of Y_1, Y_2, and Y_3 use base objects B_1, B_3 and B_4, respectively.

We also assume that processes do not accept any input from the environment when they execute any shared object implementation. This requirement, together with encapsulation, implies that the only way in which the environment, the top-level algorithm of some process, or the implementation of some shared object X can communicate with the implementation I_Y of some shared object Y (different than X) is via invocation and response events issued on Y or received by I_Y.

To summarize, the algorithm executed by every process p_i can be seen as a stack of "sub-algorithms" implementing different abstractions (cf. Figure 2.2). At the top of the stack is the top-level algorithm of p_i, which can communicate with the outside environment (e.g., a user). Below are the implementations of shared objects, forming a hierarchy. Process p_i executes only algorithm $I_X(i)$ of every shared object implementation I_X. When p_i executes I_X, p_i might perform operations on base objects, which form the shared memory and provide a means by which processes can communicate.

For example, base objects can be hardware memory locations, with operations such as *read* and *write* (or *load* and *store*). Then, at level 1, one could have simple shared objects such as locks. Shared objects at level 2 could be, for example, queues and hash tables—implemented from base objects and locks. Finally, the top level algorithm might be the user application in which the communication between processes happens via the shared objects at level 2.

2.1.3   EXECUTIONS OF CONCURRENT ALGORITHMS

We assume discrete time when representing executions. This is, of course, simply a view of the mind. In every unit of time, there is only one *active* process. The active process can, within a given unit of time, perform any finite number of local computations, and then either issue an event or execute

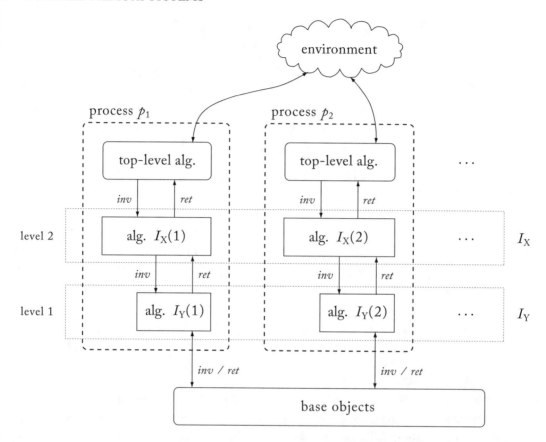

Figure 2.2: Detailed architecture of a system with two shared objects, X and Y, with implementations I_X and I_Y. Implementation I_X uses only shared object Y, and I_Y uses only base objects.

a *step*. A step is an execution of an operation on a base object, i.e., an invocation and a subsequent response of such an operation. (Hence, every operation on a base object takes at most one unit of time to execute.) Whenever a process p_i becomes active, p_i must execute an event or a step; when p_i does not have anything to execute (e.g., p_i terminated its top-level algorithm or is waiting for an input from the environment), p_i executes a *no-op* step.

Events are always local to each process. That is, an event cannot be issued by one process and received by a different process. Events simply mark times when a process starts and stops executing the implementation of a shared object. Hence, events of one process are not visible to other processes. Steps are the only means by which processes can directly communicate with each other. (An indirect communication can, in principle, happen via the environment, but this is outside the control of processes.)

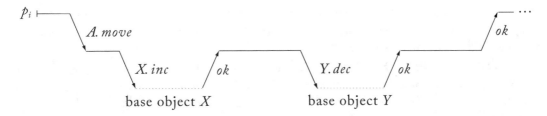

Figure 2.3: An example execution of operation *move* on shared object A by process p_i. Operation *move* is implemented using operations *inc* and *dec* of base objects X and Y.

Processes are *sequential* in that every process p_i executes, at any given time, at most one operation on at most one shared object at any level in the hierarchy. That is, if p_i invokes an operation *op* on a shared object X at level k, then p_i does not invoke any operation on any shared object at level k or higher until p_i returns from *op*.

For example, Figure 2.3 illustrates an execution of a system that consists of a shared object A implemented from base objects X and Y, at some process p_i. Initially, p_i executes its top-level algorithm. Then, p_i invokes operation *move* on A and thus starts executing the implementation I_A of A. While executing I_A, p_i executes steps $X.inc \to ok$ and $Y.dec \to ok$. Since A is at level 1 of the hierarchy (and since both X and Y are base objects), p_i cannot invoke any operation on any shared object before returning from operation *move*.

The order in which processes execute steps and events is determined by an external entity called a *scheduler*, over which processes have no control. When proving the correctness of a shared object implementation, it is useful to consider a scheduler as an adversary that acts against the implementation. A scheduler decides on a *schedule*, which is a (possibly infinite) sequence of process identifiers. A schedule assigns to every process p_i times at which p_i is active. For instance, $\langle p_1, p_2, p_1 \rangle$ is a schedule according to which process p_1 is active at time 1, then p_2 is active at time 2, and then p_1 is active at time 3.

An *execution* is the sequence of all events and steps that are issued by all processes in a given (partial or complete) run of the application. Every execution ε has an associated schedule (the schedule of ε) that corresponds to the order in which processes are active in ε. Also, every event or step in ε can be associated with its unique execution time.

2.1.4 HISTORIES

Throughout this manuscript, we focus only on what happens on the interface of a particular (shared or base) object, or inside the implementation of a given shared object. That is, we always look only at subsequences of executions, which contain only certain events or steps. (In particular, we are not interested in the communication between processes and the environment.) Intuitively, the fragments of a given execution that concern some object X form a *history* of X, or an *implementation history* of X. In this section, we give precise definitions of the notions of a history and an implementation history of an object. Before doing so, however, we introduce some additional concepts and notation, which we will use also in other chapters.

Let E be any sequence of events and steps (e.g., an execution or its subsequence). For every process p_i, we denote by $E|p_i$ the restriction of E to only events and steps executed by p_i, i.e., the longest subsequence of E that contains only events and steps of p_i. For every object X, we denote by $E|X$ the restriction of E to only invocation events issued on X and response events received from X, i.e., to only events of the form $inv_i(X.op)$ and $ret_i(X \rightarrow v)$, where p_i is any process, op is any operation of X, and v is any return value.

Consider any (pending) operation execution e (on any shared object X) in sequence $E|p_i$, for some process p_i. Every step or event in $E|p_i$ that is after the invocation event of e and, if e is not pending, before the response event of e is said to be executed *within* e. Since processes are sequential, every step or event executed within e is, in fact, a step or event of the implementation I_X of X, or of the implementation I_Y of some shared object used by I_X, or of the implementation of some shared object used by I_Y, etc.

Consider any two (pending) operation executions e and e' in E. We say that e *precedes* e' if e is not pending and the response event of e precedes the invocation event of e'. We say that e and e' are *concurrent* if neither e precedes e', nor e' precedes e. Note that all pending operation executions are pairwise concurrent.

Let X be any object, and ε be any execution. The *history H of X (in ε)* is the sequence $\varepsilon|X$. The *implementation history E of X (in ε)* is the restriction of ε to only (1) events in $\varepsilon|X$ (i.e., the history of X in ε) and (2) steps and events in ε executed within any (pending) operation execution on X. Intuitively, a history of X lists the events executed on the public interface of X, while an implementation history of X describes, in addition, what happens inside the implementation of X. When we talk about a history, or an implementation history, without specifying explicitly the containing execution ε, we mean that ε can be arbitrary.

A history H of some object X is said to be *well-formed* if, for every process p_i, $H|p_i$ is a (finite or infinite) sequence of operation executions, possibly ending with a pending operation execution. Since we assume that processes are sequential, all histories must be well-formed.

An implementation history E of a shared object X is said to be *well-formed* if, intuitively, all operations in E are properly nested at every process. More precisely, for every process p_i, $E|p_i$ is a (finite or infinite) prefix of any sequence of the form:

$$E_1 \cdot E_2 \cdot \ldots,$$

where every $E_k, k = 1, 2, \ldots$, is a sequence of the form:

$$E_k = \langle inv_i(X.op) \rangle \cdot e_1 \cdot e_2 \cdot \ldots \cdot \langle ret_i(X \rightarrow v) \rangle,$$

where op is an operation of X, v is a return value of op, and every $e_m, m = 1, 2, \ldots$, is either (1) a step or (2) a well-formed implementation history of some shared object Y such that $e_m|Y$ is a single operation execution. Within our model, all implementation histories of all shared objects are well-formed.

Example 2.1 The following is a (well-formed) history H of a shared object X, in which process p_1 executes a *read* operation (returning value 0), and process p_2 invokes a *write*(5) operation:

$$H = \langle inv_1(X.read),\ inv_2(X.write(5)),\ ret_1(0) \rangle.$$

Clearly, the operation of p_2 is pending, and the two operations in H are concurrent.

Example 2.2 Consider the execution illustrated in Figure 2.3, which involves a shared object A and two base objects: X and Y. The following is the corresponding (well-formed) implementation history of A:

$$\langle inv_i(A.move),\ X.inc_i \rightarrow ok,\ Y.dec_i \rightarrow ok,\ ret_i(ok) \rangle.$$

2.1.5 SEMANTICS OF BASE OBJECTS

Describing the semantics of a shared object X might be difficult because one has to specify what happens when several operations on X are executed concurrently by different processes. For base objects, however, the situation is much simpler. Indeed, every operation on a base object is executed as a single step, in one unit of time. Hence, since only one process can execute a step at any given time, no two operations on base objects are ever concurrent. This means that describing the semantics of a base object Y in a system with many processes boils down to describing the *sequential* behavior of Y.

We assume then that every base object Y has its *state* (also called its *value*). An operation *op* executed on Y might change the state of Y from some value s to some value s' and return a value that is a function of s. We assume, for simplicity, that all base objects are *deterministic*, i.e., that an operation *op* invoked on a base object Y in state s always returns the same value and leaves Y in the same state. Hence, given an initial value of Y, we can unambiguously determine the state of Y at every point in every execution.

The way we model shared memory corresponds to the notion of *atomicity* (or *linearizability* [Herlihy and Wing, 1990]), which says, intuitively, that every shared memory operation should appear to the processes as if it was executed instantaneously at some single and unique point in time between its invocation and response. In practice, shared memory operations provided by hardware or a run-time environment are hardly ever atomic by default. However, atomicity can be provided with use of hardware fences (memory barriers) or special language constructs. For instance, in Java, variables of primitive types declared as `volatile`, as well as objects of classes from the `java.util.concurrent.atomic` package provide atomic operations.

Atomicity of base objects helps keep the algorithms simple (devoid of technical, possibly architecture-dependent, details). It also simplifies the model and the proofs. Not surprisingly, it is a very common assumption in the theory of shared memory systems.

It is worth noting that shared objects can also be atomic. The semantics of such objects can then be described using only their sequential behavior, in the same way as for base objects. Such shared objects can be thought of in our model as base objects (e.g., when it is desirable to treat their implementations as "black boxes").

We give now several examples of base objects, including objects that are used in the algorithms presented in this manuscript. (So the reader might want to come back to this section when reading the later chapters.) Unless stated otherwise, we assume that every base object has the initial value of 0. For simplicity of algorithms, we also often assume that the domain of values of a given base object can be arbitrary (in particular, infinite).

Example 2.3   (Register)   A very simple (but ubiquitous and extremely useful) base object is a *register*.[2] Every register (base object) has two operations:

- *read*, which returns the current state (value) of the object, and

- *write*(v), which changes the state of the object to value v (and returns constant value *ok*, which we usually omit).

The following sequence is an example history of a register X (accessed by processes p_1 and p_2):

$$\langle X.read_1 \to 0, \ X.write_1(1), \ X.read_2 \to 1 \rangle.$$

Note 2.4   If a process p_i executes an operation $X.read \to v$ (on a base object X, e.g., a register), we say that p_i *reads (value v from) X*. Similarly, if p_i executes an operation $X.write(v)$, we say that p_i *writes (value v to) X*. If p_i executes any operation on X, we say that p_i *accesses X*.

Example 2.5   (Compare-and-swap)   A compare-and-swap object exports the following operations:

- *read* and *write*, with the same semantics as for registers,

- *compare-and-swap*(v, v'), which compares the state s of the object to value v, and then (a) changes the state to v' and returns *true* if $s = v$, or (b) returns *false* if $s \neq v$.

The following is an example history of a compare-and-swap base object C:

$$\langle C.compare\text{-}and\text{-}swap(0, 1) \to true, \ C.read \to 1,$$
$$C.compare\text{-}and\text{-}swap(0, 2) \to false, \ C.read \to 1 \rangle.$$

---

[2]This use of the word "register" is due to historical reasons and has little to do with processor registers or the `register` keyword in programming languages like C. A set of registers is sometimes called a *read–write shared memory*.

Example 2.6 (Test-and-set)   A test-and-set base object is similar in functionality to a compare-and-swap object. Its state is, however, binary, i.e., can be either *true* or *false*, with the initial value being *false*. It exports the following operations:

- *test-and-set*, which (a) changes the state to *true* and returns *false*, if the current state of the object is *false*, or (b) returns *true*, otherwise; and

- *reset*, which sets the state to *false* (and returns *ok*).

An example history of a test-and-set base object B follows:

$$\langle B.test\text{-}and\text{-}set \rightarrow false, \; B.test\text{-}and\text{-}set \rightarrow true, \; B.reset, \; B.test\text{-}and\text{-}set \rightarrow false \rangle.$$

Example 2.7 (Fetch-and-increment)   A fetch-and-increment base object is a basic counter. It exports two operations:

- *read*, which returns the current state (value) of the object, and

- *fetch-and-increment*, which increments the current value of the object by 1 and returns the new value.

The following is an example history of a fetch-and-increment base object V:

$$\langle V.fetch\text{-}and\text{-}increment \rightarrow 1, \; V.fetch\text{-}and\text{-}increment \rightarrow 2, \; V.read \rightarrow 2 \rangle.$$

2.1.6   CONFIGURATIONS AND INDISTINGUISHABILITY

Consider any shared object X, and any implementation history E of X (in some execution ε). The *configuration* (of X), at some point in E, is the state of all base objects that are directly or indirectly used by the implementation of X, i.e., base objects that are accessed within any operation on X by any process in any execution. Note that because every shared object encapsulates its state, if any base object Y is accessed in E, then Y is not accessed in execution ε in any step that is not in E. Therefore, since base objects are deterministic, the configuration at each point in E can be unambiguously determined (given some specified initial states of all base objects).

Consider any process p_i. Every shared object implementation, as well as the top-level algorithm of p_i, accesses some fragment of the state of p_i. Since shared objects encapsulate their state, those fragments are always disjoint. The fragment corresponding to a shared object X is called a *local state of X at p_i*. Consider any implementation history E of a shared object X, and let Y be any shared object whose events are in E (including X). Again, because of encapsulation, and since processes are deterministic, it is possible to unambiguously determine the local state of Y, at every process, at every point in E.

Let E and E' be some implementation histories of any shared object X, and let p_i be any process. We say that E and E' are *indistinguishable* for process p_i, if $E|p_i = E'|p_i$, i.e., if p_i executes the same operations on base and shared objects, and it receives the same return values from those operations, in both implementation histories. Note that the configuration after those implementation histories can be different—it is just the view of process p_i on the configuration that is the same in E and E'. That is, the local state of X, and every other shared object whose events are in E, at p_i changes in the same way in E as in E'.

2.1.7   ASYNCHRONY AND WAIT-FREEDOM

We focus in this manuscript on *asynchronous* shared-memory systems. Asynchrony means that the time between two consecutive events of any process can be arbitrary. In other words, the relative speed of processes is not bounded, and it can change arbitrarily. This captures the idea that, in general-purpose systems, a process can be, at any time, preempted or otherwise delayed, e.g., when waiting for I/O or after encountering a page fault. While real-world systems are hardly ever completely asynchronous, accounting for asynchrony helps in building reliable algorithms. Because such algorithms do not rely on any timing constraints (e.g., they can use back-off or time-out mechanisms only for boosting their performance and not for guaranteeing correctness), they still provide correct semantics when such constraints are violated. (e.g., due to the system being overloaded).

In an asynchronous system, it is often important that processes executing some implementation of a shared object do not wait for each other. That is, a process that executes an operation on a shared object X (e.g., a big data structure) and, at some point, is delayed for a long time should not inhibit the progress of concurrent operations on X executed by other processes. Such implementations are called *wait-free* [Herlihy, 1991]. Clearly, this property is not always allowed by the semantics of a shared object. For instance, a barrier object B makes sure that every process invokes an operation on B before any of them returns from its operation on B. On the other hand, an inherently blocking semantics of a shared object (e.g., a barrier) may often be replaced by special return values that mean "wait and retry later". A barrier, for example, may provide an operation that returns *true* if this operation has already been invoked by every process, or *false*, otherwise; such semantics does not inherently require processes executing the barrier implementation to block waiting for each other.

Informally, an implementation of a shared object X is wait-free if, whenever any process p_i invokes any operation on X, p_i returns from this operation within some number of its own steps, regardless of what other processes are doing. An easy way to define and reason about wait-free implementations in an asynchronous system is to assume that every process can, at any time, fail by *crashing*. When a process p_i crashes, p_i does not execute any event or step thereafter. If an implementation of a shared object X makes processes wait for each other (i.e., it is not wait-free), then a process p_i that waits for another process p_j inside an operation on X will never return from this operation if p_j crashes. This is because in an asynchronous system p_i cannot tell whether p_j has crashed or is just delayed for a long time.

We define an asynchronous system to be a one which does not put any restrictions on the schedules provided by the scheduler. That is, in an asynchronous system, every sequence of process identifiers is an allowed schedule, even if in this sequence some process identifiers appear infinitely many times, while others do not. Hence, there are executions in which some processes execute infinitely many steps and events (we call those processes *correct*), while other processes stop at some point (i.e., they *crash*).

Then, an implementation I_X of a shared object X is *wait-free* (in an asynchronous system), if, in every infinite implementation history E of X, whenever a correct process p_i invokes an operation on X, p_i returns from this operation. That is, if sub-history $E|p_i$ is infinite then $(E|p_i)|X$ either is infinite or does not end with a pending operation execution. Unless explicitly stated otherwise, we assume that every implementation of every shared object is wait-free.

2.1.8   COMPUTABILITY QUESTIONS

In an asynchronous system, not all base or shared objects are equally powerful. For instance, in a system that provides only registers as base objects, it is impossible to implement a wait-free atomic test-and-set or compare-and-swap shared object [Herlihy, 1991]. We discuss here ways to compare the computational power of shared and base objects.

Let X and Y be any objects. We say that X *can implement* Y, if there exists an implementation of Y that uses only instances of object X and registers. Instances of X are exact copies of X, i.e., base objects with the same sequential semantics, if X is a base object, or shared objects with the same implementation as X, if X is a shared object. (Note that every object X is an instance of itself.) We say that objects X and Y are *equivalent* if X can implement Y, and Y can implement X.

To compare the computational power of objects, it is useful to refer to a "benchmark" shared object called *(binary) consensus*. A consensus shared object (or, simply, consensus) allows processes to agree on a single value from a pool of values proposed by those processes. More precisely, consensus provides operation *propose(v)*, where $v \in \{0, 1\}$. When a process p_i invokes *propose(v)* on consensus C, we say that p_i *proposes* value v (to C). When p_i is returned value v' from an operation *propose(v)* on C, we say that p_i *decides* value v' (in C). Every consensus object C ensures the following properties in every history H of C:

Validity. If some process decides a value v, then some process proposes v.

Agreement. No two processes decide different values.

For $k = 1, \ldots, n$, k-*process consensus* is consensus that ensures its properties when it is accessed by at most k processes in a given execution. More precisely, every k-process consensus object C ensures validity and agreement in every history of C in which no process $p_i, i > k$, invokes operation *propose* on C. Clearly, every k-process consensus is also m-process consensus for every $m < k$.

We use the ability of a shared or base object X to implement (wait-free) k-process consensus (for a given k) as a metric of the computational power of X. It is easy to see that if X cannot implement k-process consensus, for some k, then X cannot implement (in a system of at least k processes) any shared object Y that can implement k-process consensus. The reason is straightforward: if X can implement Y and Y can implement k-process consensus, then X can also implement k-process consensus (by first implementing Y).

For example, it is known that a register can implement only 1-process consensus, a test-and-set or fetch-and-increment object can implement only 2-process consensus, while a compare-and-swap object can implement n-process consensus. This means, in particular, that test-and-set, fetch-and-increment and compare-and-swap objects cannot be implemented from only registers.

Note 2.8 The notions introduced in this section are not related to the complexity of shared object implementations. For example, even if some shared objects X and Y are equivalent, an implementation of Y from X may require infinitely many instances of X, while an implementation of X from Y may be possible using only a single instance of Y. Hence, replacing a shared object Y with an equivalent shared object X in algorithms that use Y might increase the space and/or time complexities of those algorithms.

Note 2.9 The fact that a shared object X can implement only k-process consensus, and a shared object Y can implement only m-process consensus where $m \geq k$ does not necessarily mean that Y can implement X, or that X and Y are equivalent if $m = k$. It only means that X cannot implement Y if $m > k$ (in a system of more than k processes).

2.2 SUMMARY OF NOTATION

p_i	Process
n	Number of processes
Π	Set of processes
X, Y, etc.	Shared or base object
op	Operation
$inv_i(X.op)$	Invocation event of operation op on object X by process p_i
$ret_i(X \rightarrow v)$	Response event from an operation executed by process p_i on object X, returning value v
$X.op_i \rightarrow v$	Execution of operation op on object X by process p_i, returning value v
I_X	Implementation of shared object X
$\langle e_1, e_2, \ldots \rangle$	Sequence of elements $e_1, e_2, \ldots$
$S \cdot S'$	The concatenation of sequences S and S'
ε	Execution
H	History (of an object)

E	Implementation history (of a shared object)
$H\|p_i, E\|p_i$	The restriction of (implementation) history H (E) to events (and steps) of process p_i
$H\|X, E\|X$	The restriction of (implementation) history H (E) to events issued on and received from object X

CHAPTER 3

Transactional Memory: A Primer

Transactional memory (TM) enables processes to communicate and synchronize by executing *transactions*. A transaction can issue any number of operations on *transactional objects* (or *t-objects*, for short), and then it can either *commit* or *abort*. When a transaction T commits, all its operations appear as if they were executed instantaneously (atomically), at some point within the lifespan of T. When T aborts, however, all its operations are rolled back, and their effects are not visible to any other transaction.

In this chapter, we first describe the interface of a TM and how it is used by processes (Section 3.1 and 3.2). We also define some basic notions related to transactions and t-objects. Then, we present a simplified, higher-level TM interface that is useful for describing algorithms. Finally, we discuss particularities and limitations of our model of a TM, and summarize the notation introduced in this chapter.

It is worth noting that, in this chapter, we do not discuss the exact semantics of a TM. In Chapter 4, we explain intuitively when a TM is correct, and we formalize this intuition in Chapter 7 (Part II) by introducing a correctness condition that we call *opacity*. In Part III, we describe progress guarantees that a TM can provide.

3.1 TM SHARED OBJECT

A TM can itself be implemented as a shared object with operations that allow processes to control transactions. The transactions themselves, as well as t-objects, are then "hidden" inside the TM (cf. Figure 3.1). They are, in fact, abstract notions, and it is up to the TM implementation to map them to data structures stored in local variables and base or shared objects. A process can access a t-object only via operations of the TM.

Transactions and t-objects are referred to via their identifiers from the infinite sets $Trans = \{T_1, T_2, \dots\}$ and $TObj = \{x_1, x_2, \dots\}$. For clarity of presentation, we also use (lowercase) symbols, such as x and y, to denote some (arbitrary) t-object identifiers from set $TObj$.

A TM is then a shared object with the following operations (where $x_m \in TObj$ and $T_k \in Trans$):

- *texec*$(T_k, x_m.op)$, which executes operation op on t-object x_m within transaction T_k, and returns the return value of op or a special value A_k;

- $tryC(T_k)$, which attempts to commit transaction T_k, and returns either A_k or C_k; and

- $tryA(T_k)$, which aborts transaction T_k, and always returns value A_k.

The special value A_k that can be returned by the operations of a TM indicates that transaction T_k has been aborted. Value C_k returned by operation $tryC(T_k)$ means that transaction T_k has indeed been committed. A response event with a return value A_k or C_k is called, respectively, an *abort event* or *commit event* (of transaction T_k). A TM can also provide an operation *init*, which we discuss in Section 3.1.2.

It is worth noting that every operation of a TM (except for *init*) can return a special value A_k, for any transaction T_k. Hence, the TM is allowed to force T_k to abort. This is crucial—if only operation *tryA* could return A_k, then the TM could not use any optimistic concurrency control scheme, which would hamper significantly the parallelism of transactions. (In fact, it would be then impossible to implement a TM in an asynchronous system—cf. Chapter 14.)

Consider any execution ε, and any process p_i that invokes in ε, at some time t, any operation $texec(T_k, \ldots)$, $tryC(T_k)$, or $tryA(T_k)$, on some TM object M, for some $T_k \in Trans$. Then, we say that p_i *executes transaction* T_k from time t until p_i receives a commit or an abort event of T_k from M.

For simplicity, we put certain restrictions on how processes are allowed to use the interface of any TM object M, in any execution ε. In particular, we require that, intuitively, every transaction $T_k \in Trans$ is executed, in M, by at most one process, and that transactions executed by a single process are not "nested", i.e., that every process executes, in M, at most one transaction at any given time. We define those restrictions precisely in Section 3.2.4 after we introduce additional terminology related to histories of TM objects.

Note 3.1 This abstract view of a TM simplifies the reasoning about executions in which processes access both base or shared objects and t-objects, or even t-objects of different TMs. It also allows reusing much of the terminology introduced in the previous chapter. This model also has some limitations, which we discuss in Section 3.4.

3.1.1 TRANSACTIONS

Even though transactions are fully controlled by processes, and exist only inside a TM, it is convenient to talk about them as if they were separate and independent entities. We thus say that a transaction T_k performs some action, meaning that the process executing T_k performs this action within the transactional context of T_k, i.e., using T_k as a transaction identifier. More precisely, when a process p_i invokes, returns from, or executes any operation $texec(T_k, x_m.op) \rightarrow v$, $tryC(T_k) \rightarrow v$, or $tryA(T_k) \rightarrow v$ on a TM, we say that transaction T_k invokes, returns from, or executes operation $x_m.op \rightarrow v$, $tryC \rightarrow v$, or $tryA \rightarrow v$, respectively. Also, when p_i executes a step or event (of the TM implementation) within any of those operations, we say that T_k executes this step or event.

Let M be any TM. A transaction T_k *starts* (within M) when T_k invokes its first operation. When T_k is returned value C_k from operation *tryC*, we say that T_k *commits*. When T_k is returned

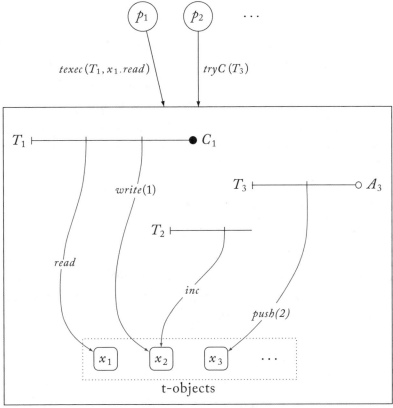

Figure 3.1: A logical view of a TM. Transactions and t-objects are "hidden" inside a TM shared object. Processes control transactions via operations of the TM (*texec*, *tryC*, and *tryA*).

value A_k from any operation of M, we say that T_k *aborts*. Once a transaction T_k commits or aborts, T_k is not allowed to perform any further actions. Hence, if a process p_i wants to retry the computation of an aborted transaction, p_i starts a new transaction with a new transaction identifier.

3.1.2 T-OBJECTS AND THEIR SEMANTICS

Every t-object provides a number of operations. We describe the semantics of a t-object (i.e., its operations) using the notion of a *sequential specification*. Intuitively, the sequential specification of a t-object x lists all (possibly infinite) sequences of operations on x that are considered correct when executed by a single transaction. More precisely, the sequential specification of x is a prefix-closed set of sequences of the form:

$$\langle \alpha_1 \rightarrow v_1, \ \alpha_2 \rightarrow v_2, \ \ldots \rangle,$$

where each α_k, $k = 1, 2, \ldots$, is an operation of x, and each value v_k, which must not belong to the set $\{A_1, A_2, \ldots\}$ of special return values, is a possible return value of α_k. (A set Q of sequences is prefix-closed if, whenever a sequence S is in Q, every prefix of S is also in Q.)

Example 3.2   (T-variables)   A very important class of t-objects consists of those that provide only *read* and *write* operations (like registers). We call those t-objects *t-variables*. The sequential specification of a t-variable x, with domain D and initial value $v_0 \in D$, is the set of sequences of the form:

$$\langle \alpha_1 \rightarrow v_1, \ \alpha_2 \rightarrow v_2, \ \ldots \rangle,$$

where each $\alpha_k \rightarrow v_k$, $k = 1, 2, \ldots$, is one of the following:

- $write(v'_k) \rightarrow ok$, where $v'_k \in D$, or

- $read \rightarrow v_k$, and either (a) the latest *write* operation preceding $read \rightarrow v_k$ is $write(v_k)$, or (b) no *write* operation precedes $read \rightarrow v_k$ and $v_k = v_0$ (the initial value of x).

For instance, the following sequences are some elements of the sequential specification of a t-variable with the initial value 0 (we omit the *ok* return values of *write* operations):

$$\langle read \rightarrow 0 \rangle,$$
$$\langle write(1), \ read \rightarrow 1 \rangle,$$
$$\langle write(1), \ write(2), \ read \rightarrow 2, \ write(3), \ read \rightarrow 3 \rangle.$$

Unless stated otherwise, we assume that the domain of every t-variable is the set of natural numbers (including 0), and the initial value of every t-variable is 0. We denote by Seq_{tvar} the sequential specification of such (default) t-variables.

Let x be any t-object with a sequential specification Q, and op be any operation of x. We say that operation op of x is *read-only* if, for every finite sequence S_1, there exists a value v, such that, for every (finite or infinite) sequence S_2, if sequence $S_1 \cdot S_2$ is in set Q, then the following sequence:

$$S_1 \cdot \langle op \rightarrow v \rangle \cdot S_2$$

is also in set Q. That is, intuitively, a read-only operation does not impact the return values of the following operations. We say that operation op is an *update* operation if op is not read-only. For instance, if x is a t-variable, then *read* is a read-only operation of x and *write* is an update operation of x.

A TM can provide an operation *init* that lets processes decide on the semantics of every t-object *before* any transaction starts. This operation takes as an argument a function that maps every t-object identifier $x_m \in TObj$ to the desired sequential specification of x_m. If a TM does not provide operation *init* or if no process invokes this operation, all t-objects are assumed to be t-variables (with sequential specification Seq_{tvar}).

3.2   TM HISTORIES

A *TM history* is a history of a TM shared object. Let H be any TM history, and T_k be any transaction (identifier). We denote by $H|T_k$ the restriction of H to invocations and responses of TM operations (*texec*, *tryC*, and *tryA*) executed by T_k. We say that transaction T_k is in H if $H|T_k$ is a non-empty sequence, i.e., if H contains at least one event of T_k.

Let H be any TM history, and x be any t-object. An operation $x.op$ executed in H by any transaction T_k is said to be *successful* if op returns a value different than A_k. We denote by $H|x$ the sequence of successful operations executed on x in H (by all transactions). For instance, if

$$H = \langle texec(T_1, x.read) \rightarrow 0,\ texec(T_1, y.read) \rightarrow 0,\ texec(T_2, x.write(1)) \rightarrow ok,\ C_2 \rangle,$$

then

$$H|x = \langle read \rightarrow 0,\ write(1) \rightarrow ok \rangle.$$

We denote by $Seq_H(x)$ the sequential specification of t-object x in TM history H. That is, if H begins with an operation $init(s)$, then $Seq_H(x) = s(x)$; otherwise, $Seq_H(x) = Seq_{\mathrm{tvar}}$.

When referring to TM histories, we often, when there is no ambiguity, use a simplified notation for events and executions of TM operations. We write $x.op_k \rightarrow v$ instead of $M.texec_i(T_k, x.op) \rightarrow v$, where M is some TM shared object and p_i is a process that executes transaction T_k, or $inv_k(x.op)$ and $ret_k(x \rightarrow v)$ instead of, respectively, $inv_i(M.texec(T_k, x.op))$ and the subsequent $ret_i(M \rightarrow v)$. Hence, we use the same notation for a transaction T_k accessing t-object x as for process p_k accessing shared object x.

Similarly, we write $tryC(T_k)$ and $tryA(T_k)$ instead of $M.tryC(T_k)$ and $M.tryA(T_k)$. When not ambiguous, we also simply write C_k and A_k to denote operation executions $tryC(T_k) \rightarrow C_k$ and $tryA(T_k) \rightarrow A_k$, respectively. Moreover, we omit those elements of the notation that are clear from the context or that can be arbitrary.

We illustrate TM histories using diagrams such as the one in Figure 3.2. The history H depicted in this figure is the following (using our simplified notation):

$$H \quad = \quad \langle x.write(1)_1,\ x.read_3 \rightarrow 0,\ y.write(1)_1,\ inv(tryC(T_3)),\ C_1,$$
$$x.read_2 \rightarrow 1,\ y.write(2)_2,\ A_2 \rangle.$$

Note that, for simplicity, operation executions are usually represented by single line ticks in the diagrams even though they are, in fact, two separate events (an invocation and a response).

Let E be any implementation history of any TM shared object M. For simplicity of notation, whenever we use E in a context that requires a TM history, we assume that E refers to TM history $E|M$. For instance, when we say that a transaction T_i is in E, we mean that T_i is in $E|M$.

3.2.1   STATUS OF TRANSACTIONS

Let H be any TM history, and T_k be any transaction in H. We say that transaction T_k is *committed* in H, if $H|T_k$ contains operation $tryC(T_k) \rightarrow C_k$. We say that transaction T_k is *aborted* in H if $H|T_k$

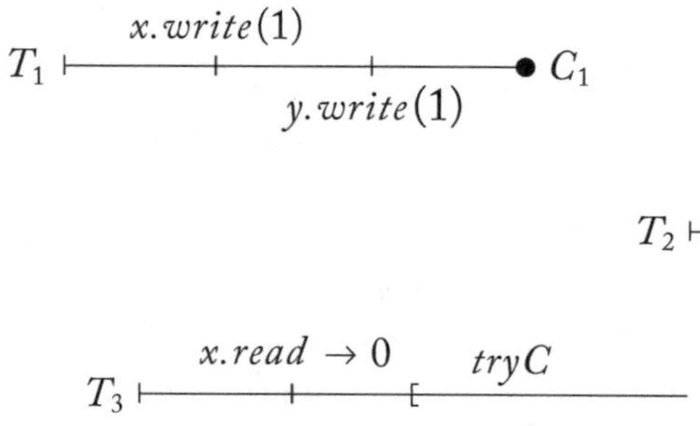

Figure 3.2: An example TM history H

contains response event $ret(A_k)$ from any TM operation. We say that transaction T_k is *forceably aborted* in H if T_k is aborted in H, but $H|T_k$ does not contain any invocation of operation $tryA(T_k)$. That is, T_k is aborted but did not request to be aborted.

A transaction (in H) that is committed or aborted is called *completed*. A transaction that is not completed is called *live*. TM history H is called *complete* when there is no live transaction in H.

Finally, transaction T_k is said to be *commit-pending* in TM history H, if sub-history $H|T_k$ has a pending operation $tryC(T_k)$. That is, T_k has invoked operation $tryC(T_k)$ but has not received any response from this operation.

For example, in the TM history H depicted in Figure 3.2, transaction T_1 is committed, T_2 is aborted (but not forceably aborted because T_2 invokes operation $tryA$), and T_3 is live and commit-pending.

3.2.2 REAL-TIME ORDER

For every TM history H, there is a partial order $\prec_H$ that represents the *real-time order* of transactions in H. For all transactions T_k and T_m in H, if T_k is completed and the last event of T_k precedes the first event of T_m in H, then $T_k \prec_H T_m$. We say then that T_k *precedes* T_m in H. We say that transactions T_k and T_m are *concurrent* in H if $T_k \nprec_H T_m$ and $T_m \nprec_H T_k$. We say that a TM history S is *sequential* if no two transactions are concurrent in S.

For example, in the TM history H depicted in Figure 3.2, transaction T_1 precedes T_2, while T_3 is concurrent to T_1 and T_2. That is, $\prec_H = \{(T_1, T_2)\}$. Clearly, H is not sequential.

3.2.3 CONFLICTS

Let H be any TM history, and T_k be any transaction in H. We say that transaction T_k *reads* (respectively, *writes* or *updates*) a t-object x (in H) when T_k invokes a read-only (respectively, update) operation on x. We say that T_k *accesses* x when T_k invokes any operation on x.

The *read set* of transaction T_k in H, denoted by $RSet_H(T_k)$, is the set of t-objects that T_k reads in history H. Analogously, the *write set* of T_k, denoted by $WSet_H(T_k)$, is the set of t-objects that T_k updates in H. The union of sets $RSet_H(T_k)$ and $WSet_H(T_k)$ is denoted by $RWSet_H(T_k)$.

Intuitively, two concurrent transactions *conflict on a t-object x* if both of them access x and at least one of them writes x. More precisely, let H be any TM history, T_k and T_m be any two transactions in H, and x be any t-object. We say that T_k and T_m conflict on t-object x in H if (1) T_k and T_m are concurrent in H, and (2) either $x \in WSet_H(T_k) \cap RWSet_H(T_m)$ or $x \in RWSet_H(T_k) \cap WSet_H(T_m)$. We say that T_k *conflicts* with T_m if T_k and T_m conflict on any t-object.

For example, consider the TM history H depicted in Figure 3.2. Then, e.g., $WSet_H(T_1) = \{x, y\}$, $RSet_H(T_2) = \{x\}$, and $RWSet_H(T_2) = \{x, y\}$. Transactions T_1 and T_3 conflict on t-object x. Note, however, that T_1 does not conflict with T_2 because T_1 and T_2 are not concurrent. Also, T_3 does not conflict with T_2 since both T_3 and T_2 only read t-object x.

3.2.4 RESTRICTIONS

We put the following restrictions on the way in which processes use any TM shared object M, in any history H of M:

1. Every transaction T_k in H is executed by exactly one process, i.e., $H|T_k$ is a subsequence of $H|p_i$ for some process p_i;

2. Every process p_i executes transactions sequentially, i.e., sub-history $H|p_i$ is sequential; and

3. There is at most one execution of operation *init* in H, and it precedes all other operations on M.

If processes do not observe the above restrictions, the behavior of a TM is undefined. We focus in this manuscript only on those TM histories in which those restrictions are observed.

3.3 HIGH-LEVEL TM API

It is cumbersome and not very readable to describe algorithms that involve TMs using directly operations *texec*, *tryC*, and *tryA*. The simplified notation helps, but one still has to deal with the special return values A_1, A_2, ... We describe here a high-level TM interface, illustrated by the example code in Figure 3.3, that makes the task much easier.

The key element of the high-level TM interface is an **atomic** block. The code inside any **atomic** block B is executed by some transaction T_k, with all invocations of operations on t-objects (i.e., variables that are defined to be t-objects) in B converted to corresponding calls to operations of a TM. The TM shared object can be specified with a **using** statement; if it is not specified, we assume that there is only one TM in the system. An **abort** statement inside B aborts transaction T_k. Whenever T_k is aborted (explicitly using an **abort** statement or forceably), execution of B is terminated and the code inside the **on abort** block that follows B (if any) is executed. We assume that B is not automatically restarted upon the abort of T_k—the execution simply continues at the code that directly follows B.

```
1  atomic using M
2  |   v ← x.read;
3  |   if v = 0 then abort ;
4  |   x.write(v + 1);
5  on abort failed ← true;
```

Figure 3.3: An illustration of a high-level TM interface (M is a TM, x is a t-variable, and both v and *failed* are local variables)

```
1  T_k ← get a new unique transaction id;
2  v ← M.texec(T_k, x.read);
3  if v = A_k then goto line 12;
4  if v = 0 then
5  |   M.tryA(T_k);
6  |   goto line 12;
7  s ← M.texec(T_k, x.write(v + 1));
8  if s = A_k then goto line 12;
9  s ← M.tryC(T_k);
10 if s = A_k then goto line 12;
11 goto line 13;
12 failed ← true;
13 ...
```

Figure 3.4: The code from Figure 3.3 translated to the low-level TM API (i.e., operations of a TM shared object)

For example, consider the code in Figure 3.3. The only t-object accessed inside the **atomic** block is t-variable x (other variables are local). The calls to operations *read* and *write* on x will be converted to invocations of operation *texec* on TM shared object M. When a transaction executing the **atomic** block aborts, local variable *failed* is set to *true*. Figure 3.4 shows what the code in Figure 3.3 looks like after the transformation to the low-level TM interface (using explicitly TM operations).

Some existing TMs, indeed, use a similar high-level API. This interface is typically implemented as an extension to a compiler of a general-purpose programming language (e.g., C++ or Java). The modified compiler transforms all operations inside **atomic** blocks so that they use a low-level TM API (calls to TM library functions, as in Figure 3.4).

3.4 DISCUSSION

Every model represents only a single, simplified view of a given system. Our model of a TM is no different: it aims at being close to interfaces of real TM implementations; however, it omits certain aspects that we consider outside the scope of this manuscript but that are important in practical TM implementations. In this section, we discuss those aspects, and also highlight an alternative way of representing transactions.

3.4.1 NESTED TRANSACTIONS

Some TMs allow transactions to be nested. That is, a transaction T_k can create child transactions. A child transaction T_m of T_k can commit before T_k commits, in which case the operations of T_m become visible to other child transactions of T_k. When T_k commits, the effects of T_m become visible to all transactions. However, if T_k aborts, all its child transactions are rolled back together with T_k.

The simplest form of transaction nesting is *flat nesting*. When a TM uses flat nesting, operations of child transactions of a transaction T_k become part of T_k, and an abort of any child transaction of T_k results in T_k being also aborted. Flat nesting maps in a straightforward way to our model of a TM, even though the model does not introduce the notion of child transactions.

When a TM uses *closed nesting*, an abort of a child transaction T_m of a transaction T_k causes only the operations of T_m being rolled back. Transaction T_k can still continue its execution, create new child transactions, and commit. *Parallel nesting* adds to closed nesting the possibility of child transactions of T_k to be concurrent.

Adding support for closed or even parallel nesting to our model does not pose significant difficulties. However, it would make the model much more complex, while not giving more insight into the problems that we discuss in this manuscript.

3.4.2 NON-TRANSACTIONAL ACCESS TO T-OBJECTS

In our model, t-objects are encapsulated inside a TM shared object. This means that t-objects of a TM can be accessed only by transactions executed by this TM. In real TMs, t-objects are often not isolated—they are objects or memory words that are directly accessible to processes. Hence, it is possible to have executions in which processes access the same t-objects inside and outside of transactions. Defining the semantics of such "mixed" executions requires taking into account both usability issues (avoiding counter-intuitive scenarios but, at the same time, giving users freedom to mix transactions and non-transactional code) as well as engineering problems (avoiding excessive overhead on non-transactional code but, at the same time, making transactions efficient). We do not cover this topic in this manuscript; however, we discuss it in Chapter 10.

3.4.3 FALSE CONFLICTS

According to our definition of a conflict, two transactions T_k and T_m cannot conflict if they do not access some common t-object. In some TM implementations, however, t-objects are divided into groups and conflicts are detected at the level of those groups. For example, each group G of t-objects may be protected by a single lock L_G and any transaction that wants to access a t-object in G might have to acquire lock L_G. Hence, if two transactions access two different t-objects, say x and y, but both x and y happen to be in the same group, the two transactions will indeed have a conflict, the same as if both accessed, e.g., t-object x. Such conflicts, which exist only because the TM implementation does not do fine-grained (per t-object) conflict detection, are called *false conflicts*.

For simplicity, we do not take false conflicts into account in our model. However, all the definitions in this manuscript that rely on the notion of a conflict can be easily extended to handle false conflicts. A straightforward way of doing so is introducing an explicit function h (dependent on the TM implementation) that maps every t-object to its group. Then, we can re-define read set $RSet_H(T_k)$ and write set $WSet_H(T_k)$ of a transaction T_k (in a TM history H) to contain not only every t-object x, respectively, read or written by T_k in H, but also every t-object y such that $h(x) = h(y)$. So-defined notions of read and write sets give a definition of a conflict that includes false conflicts.

3.4.4   A TRANSACTION ABSTRACTION

We could think of a transaction T_k as a block of code, in some domain-specific language, that is submitted by a process p_i to a TM for execution. Then, p_i would wait until its transaction T_k commits, after which p_i would receive the return value of T_k (if any). This is, however, *not* the way in which most TM implementations work. In a typical TM, and in our model, a process p_i executes its transaction T_k interactively: p_i issues each operation of T_k, and then p_i requests the TM to commit or abort T_k. This model of interaction between processes and a TM has an important consequence. Process p_i observes the result (return value) of every operation of T_k even if T_k is (later) aborted. Hence, when defining what it means for a TM to be correct (see Part II of this manuscript), we need to specify which interleavings of operations of different transactions (processes) are considered correct. We cannot simply assume that a transaction executes in isolation. Also, because aborts of transactions cannot, in general, be hidden from process p_i, we cannot focus exclusively on transactions that are committed.

3.5   SUMMARY OF NOTATION

$T_1, T_2, \dots$	Transaction (identifier)
Trans	Set of transactions (transaction identifiers)
$x_1, x_2, \dots$	T-object / t-variable (identifier)
x, y, etc.	Idem (shorthand notation)
TObj	Set of t-objects (t-object identifiers)
M	TM shared object
H	TM history

S	Sequential TM history
$H\|T_k$	Restriction of H to events of transaction T_k
$H\|x$	Sequence of successful operations executed on t-object x in H
$RSet_H(T_k)$	Read set of transaction T_k
$WSet_H(T_k)$	Write set of transaction T_k
$RWSet_H(T_k)$	Union of $RSet_H(T_k)$ and $WSet_H(T_k)$
$Seq_H(x)$	Sequential specification of t-object x in H
A_k	Special return value (= T_k has aborted), *or* a shorthand notation for $M.tryA(T_k) \rightarrow A_k$
C_k	A return value of operation $tryC(T_k)$ (= T_k has committed), *or* a shorthand notation for $M.tryC(T_k) \rightarrow C_k$
$x.op_k \rightarrow v$	Shorthand notation for $M.texec(T_k, x.op) \rightarrow v$, i.e., execution of operation op on t-object x by transaction T_k, returning value v
$inv_k(x.op)$	Shorthand notation for $inv(M.texec(T_k, x.op))$, i.e., invocation of operation op on t-object x by transaction T_k
$ret_k(x \rightarrow v)$	Shorthand notation for a response from an operation executed by transaction T_k on t-object x and returning value v

CHAPTER 4

TM Correctness Issues

A transaction is a very simple, yet very powerful abstraction. To an application, all operations of a *committed* transaction appear as if they were executed instantaneously at some single and unique point in time. All operations of an *aborted* transaction, however, appear as if they never took place. From a programmer's perspective, transactions are like critical sections protected by a global lock: a TM provides an illusion that all transactions are executed sequentially, one by one, and aborted transactions are entirely rolled back.

However, hardly any TM implementation runs transactions sequentially. Indeed, a TM is supposed to make use of the parallelism provided by the underlying multi-processor architecture, and so it should not limit the parallelism of transactions executed by different processes. A real TM history thus often contains sequences of interleaved events from many concurrent transactions. Some of those transactions might be aborted because aborting a transaction is sometimes a necessity for optimistic TM protocols. Not surprisingly, the question of whether a transactional history is correct becomes, in general, tricky.

Deciding whether a given TM history H is correct or not goes usually through finding a sequential history S that is correct and that "looks like" H. The crux of the problem is defining precisely what the notion of "looks like" really means and when a sequential history that contains aborted and live transactions is correct. We address this problem in Chapter 7 by defining a correctness condition called *opacity*. Before we do so, however, we highlight in the following sections the intuitive requirements that a TM implementation should satisfy, and that opacity formally captures.

4.1 ATOMICITY OF COMMITTED TRANSACTIONS

A committed transaction should appear as if it executed all its operations instantaneously, or *atomically*. In other words, every committed transaction T_i should appear as if no other transaction executed concurrently to T_i. Thus, for any TM history H that contains only committed transactions, we should be able to find a total order $\ll$ that represents the order in which the transactions in H appear to be executed. That is, if transactions from history H are indeed executed sequentially in order $\ll$, then they must get the same return values from their operations as in H. (Note that there are certain restrictions on $\ll$, which we discuss in the next section.)

Consider, for example, TM history H_1 depicted in Figure 4.1a, in which transactions T_1, T_2, and T_3 access t-variables x and y (both initialized to 0). The transactions in H_1 indeed appear as if they executed sequentially: first T_3, then T_1, and finally T_2. Hence, H_1 seems, intuitively, correct.

(a) TM history H_1

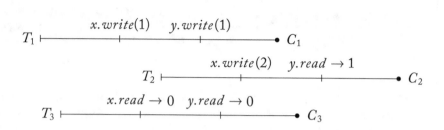

(b) TM history H_2

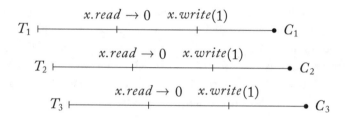

(b) TM history H_3

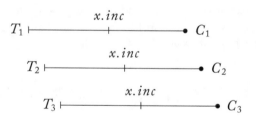

Figure 4.1: Example TM histories

Consider, however, TM history H_2 depicted in Figure 4.1b. In H_2, transactions T_1, T_2, and T_3 read value 0 from t-variable x, and then write 1 to x. Since it is not possible to find a sequential order in which the transactions in H_2 could appear to happen, H_2 is incorrect. In order for H_2 to be correct, at least two of the three transactions in H_2 would have to be aborted.

The situation illustrated by TM history H_2 can arise, for instance, if transactions T_1, T_2, and T_3 try to increment the value of a t-variable x by first reading x and then writing to x, as in the following code:

atomic

$\quad \lfloor \quad v \leftarrow x.read;$

$\qquad x.write(v + 1);$

If several transactions execute the above **atomic** block concurrently, and indeed all of them return value $v = 0$ from the *read* operation on x, as in H_2, then only one of those transactions can commit. This is regardless of whether value v is ever used after the *write* operation on x. Consider, however, the following code:

atomic

$\quad \lfloor \quad x.inc;$

and assume that operation *inc* does not return any meaningful value (it just increments the value of x). If the TM understands the semantics of operation *inc*, then many transactions can execute the above **atomic** block concurrently and commit. For instance, TM history H_3 depicted in Figure 4.1 is correct. This example shows the importance of supporting operations beyond *read* and *write*. Opacity is indeed defined for histories that involve arbitrary t-objects, not only t-variables.

4.2   REAL-TIME ORDER

Consider a transaction T_i that updates a t-object x and commits. Now, consider another transaction T_k that starts after T_i commits. Can T_k still observe the old state of x, from before the update of T_i? By analogy to critical sections, we should say "no"—the real-time order of transactions should be respected by a TM. Indeed, T_k returning an outdated state of x might seem counterintuitive to a programmer.

Violating the real-time order can also lead to subtle bugs. For instance, let processes p_1 and p_2 execute the algorithm shown in Figure 4.2, in which transactions are used to implement an optimistic locking mechanism that protects accesses to an external device. Process p_1 uses two **atomic** blocks to, respectively, acquire and release a lock implemented by t-variables *locked* and *version*. Process p_2 waits until the lock is unlocked (i.e., *locked = false*), and then optimistically reads data from the external device. Afterwards, p_2 checks whether t-variables *locked* and *version* have not changed since the last transaction of p_2. If this is indeed the case, p_2 can be sure that p_1 did not write to the external device while p_2 was reading data from this device, and so p_2 can safely process the data. Note that the protocol should work because each time p_1 releases the lock, it also increases the value of t-variable *version*.

This intuition is, however, violated when the TM does not respect the real-time order of transactions. It is easy to see that if p_2 can observe outdated values of t-variables *locked* and *version* in its transactions, then this locking protocol does not work. For instance, consider the following scenario: (1) p_2 reaches line 5, then (2) p_1 acquires the lock and reaches line 5, then (3) both processes access the external device concurrently, and, finally, (4) p_2 reads (outdated) value *false* from t-variable *locked* in line 7 and thus reaches line 11. In this case, p_2 may process data that is inconsistent.

Process p_1:

    ▶ Lock the device

1 **atomic**
2   **if** *locked.read* **then abort** ;
3   *locked.write*(*true*);
4 **on abort goto** *line 1*;

5 *device.write-data*();

    ▶ Release the lock

6 **atomic**
7   *version.inc*;
8   *locked* ← *false*;

Process p_2:

    ▶ Check the lock

1 **atomic**
2   **if** *locked.read* **then abort** ;
3   v_1 ← *version.read*;
4 **on abort goto** *line 1*;

    ▶ Optimistically read data from the device

5 *data* ← *device.read-data*();

    ▶ Check the lock again

6 **atomic**
7   *l* ← *locked.read*;
8   v_2 ← *version.read*;
9   **if** *l* **or** $v_1 \neq v_2$ **then abort** ;
10 **on abort goto** *line 1*;

    ▶ The optimistic read was safe

11 *process-data*(*data*);

Figure 4.2: An optimistic locking mechanism protecting accesses to an external device using a TM

4.3 PRECLUDING INCONSISTENT VIEWS

A more subtle issue is related to the state accessed by *live* transactions, i.e., transactions that did not commit or abort yet. Because a live transaction can always be later aborted, and its updates discarded, one might naively assume that the remedy to a transaction that accesses an inconsistent state is to abort it. However, a transaction that accesses an inconsistent state can cause various problems, even if it is later aborted.

To illustrate this, consider two t-variables, x and y. A programmer may assume that y is always equal to x^2, and $x \geq 2$. Clearly, the programmer will then take care that every transaction, when executed as a whole, preserves the assumed invariants. Assume the initial value of x and y is 4 and 16, respectively. Let T_1 be a transaction that performs the following operations:

    $x.write$(2);
    $y.write$(4);
    $tryC \rightarrow C_1$;

Consider another transaction T_2 that is executed by some process p_i concurrently with T_1. Then, if T_2 reads the old value of x (4) and the new value of y (also 4), the following problems may occur, even if T_2 is to be aborted later:

1. If p_i tries to compute the value of $1/(y - x)$, then a "divide by zero" exception will be thrown, which can crash the process executing the transaction or even the entire application.

2. If p_i enters the following loop:

    $v_x \leftarrow x.read;$
    $v_y \leftarrow y.read;$
    while $v_x \neq v_y$ **do**
    $\quad array[v_x] \leftarrow 0;$
    $\quad v_x \leftarrow v_x + 1;$

    (where v_x, v_y, and *array* are variables local to p_i), and indeed p_i reads $v_x = v_y = 4$, then unexpected memory locations could be overwritten, not to mention that the loop would need to span the entire value domain. (Note that this situation does not necessarily result in a "segmentation fault" signal that is usually easy to catch. Basically, the loop may overwrite memory locations of variables that belong to the application executing the loop.)

Process p_i, while executing transaction T_2, could also enter a code path that it was never supposed to enter. Then, p_i could, for example, perform direct (and unexpected) I/O operations, which would not be rolled back upon the abort of T_2.

When programs are run in managed environments, these problems can be solved by carefully isolating transactions (i.e., processes executing those transactions) from the outside world (sandbox-ing). However, sandboxing is often expensive and applicable only to specific run-time environments. Sandboxing would, for instance, be difficult to achieve for applications written in low-level languages (like C or C++) and executed directly by an operating system.

It is indeed possible to implement a TM that will completely isolate aborted transactions from the outside world. Then, such transactions might not even be visible to the application, and so they can be returned arbitrary values from their operations. Note, however, that all transactions that *are* visible to the user should still observe consistent states. Therefore, if we consider the interface between the application and the TM at a bit higher level, we still require the same, strong semantics as for TMs that do not provide any transaction sandboxing. In this sense, sandboxing can be thought of as a method for implementing a TM that, from the application's perspective, gives the strong guarantees that we formalize in the following chapters.

CHAPTER 5

Implementing a TM

In this chapter, we describe the basic idea that underlies most (software) TM implementations. We first present a TM algorithm that uses a simple 2-phase locking protocol. We then describe a more sophisticated TM algorithm that better reflects most recent TM implementations. We discuss its advantages and issues as compared to "bare" 2-phase locking TM. Finally, we give an overview of common implementation techniques that go beyond the two TM algorithms we present in this chapter.

This chapter can be viewed as a rather informal introduction to common TM implementation techniques. The TM algorithms we present here are meant only to illustrate the main, high-level idea of implementing a TM with given properties. We ignore here low-level details and optimizations of real TM implementations, most of which are related to the limitations of particular hardware platforms.

The correctness of the TM algorithms presented in this chapter is proved later, in Chapter 8. Progress properties of two classes of TM implementations that we discuss here—lock-based and obstruction-free TMs—are defined precisely in Part III. Finally, precise definitions of individual TM implementation techniques that we describe intuitively in this chapter are given when they are needed for any formal proof.

It is also worth noting that the TM algorithms we show here implement only t-variables (i.e., t-objects that support only operations *read* and *write*). This is indeed for simplicity—the purpose of this chapter is to give a high-level overview of the TM implementation techniques, not a detailed survey of existing TM algorithms. In fact, those TMs that do support arbitrary t-objects often use similar algorithms to the ones we present in this chapter. While it is possible to exploit, e.g., commutativity of operations of certain t-objects, in order to allow more parallelism between transactions, the techniques for doing so are usually complex and well beyond the scope of this manuscript.

5.1 GENERAL IDEA

Most TM algorithms can be viewed as variants of the well-known (strict) 2-phase locking protocol. The basic idea of this protocol is the following: Every t-variable x_m is protected by a lock $L[m]$. Access to x_m is, at any time, restricted to a single writer or multiple readers. When a transaction T_k wants to write to a t-variable x_m, T_k first acquires lock $L[m]$ in *exclusive* mode. We say then that T_k *acquires x_m (for writing)*. Until T_k commits or aborts, no other transaction can access x_m.

When transaction T_k wants to read x_m, T_k acquires $L[m]$ in *shared* mode. We say then that T_k *acquires* x_m *for reading*. Many transactions can read x_m concurrently with T_k; however, only one transaction (e.g., T_k) may later write to x_m, by upgrading lock $L[m]$ to exclusive mode.

The commit phase of T_k (i.e., operation $tryC(T_k)$) consists only of releasing all (shared and exclusive) locks acquired by T_k. If T_k wants to abort, T_k has to first rollback all its writes to t-variables before releasing locks.

An obvious problem with this scheme is a possibility of a deadlock. Avoiding deadlocks is infeasible here because transactions may access t-variables in any order, and this order is not known in advance to a TM. A simple way of dealing with deadlocks is using *timeouts* when acquiring locks. If a transaction T_k times out when trying to acquire a lock, T_k aborts. Instead of locks and additional timeout mechanisms, TM implementations usually use *try-locks*—objects that we introduce in the following section and whose implementation can be as simple as a single *test-and-set* operation.

5.1.1   (READ-WRITE) TRY-LOCKS

Roughly speaking, a try-lock is a lock whose operations are wait-free. That is, intuitively, a process p_i that tries to acquire a try-lock L is not blocked indefinitely waiting for L to be released; instead, if acquiring L by p_i is not possible, p_i is eventually returned a "failed" value. When p_i fails to acquire L, p_i can try again later, or, e.g., abort its current transaction. Those try-locks that can be acquired in shared and exclusive modes are called *read-write try-locks*; other try-locks support only the exclusive mode.

More precisely, every read-write try-lock object L has the following operations:

- *trylock-shared* for acquiring L in shared mode,

- *trylock* for acquiring L in exclusive mode, and

- *unlock* for releasing L.

Operations *trylock-shared* and *trylock* of L return *true* on success, or *false* on failure. When a process p_i is returned *true* from operation *trylock-shared* or *trylock* on L, we say that p_i *acquires* L in, respectively, shared or exclusive mode. Then, p_i *holds* L (in shared or exclusive mode, respectively) until p_i invokes operation *unlock* on L (i.e., until p_i *releases* L). If L is a non-read-write try-lock, i.e., if L can be acquired only in exclusive mode, we usually say that a process p_i acquires or holds L, without adding the redundant "in exclusive mode".

Every (read-write) try-lock L ensures the following property in every history H of L:

Mutual exclusion. If a process p_i holds L in exclusive mode at some point in H, then no other process holds L (in shared or exclusive mode) at this point in H.

For simplicity, we consider only (read-write) try-locks that are not reentrant. That is, a process p_i that holds a (read-write) try-lock L in exclusive mode is not allowed to invoke operations *trylock-shared* or *trylock* on L until p_i first releases L. When p_i holds L in shared mode, p_i cannot invoke operation *trylock-shared* on L; however, p_i can try to "upgrade" L by executing operation *trylock* on L (which, clearly, may not always succeed, e.g., if other processes also hold L in shared mode at the same time). Even if p_i first acquires L in shared mode and then "upgrades" L to exclusive mode, by invoking operation *unlock* on L process p_i releases L, and not, e.g., "downgrades" L back to shared mode.

We also assume, for simplicity, that only a process that holds a (read-write) try-lock L (in shared or exclusive mode) can invoke operation *unlock* on L.

Note 5.1   We did not state when operations *trylock-shared* and *trylock* are allowed to return *false*. For instance, a trivial implementation of a (read-write) try-lock that always returns *false* from those operations would ensure the mutual exclusion property. For the purpose of this section, it is sufficient to assume that (read-write) try-locks are somehow "best-effort"—their operations return *true* in "most" cases when it does not violate the mutual exclusion property. We are more precise on this issue in Chapter 12, when we discuss the progress properties of lock-based TM implementations. Indeed, the two TM algorithms that we present in this chapter remain correct (as defined in Chapter 7) even if they use (read-write) try-locks whose operations *trylock-shared* and *trylock* often, or always, return *false*.

5.1.2   2-PHASE LOCKING TM ALGORITHM

A TM algorithm $\mathcal{A}_{2PL}$ that is based on the 2-phase locking protocol is shown in Figure 5.1 (we prove its correctness in Chapter 8). The state of every t-variable x_m is stored in register $TVar[m]$. The read-write try-lock that protects accesses to x_m is $L[m]$.

The code of the TM algorithm is executed by every process p_i that invokes an operation on the TM. Variables *rset* and *wset*, local to p_i, track the t-variables, respectively, read and written by the current transaction T_k at p_i. The local array *oldval* stores the original values of t-variables written by T_k, which are restored (in line 21) when T_k aborts.

5.2   AN IMPROVED TM ALGORITHM

In this section, we present a TM algorithm $\mathcal{A}_{IR}$ that uses 2-phase locking only for transactional writes and handles transactional reads in an optimistic way. Before we do so, however, we explain what the main problem with algorithm $\mathcal{A}_{2PL}$ is, i.e., with using locks also for reading. Then, we explain the role of *validation* of transactional reads when those reads are optimistic.

In a multi-processor system, a change to the state of a base object at one processor may cause invalidation of cache lines of other processors. If the same base object B is concurrently updated by many processors, the ownership of the corresponding cache line "bounces" between processors, causing possibly high traffic on the inter-processor bus and often significantly increasing the time that each processor needs to execute its operation on B. On the other hand, if the processors access B

uses: $L[1, \ldots]$—read-write try-locks, $TVar[1, \ldots]$—registers (other variables are process-local)

initially: $TVar[1, \ldots] = 0$, $L[1, \ldots]$ unlocked, $rset = wset = \emptyset$ at every process

1 **operation** $x_m.read_k$

2   **if** $m \notin rset \cup wset$ **then**

       ▶ Acquire read-write try-lock $L[m]$ of x_m in shared mode

3       $locked \leftarrow L[m].trylock\text{-}shared$;

4   **if not** $locked$ **then return** $abort(T_k)$;

5       $rset \leftarrow rset \cup \{m\}$;

6   **return** $TVar[m].read$;

7 **operation** $x_m.write(v)_k$

8   **if** $m \notin wset$ **then**

       ▶ Acquire read-write try-lock $L[m]$ of x_m in exclusive mode

9       $locked \leftarrow L[m].trylock$;

10   **if not** $locked$ **then return** $abort(T_k)$;

11      $wset \leftarrow wset \cup \{m\}$;

12      $oldval[m] \leftarrow TVar[m].read$;

13    $TVar[m].write(v)$;

14   **return** ok;

15 **operation** $tryC(T_k)$

16    $unlock\text{-}all()$;

17   **return** C_k;

18 **operation** $tryA(T_k)$

19   **return** $abort(T_k)$;

20 **function** $abort(T_k)$

    ▶ Rollback changes

21   **foreach** $m \in wset$ **do** $TVar[m].write(oldval[m])$;

22    $unlock\text{-}all()$;

23   **return** A_k;

24 **function** $unlock\text{-}all()$

    ▶ Release all try-locks

25   **foreach** $m \in rset \cup wset$ **do** $L[m].unlock$;

26    $wset \leftarrow rset \leftarrow \emptyset$;

Figure 5.1: Algorithm $\mathcal{A}_{2PL}$ that implements a TM shared object using the 2-phase locking protocol

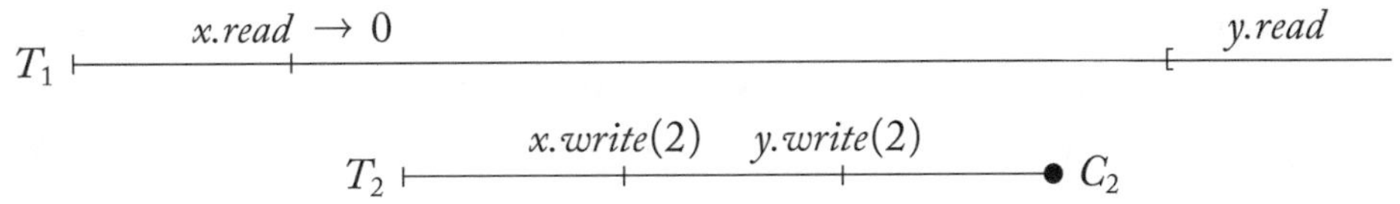

$$T_1 \vdash \xrightarrow{\quad x.read \ \to \ 0 \quad} \hspace{4cm} \xrightarrow{\quad y.read \quad}$$

$$T_2 \vdash \xrightarrow{\quad x.write(2) \quad y.write(2) \quad} \bullet \ C_2$$

Figure 5.2: An illustration of the problem a TM implementation must deal with when using invisible reads

without changing the state of B, their operations can proceed in parallel, requiring little (or no) communication between processors.

In the 2-phase locking TM algorithm presented in the previous section, any transaction that *reads* a t-variable x_m has to acquire read-write try-lock $L[m]$ (in shared mode). Hence, reads of t-variables are implemented using operations that *change* the state of some base objects. This TM implementation technique is called *visible reads*—indeed, a transaction that attempts to write to a t-variable x_m knows of concurrent transactions that have acquired x_m for reading.

Visible reads have the disadvantage of causing cache "bouncing" when many transactions concurrently read the same t-variables. This may become a serious performance bottleneck in workloads that are dominated by reads. A solution is to make reads *invisible*, i.e., ensure that the implementation of a *read* operation on a t-variable does not change the state of any base object.

A difficulty in implementing a TM that uses invisible reads is that transactions that write to a t-variable x are not aware of the concurrent transactions that read or that are about to read x. Thus, a transaction T_k that reads two or more t-variables, say x and y, has to make sure that the values read from x and y are *consistent*. For example, consider the following history H, illustrated in Figure 5.2, of some TM implementation that uses invisible reads:

$$
\begin{aligned}
H \ = \ \langle & x.read_1 \to 0, \\
& x.write(2)_2, \ y.write(2)_2, \ C_2, \\
& inv_1(y.read) \rangle.
\end{aligned}
$$

Transaction T_1 reads value 0 from t-variable x. Then, transaction T_2 writes value 2 to t-variables x and y. Because T_2 does not see the read of T_1, T_2 can possibly execute both its writes and commit. Now, when T_1 invokes operation *read* on y, T_1 cannot be returned value 2 written to y by T_2—this would violate the intuitive correctness requirement (formalized in Chapter 7) that transactions appear as if they executed sequentially. Transaction T_1 must be returned either 0 or A_1 (abort event) from the *read* operation on y.

Consider, however, a history H' that is the same as H except that in H' transaction T_2 does not write to x, only to y. In H', T_1 can read value 2 from y—then T_1 appears as if it executed entirely after T_2. To distinguish history H' from H, transaction T_1 can, e.g., go back to t-variable x and re-read its value.

Checking whether the value that is to be returned from a *read* operation of a transaction T_k is consistent with the values returned from the previous reads executed by T_k is called *validation*. When validation of T_k fails (i.e., when T_k would not be returned a consistent value from its *read* operation), transaction T_k is aborted.

Algorithm $\mathcal{A}_{IR}$ depicted in Figures 5.3 and 5.4 illustrates how the 2-phase locking protocol can be combined with the invisible reads strategy. It also shows a basic validation technique, called *incremental validation*, that consists in re-reading all the t-variables in the current read set of a transaction.

The basic idea is the following: As in the 2-phase locking protocol, a transaction T_k that invokes operation *write* on a t-variable x_m for the first time needs to acquire try-lock $L[m]$ (in exclusive mode; shared mode is not used in this algorithm, and so $L[m]$ does not have to be a read-write try-lock). The current value of x_m, stored in register $TVar[m]$, is then saved in local array *oldval*, and the new value of x_m (the parameter of the *write* operation) is stored in $TVar[m]$. The main difference from the 2-phase locking TM given in the previous section is that $TVar[m]$ contains not only the current value of x_m but also two additional fields: the timestamp (version number) of x_m and a *locked* flag. We explain the use of those fields in the following paragraphs.

When transaction T_k invokes operation *read* on a t-variable x_m, T_k first reads from register $TVar[m]$ the current value, timestamp, and the *locked* flag of x_m. If x_m has been written by T_k before (i.e., $m \in wset$), T_k simply returns the value of x_m—no other steps are necessary because T_k already holds a lock on x_m.

If t-variable x_m is locked by a transaction T_l different than T_k, then T_k aborts—the current value of x_m cannot be returned by any *read* operation of T_k if T_l aborts or writes a new value to x_m before committing. To check whether x_m is currently acquired by any transaction, T_k reads the *locked* flag of x_m. This flag is always *true* when some transaction holds $L[m]$ and has already written a new value to register $TVar[m]$. If T_k reads *true* from the *locked* flag of x_m, T_k aborts.

Transaction T_k also performs validation before returning from the *read* operation on x_m (implemented by function *validate*). Validation consists in checking, for every t-variable x_l in set *rset*, whether the value of $TVar[l]$ has changed since T_k first read $TVar[l]$. That is, in each read of T_k, we validate all the preceding reads of T_k. The value of register $TVar[l]$ contains a monotonically increasing timestamp that ensures uniqueness of every value of $TVar[l]$ (at any point in time) with respect to the previous values of $TVar[l]$.

To understand the role of timestamps, consider the following TM history illustrated in Figure 5.5:

$$
\begin{aligned}
H \quad = \quad & \langle x_1.read_1 \rightarrow 0,\ inv_1(x_2.read), \\
& x_1.write(1)_2,\ x_2.write(1)_2,\ C_2, \\
& x_1.write(0)_3,\ x_2.write(0)_3,\ C_3, \\
& ret_1(v) \rangle.
\end{aligned}
$$

Assume that the TM does not use timestamps, e.g., that the timestamp value in every register $TVar[l]$ is always 0. In H, transaction T_1 reads 0 from t-variable x_1 and then invokes operation *read* on t-

uses: $L[1, \ldots]$—try-locks, $TVar[1, \ldots]$—registers (other variables are process-local)
initially: $TVar[1, \ldots] = (0, 0, \text{false})$, $L[1, \ldots]$ unlocked, $rset = wset = \emptyset$ at every process

1   **operation** $x_m.read_k$
2       $(v, ts, locked) \leftarrow TVar[m].read$;
3   **if** $m \in wset$ **then return** v;
     ▶ Abort if x_m is locked or if validation fails
4   **if** $locked$ **or not** $validate()$ **then return** $abort(T_k)$;
5   **if** $m \notin rset$ **then**
6          $readts[m] \leftarrow ts$;
7          $rset \leftarrow rset \cup \{m\}$;
8   **return** v;

9   **operation** $x_m.write(v)_k$
10   **if** $m \notin wset$ **then**
        ▶ Acquire try-lock $L[m]$ of x_m
11         $locked \leftarrow L[m].trylock$;
12   **if not** $locked$ **then return** $abort(T_k)$;
        ▶ Save the current value of x_m and its new timestamp
13         $(v', ts, locked) \leftarrow TVar[m].read$;
14         $oldval[m] \leftarrow v'$;
15         $oldts[m] \leftarrow ts$;
16         $wset \leftarrow wset \cup \{m\}$;
17      $TVar[m].write((v, oldts[m], true))$;
18   **return** ok;

19 **operation** $tryC(T_k)$
20   **if not** $validate()$ **then return** $abort(T_k)$;
     ▶ Release all try-locks
21   **foreach** $m \in wset$ **do**
22         $(v, ts, locked) \leftarrow TVar[m].read$;
23         $TVar[m].write((v, ts + 1, false))$;
24         $L[m].unlock$;
25      $wset \leftarrow rset \leftarrow \emptyset$;
26   **return** C_k;

Figure 5.3: TM algorithm $\mathcal{A}_{IR}$ that uses invisible reads (continues in Figure 5.4)

```
27  operation tryA(T_k)
28  │    return abort(T_k);

29  function abort(T_k)
30  │    foreach m ∈ wset do
     │         ► Rollback changes and release all try-locks
31  │         TVar[m].write((oldval[m], oldts[m], false));
32  │         L[m].unlock;
33  │    wset ← rset ← ∅;
34  │    return A_k;

35  function validate()
36  │    foreach m ∈ rset do
37  │         (v, ts, locked) ← TVar[m];
38  │         if (locked and m ∉ wset) or ts ≠ readts[m] then return false;
39  │    return true;
```

Figure 5.4: The second part of algorithm $\mathcal{A}_{\mathrm{IR}}$ (continues from Figure 5.3)

variable x_2. Transactions T_2 and T_3, each writing to both x_1 and x_2, execute concurrently to the latter *read* operation of T_1 and commit. Assume that T_2 executes and commits just before T_1 executes the *read* operation on register $TVar[2]$ in line 2. Transaction T_1 will then read value $(1, 0, false)$ from $TVar[2]$ and enter the validation phase (function *validate*). Assume that transaction T_3 executes and commits just before T_1 reads register $TVar[1]$ in line 37. Then, T_1 will read value $(0, 0, false)$ from $TVar[1]$, i.e., the initial value of register $TVar[1]$. Hence, the validation of T_1 will succeed and T_1 will return value $v = 1$ from its *read* operation on x_2. But then, the history is incorrect: T_1 reads $x_1 = 0$ and $x_2 = 1$, while every transaction that writes to x_1 or x_2 preserves the invariant $x_1 = x_2$. When timestamps are used, transaction T_3 writes value $(0, 2, false)$ to register $TVar[1]$ (instead of value $(0, 0, false)$), causing the validation of transaction T_1 to fail.

    When transaction T_k invokes operation $tryC(T_k)$ of the TM, T_k first performs validation and then releases all try-locks. Operation $tryA(T_k)$ consists in rolling back all the changes of T_k and releasing try-locks—as in algorithm $\mathcal{A}_{2\mathrm{PL}}$.

5.3 ALTERNATIVE IMPLEMENTATION TECHNIQUES

5.3.1 OBSTRUCTION-FREE MECHANISMS

The two TM algorithms that we showed in this chapter use try-locks. This makes them vulnerable to crashes of processes. On the one hand, operations of those TMs are wait-free: a transaction T_k, executed by some process p_i, that invokes any operation of those TMs will eventually return from

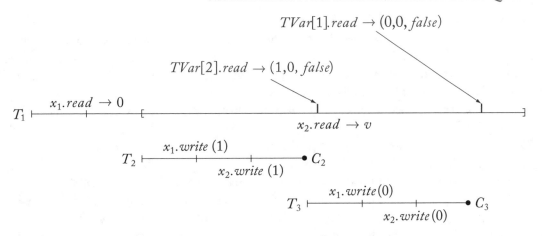

Figure 5.5: An illustration of the role of timestamps in TM algorithm $\mathcal{A}_{IR}$ (the square brackets delimit the execution of operation $x_2.read \rightarrow v$)

this operation even if all processes, except p_i, crash. However, on the other hand, if T_k acquires a try-lock on some t-variable x_m and then process p_i crashes, every transaction that accesses x_m thereafter will get aborted. This is because this try-lock will never get released. In a sense, TMs that use try-locks ensure progress of the individual operations of transactions but not of the entire transactions when processes can crash.

There are indeed TM implementations that can make progress with crashes of processes. An important class of those implementations consists of TMs that are *obstruction-free* [Herlihy et al., 2003a,b]. Intuitively, an obstruction-free TM guarantees that every transaction T_k that executes alone, i.e., with no other transaction taking steps concurrently, can commit. That is, if T_k has no concurrent transactions, or all transactions concurrent to T_k are suspended while T_k executes (i.e., due to delays or crashes of processes), then T_k cannot be forceably aborted.

We define precisely obstruction-free TMs in Chapter 13. We also give there two example algorithms that implement obstruction-free TMs.

5.3.2   VALIDATION HEURISTICS

The TM algorithm that we showed in Section 5.2 uses incremental validation. That is, a transaction T_k that invokes a *read* operation re-reads all the t-variables on which T_k invoked operation *read* before. Hence, if T_k reads s t-variables, T_k needs to execute $O(s^2)$ steps of the TM implementation, which might be very expensive if s is very large. It is thus desirable to limit the cases in which incremental validation is performed, or even eliminate it entirely.

A simple idea, used for instance by RSTM [Marathe et al., 2006], is to use a global counter V (a fetch-and-increment base object) that is incremented by every transaction that commits (e.g., before it releases its try-locks). Then, incremental validation can be skipped in a *read* operation of a transaction T_k if the value of counter V has not changed since the last *read* operation of T_k (meaning that no transaction committed its changes to t-variables since then). This method is rather coarse-grained: a transaction T_k will execute the incremental validation even if transactions that committed since the last *read* operation of T_k do not have any conflict with T_k.

A more fine-grained scheme, called *time-based validation*, is used by TM implementations such as TL2 [Dice et al., 2006], TinySTM [Felber et al., 2008], and SwissTM [Dragojević et al., 2009]. In this scheme, the global counter V is used to generate timestamps for t-variables. Any transaction T_k in its commit phase (operation *tryC*) first obtains its *write timestamp* by performing operation *fetch-and-increment* on V. Then, T_k updates the timestamp of every t-variable in its write set using its write timestamp. For instance, in the TM algorithm shown in Figure 5.3, the write timestamp of T_k would be written to register $TVar[m]$, for every $m \in wset$, in line 23.

With this scheme, the timestamp of a t-variable x_m corresponds to the logical time of the latest (committed) update to x_m. A transaction T_k can then skip the incremental validation in operation *read* on a t-variable x_m, if the timestamp of x_m is lower than the value that T_k read from V at its beginning or before its latest incremental validation. Indeed, then x_m could not have changed since the last read of counter V by T_k.

In Section 12.2, we show the algorithm underlying the TL2 TM implementation. TL2 uses time-based validation. However, it does not execute incremental validation at all—if a transaction T_k reads a t-variable x_m with the timestamp higher or equal to the value of V read by T_k in its first operation, then T_k immediately aborts.

5.3.3   CONTENTION MANAGEMENT

In the TM algorithms presented in this chapter, a transaction that cannot acquire a try-lock or that fails in its validation phase, immediately aborts. Hence, it may happen that processes, repeatedly trying to commit some transactions, cause high contention of those transactions. In an extreme case, it may happen that due to frequent conflicts no transaction will be able to commit—a situation called *livelock*. It is also possible that *some* processes may be unable to commit any transaction, or that some transactions (e.g., very long ones) may be always forceably aborted.

Reducing contention and preventing starvation of processes or individual transactions may be delegated to a logically separate TM module called a *contention manager*. There are two means by which a contention manager can influence the algorithm of a TM. First, it can delay some transactions. For example, an exponential or randomized back-off used for transactions that are about to abort can reduce contention. Second, a contention manager can arbitrate conflicts between transactions. That is, when a transaction T_k fails to acquire a try-lock on a t-variable x_m, the contention manager can decide to abort T_k (as we do in the TM algorithms in this chapter), make T_k wait for some time and then retry acquiring the try-lock, or even cause the transaction that currently holds the try-lock to be (eventually) aborted. Such arbitration of conflicts can give priority to some transactions (e.g., long ones), thus helping reduce the likelihood of starvation.

For the purpose of this manuscript, we treat a contention manager as an integral part of a TM algorithm. This means that all the assumptions we make and properties we define should apply to the entire TM, including the contention manager. This is generally not an issue except for the assumption that operations of a TM are wait-free. Indeed, there are a few contention managers (e.g., Greedy [Guerraoui et al., 2005b]) that can make transactions wait for each other indefinitely long. Such contention managers are, however, used to provide strong liveness guarantees that we capture in the theoretical framework described in Chapter 14. This framework does *not* assume wait-freedom of individual TM operations.

5.3.4   MULTI-VERSION SCHEMES

The TM algorithms we showed before use, for each t-variable x_m, a single base object $TVar[m]$ that holds the latest committed value of x_m. If a transaction T_k writes value v to x_m and commits, only value v is stored in $TVar[m]$ and thus visible to all transactions. The old values of x_m are lost, possibly retained only in process-local variables.

Consider the following history that has already been discussed in Section 5.2 and illustrated in Figure 5.2:

$$H = \langle x.read_1 \to 0,$$
$$x.write(2)_2, \ y.write(2)_2, \ C_2,$$
$$inv_1(y.read) \rangle.$$

Transaction T_1 can only return either 0 or A_k from its *read* operation on y. It would be desirable if T_1 returned 0—only then T_1 can eventually commit. However, before T_1 invokes *read* on y, transaction T_2 writes to y a new value and commits. Then, if the TM does not retain the old value of y, T_1 cannot return 0 from its *read* operation on y and has to abort.

Multi-version TM implementations keep a log of past values for every t-variable. Such TMs would allow transaction T_1 in history H to read value 0 from y and eventually commit. In fact, if every such log holds *all* the past values of a given t-variable, then every transaction that invokes only *read* operations can always commit. This is especially advantageous for systems in which long read-only transactions are frequent.

However, the cost of maintaining logs for all t-variables can be high. It is thus not surprising that only few TM implementations are multi-version—we know only of JVSTM [Cachopo and Rito-Silva, 2005] and LSA-STM [Riegel et al., 2006]. In obstruction-free TMs, and some lock-based TMs such as SwissTM, many values of a single t-variable x_m can be stored in base objects at the same time. However, those TMs are not considered multi-version because at any given time only a single value written to x_m by a *committed* transaction is stored in base objects. For instance, in history H we discussed before (Figure 5.2), the old value of t-variable y would be lost in those TMs by the time transaction T_1 invokes operation *read* on y.

5.3.5   DEFERRED UPDATES

So far, we assumed that a transaction T_k acquires a lock on t-variable x_m within a *write* operation on x_m. Both algorithms that we presented in this chapter follow this assumption. However, TMs can also acquire t-variables *lazily*—a scheme also called *deferred updates*. In such TMs, a transaction T_k that invokes a *write* operation on a t-variable x_m simply adds x_m to its write set and stores locally the new value of x_m. Only when T_k enters its commit phase (operation $tryC(T_k)$), T_k acquires all t-variables in its write set (e.g., by acquiring respective try-locks) and writes new values of those t-variables. This scheme is used, e.g., by TL2 [Dice et al., 2006], the algorithm of which we give in Section 12.2.

CHAPTER 6

Further Reading

6.1 SHARED MEMORY SYSTEMS

Our model of an asynchronous shared memory system is inspired by the books of Attiya and Welch [2004] and Lynch [1996]. The models used in those works are, however, more general, since they capture also message-passing systems, failures beyond crashes, nondeterministic algorithms, etc.

The atomicity of registers was formalized by Lamport [1986]. The atomicity of general objects was defined, under the notion of *linearizability*, by Herlihy and Wing [1990]. The model we consider for base objects is stronger than the one used for defining linearizability because we assume that operations on base objects are never concurrent. Lynch [1996, Chapter 13.1.4] shows a general transformation from the stronger model to the weaker one, and it defines conditions under which this transformation is possible.

Wait-freedom was defined by Herlihy [1991]. He also proposed, in the same paper, a way to measure the computational power of an object using consensus. He determined there the computational power of objects such as test-and-set and compare-and-swap. The consensus problem was first defined by Lamport et al. [1980].

Fischer et al. [1985] were the first to prove that implementing consensus in an asynchronous message-passing system (in which at least one process can crash) is impossible. The same proof technique was subsequently used by Loui and Abu-Amara [1987] to prove that it is impossible to implement consensus, for 2 or more processes, in an asynchronous shared-memory system that provides only registers.

Scott and Scherer [2001] gave several implementations of try-locks, and they discussed related issues. The general problem of mutual exclusion in systems with multiple processes dates back at least to year 1962 [Dijkstra, 1965]. A good overview of various algorithms implementing locks can be found in the book by Raynal [1986].

6.2 TRANSACTIONAL MEMORY

Transactional memory was first proposed by Herlihy and Moss [1993] as an extension to the cache-coherency protocol in multi-processor systems. The first software TM algorithm was described by Shavit and Touitou [1995]. The limitation of this TM was that it supported only predefined transactions. The first software TM that allowed dynamic transactions was DSTM by Herlihy et al. [2003a]. Since then, all TM implementations handle dynamic transactions. Integrating TM operations in a programming language, using **atomic** blocks, was first proposed by Harris and Fraser [2003].

Clearly, transactional protocols had been used in databases and distributed systems long before the first TM was proposed. An excellent overview of concepts and techniques related to transactions (including concepts that we do not discuss in detail, e.g., transaction nesting) can be found in the books of Weikum and Vossen [2001] and of Gray and Reuter [1992].

Herlihy et al. [2003a] were the first to argue that all transactions in a TM, including the aborted ones, should observe a consistent state of the system. A similar argument was given before for distributed transactional systems, e.g., by Lynch et al. [1994]. We gave some examples to support this argument in Section 4.3; others can be found in the paper by Spear et al. [2006].

The 2-phase locking protocol that we referred to in Chapter 5 was first presented by Eswaran et al. [1976]. The first TM with dynamic transactions, DSTM [Herlihy et al., 2003a], was obstruction-free—it did not use locks. Ennals [2006] argued that TM implementations should not be obstruction-free because they have too high overhead. Since then, most software-based TMs use locks and a variant of the 2-phase locking protocol, e.g., TL2 [Dice et al., 2006], TinySTM [Felber et al., 2008], BartokSTM [Harris et al., 2006], McRT-STM [Adl-Tabatabai et al., 2006], and SwissTM [Dragojević et al., 2009].

The invisible reads strategy was first used, together with incremental validation, in DSTM. Spear et al. [2006] and Dice et al. [2006] proposed strategies for avoiding incremental validation using a global counter and a time-based validation, respectively.

TM contention managers were first used in DSTM. Various contention management strategies were proposed, e.g., by Scherer and Scott [2004, 2005] and Guerraoui et al. [2005a,b,c].

The first TM implementation that used a multi-version scheme was JVSTM [Cachopo and Rito-Silva, 2005].

Harris et al. [2010] give in their book a fairly comprehensive overview of the TM literature. They focus on practical aspects, and, in particular, on TM implementations.

PART II

Safety

CHAPTER 7

Opacity

In this chapter, we define opacity—a correctness condition for TMs that captures the intuitive requirements described in Chapter 4. We first give a step-by-step introduction to opacity, then we give its formal definition, and, finally, we illustrate it with a few examples. In Chapter 8, we show how to prove that a TM implementation indeed ensures opacity, using, as an example, the two TM algorithms introduced in Chapter 5. In Chapter 9, we compare opacity to the classical atomicity property of database transactions and prove that the difference here is fundamental—ensuring opacity can be inherently more expensive than ensuring traditional (database) atomicity.

7.1 OPACITY STEP BY STEP

To help understand the definition of opacity, we first illustrate it using very simple TM histories, and then we increase the complexity of those histories step by step. The precise definitions of the terms that correspond to the steps described here are given in the following section.

Opacity is simple to express and verify for sequential TM histories in which every transaction, except possibly the last one, is committed. Basically, if S is such a history, then S is considered correct, and called *legal*, if, for every t-object x, the sub-history $S|x$ respects the semantics of x, i.e., $S|x$ conforms to the sequential specification of x. For example, in the TM history S shown in Figure 7.1a, transaction T_1 writes value 1 to t-variable x. Then, all subsequent reads of x in S, performed by T_1 or by a following transaction (e.g., T_2), until the next write of x, return value 1.

The situation becomes more difficult if S is sequential but contains some aborted transactions followed by other transactions. This is indeed very common in real TM executions. For example, in TM history S shown in Figure 7.1b, aborted transaction T_2 writes value 1 to t-variable x (and no other transaction writes 1 to x). Then, only T_2 can read 1 from x thereafter. A read operation on x executed by transaction T_3 that follows T_2 returns the last value written to x by the latest preceding *committed* transaction (T_1 in our example).

In general, when considering a transaction T_i (committed or aborted) in a sequential TM history S, we have to remove all aborted transactions that precede T_i in S. We then say that T_i is *legal* in S if T_i, together with all committed transactions preceding T_i in S, form a legal history. For an arbitrary sequential TM history S to be correct, all transactions in S must be legal.

To determine the correctness of an arbitrary TM history H, we ask whether H "looks like" some sequential TM history S that is correct (i.e., in which every transaction is legal). More precisely, history S should contain the same transactions, performing the same operations and receiving the same return values from those operations, as history H. We say then that H is *equivalent* to S. Equivalent TM histories differ only in the relative position of events of *different* transactions. Sequential history S should also preserve the real-time order of transactions in H. That is, if a transaction T_i precedes a transaction T_k in H, then T_i must also precede T_k in S. We call S a *witness history* of H. For instance, TM history H, shown in Figure 7.1c, is equivalent to sequential TM history S in Figure 7.1b. The real-time order of transactions in H is preserved in S: in both histories, transaction T_1 precedes transaction T_3.

There is, however, one problem with finding a sequential history that is equivalent to a given TM history H: if two or more transactions are live in H, then there is no sequential history that is equivalent to H. Basically, if S is a sequential TM history, then $\prec_S$ must be a total order; however, if a transaction T_i precedes a transaction T_k in S, i.e., if $T_i \prec_S T_k$, then T_i must be committed or aborted. To solve the problem, observe the following, assuming that T_i is any live transaction in some TM history H:

1. Until transaction T_i invokes operation $tryC(T_i)$ in history H, it is undecided whether T_i wants to commit. Indeed, T_i may be about to invoke operation $tryA(T_i)$ instead of $tryC(T_i)$, in which case no operation of T_i may be visible to other transactions. Hence, the semantics of a live transaction that is not commit-pending is effectively the same as of an aborted transaction.

2. If transaction T_i invokes operation $tryC(T_i)$ in history H, but this operation is still pending in H, then it is uncertain what the response from this operation will be: C_i or A_i. However, the implementation of operation $tryC(T_i)$ might have already reached a point at which it is decided that T_i will commit. Then, T_i is effectively committed, and its operations may be visible to other transactions. This point is not directly visible in TM history H because a history shows only what happens at the public interface of a shared object. Hence, the semantics of a commit-pending transaction may be the same as either the semantics of a committed transaction or the semantics of an aborted transaction.

Therefore, we can safely transform an arbitrary TM history H into a *complete* TM history H' by aborting every live and non-commit-pending transaction in H, and either aborting or committing every commit-pending transaction in H.

For example, in TM history H depicted in Figure 7.1d, transactions T_2 and T_3 are both live (but only T_3 is commit-pending). Hence, before finding a sequential history that "looks like" H, we can, for instance, abort transaction T_2 and commit transaction T_3, obtaining the TM history depicted in Figure 7.1c. Alternatively, we can abort both T_2 and T_3.

7.2 DEFINITION OF OPACITY

In this section, we first give precise definitions of the terms that we explained intuitively in the previous section. The definition of opacity is split, for simplicity, into two parts. First, we define *final-state opacity*. This property captures the essence of opacity, but it is not a safety property: it is possible for a final-state opaque TM history to have a prefix that violates final-state opacity. Second,

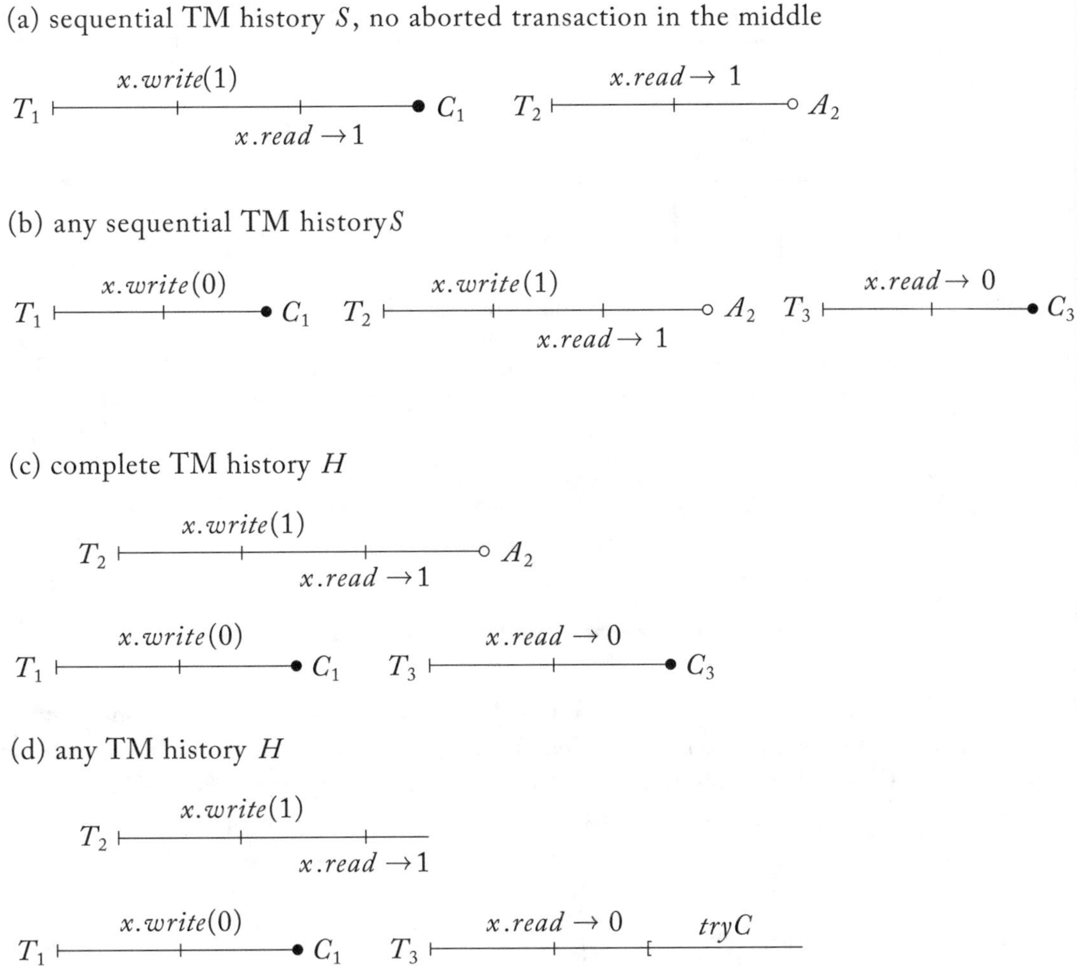

(a) sequential TM history S, no aborted transaction in the middle

$$T_1 \vdash\!\!\!\begin{array}{c} x.write(1) \\ \overline{} \\ x.read \to 1 \end{array}\!\!\!\bullet C_1 \qquad T_2 \vdash\!\!\!\begin{array}{c} x.read \to 1 \\ \overline{} \end{array}\!\!\!\circ A_2$$

(b) any sequential TM history S

$$T_1 \vdash\!\!\!\begin{array}{c} x.write(0) \\ \overline{} \end{array}\!\!\!\bullet C_1 \quad T_2 \vdash\!\!\!\begin{array}{c} x.write(1) \\ \overline{} \\ x.read \to 1 \end{array}\!\!\!\circ A_2 \quad T_3 \vdash\!\!\!\begin{array}{c} x.read \to 0 \\ \overline{} \end{array}\!\!\!\bullet C_3$$

(c) complete TM history H

$$T_2 \vdash\!\!\!\begin{array}{c} x.write(1) \\ \overline{} \\ x.read \to 1 \end{array}\!\!\!\circ A_2$$

$$T_1 \vdash\!\!\!\begin{array}{c} x.write(0) \\ \overline{} \end{array}\!\!\!\bullet C_1 \quad T_3 \vdash\!\!\!\begin{array}{c} x.read \to 0 \\ \overline{} \end{array}\!\!\!\bullet C_3$$

(d) any TM history H

$$T_2 \vdash\!\!\!\begin{array}{c} x.write(1) \\ \overline{} \\ x.read \to 1 \end{array}$$

$$T_1 \vdash\!\!\!\begin{array}{c} x.write(0) \\ \overline{} \end{array}\!\!\!\bullet C_1 \quad T_3 \vdash\!\!\!\begin{array}{c} x.read \to 0 \quad tryC \\ \overline{} \end{array}$$

Figure 7.1: An illustration of the four different kinds of histories considered in the step-by-step introduction to opacity (Section 7.1)

we say that a TM history is opaque if all its prefixes are final-state opaque. We show that, when proving correctness of TM implementations, it is sufficient to focus on final-state opacity, which is simpler than opacity.

Let S be any sequential TM history such that every transaction in S, except possibly the last one, is committed. We say that S is *legal* if, for every t-object x, the sequence $S|x$ is in set $Seq_S(x)$ (the sequential specification of x in S).

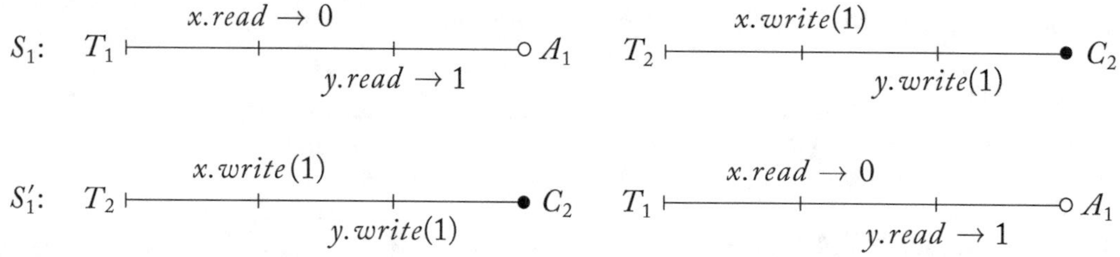

Figure 7.2: Sequential histories S_1 and S_1' (x and y are t-variables)

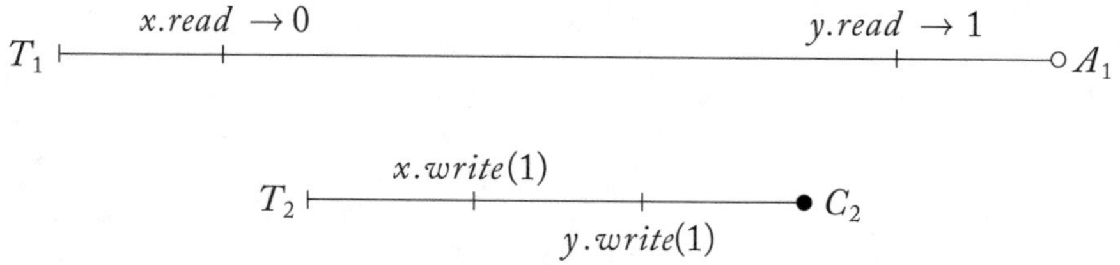

Figure 7.3: TM history H_1 that violates opacity (assuming x and y are t-variables)

Let S be any complete sequential TM history. We denote by $visible_S(T_i)$ the longest subsequence S' of S such that, for every transaction T_k in S', either (1) $k = i$, or (2) T_k is committed and $T_k \prec_S T_i$. We say that a transaction T_i in S is *legal in S*, if TM history $visible_S(T_i)$ is legal. For example, consider (sequential, complete) histories S_1 and S_1' depicted in Figure 7.2. Then:

$$
\begin{aligned}
visible_{S_1}(T_1) &= S_1|T_1 \\
&= \langle x.read_1 \rightarrow 0,\ y.read_1 \rightarrow 1,\ A_1 \rangle, \\
visible_{S_1}(T_2) &= S_1|T_2 \\
&= \langle x.write(1)_2,\ y.write(1)_2,\ C_2 \rangle, \\
visible_{S_1'}(T_1) &= S_1', \text{ and} \\
visible_{S_1'}(T_2) &= S_1'|T_2 \\
&= visible_{S_1}(T_2).
\end{aligned}
$$

History $visible_{S_1}(T_2)$ (and so also the equal history $visible_{S_1'}(T_2)$) is legal because:

$$
\begin{aligned}
visible_{S_1}(T_2)|x &= \langle write(1) \rangle \in Seq_{S_1}(x), \text{ and} \\
visible_{S_1}(T_2)|y &= \langle write(1) \rangle \in Seq_{S_1}(y).
\end{aligned}
$$

Hence, transaction T_2 is legal in history S_1 (and in S_1'). However, histories $visible_{S_1}(T_1)$ and $visible_{S_1'}(T_1)$ are not legal (assuming the initial value of x and y is 0) because:

$$
visible_{S_1}(T_1)|y = \langle read \rightarrow 1 \rangle \notin Seq_{S_1}(y), \text{ and}
$$

$$visible_{S_1'}(T_1)|x = \langle write(1),\ read \to 0 \rangle \quad \notin \quad Seq_{S_1'}(x).$$

Hence, transaction T_1 is not legal in S_1 and in S_1'.

We say that TM histories H and H' are *equivalent*, and we write $H \equiv H'$, if, for every transaction $T_i \in Trans$, $H|T_i = H'|T_i$. We say that a TM history H' *preserves the real-time order* of a TM history H if $\prec_H \subseteq \prec_{H'}$. That is, if $T_i \prec_H T_j$, then $T_i \prec_{H'} T_j$, for all transactions T_i and T_j in H. For example, TM histories S_1 and S_1' (Figure 7.2) are both equivalent to TM history H_1 depicted in Figure 7.3, and both preserve (trivially) the real-time order of H_1 (since $\prec_{H_1} = \emptyset$).

Intuitively, a *completion* of a finite TM history H is any TM history H' obtained from H by (1) aborting every live and non-commit-pending transaction in H and (2) aborting or committing every commit-pending transaction in H. More formally, a completion of H is any (well-formed) complete TM history H' such that (a) H is a prefix of H', and (b) for every transaction T_i in H, sub-history $H'|T_i$ is equal to one of the following histories:

1. $H|T_i$ (when T_i is completed),

2. $H|T_i \cdot \langle tryA(T_i) \to A_i \rangle$ (when T_1 is live and there is no pending operation in $H|T_i$),

3. $H|T_i \cdot \langle ret(A_i) \rangle$ (only when T_i is live and there is a pending operation in $H|T_i$), or

4. $H|T_i \cdot \langle ret(C_i) \rangle$ (only when T_i is commit-pending).

(Note that cases 3 and 4 partially overlap: if T_i is commit-pending, then either of those cases can be applied.) For example, possible completions of TM history H depicted in Figure 7.1d include the history in Figure 7.1c and history $H \cdot \langle tryA(T_2) \to A_2,\ ret(A_3) \rangle$.

Definition 7.1 (Final-state opacity).   A finite TM history H is *final-state opaque* if there exists a sequential TM history S equivalent to any completion of H, such that (1) S preserves the real-time order of H, and (2) every transaction T_i in S is legal in S. The sequential history S in the above definition is called a *witness history* of TM history H.

Definition 7.2 (Opacity).   A TM history H is *opaque* if every finite prefix of H (including H itself if H is finite) is final-state opaque.

Definition 7.3 (Opacity of a TM).   A TM object M is *opaque* if every history of M is opaque.

Since the set of histories of every object is prefix-closed, by Definition 7.2 and Definition 7.3, we immediately obtain the following result:

Observation 7.4 (Opacity of a TM)   A TM object M is opaque if, and only if, every finite history of M is final-state opaque.

Note 7.5   Final-state opacity is not a safety property. That is, the set of TM histories that are final-state opaque is not prefix-closed. For example, while the following TM history is final-state opaque:

$$H = \langle x.write(1)_1, \; x.read_2 \rightarrow 1, \; C_1, \; C_2 \rangle,$$

the prefix

$$H' = \langle x.write(1)_1, \; x.read_2 \rightarrow 1 \rangle$$

of H is not final-state opaque (assuming x is a t-variable with the initial value 0) because, in H', transaction T_2 reads a value written by transaction T_1 that is neither committed nor commit-pending. Opacity, however, is a safety property.

Note 7.6   The way we define the real-time ordering between transactions introduces a subtlety to the definition of opacity. Basically, the following situation is possible (and considered correct): a transaction T_1 updates some t-object x and then some other transaction T_2 concurrent to T_1 observes an old state of x (from before the update of T_1) even after T_1 commits. For example, consider the following TM history H_2 illustrated in Figure 7.4 (x and y are t-variables):

$$H_2 \;=\; \langle x.read_1 \rightarrow 0, \; x.write(5)_2, \; y.write(5)_2, \; C_2, \; y.read_3 \rightarrow 5, \; y.read_1 \rightarrow 0 \rangle.$$

In history H_2, transaction T_1 appears to happen before T_2 because T_1 reads the initial values of t-variables x and y that are modified by T_2. Transaction T_3, on the other hand, appears to happen after T_2 because it reads the value of y written by T_2. It is straightforward to verify that the sequential history

$$\begin{aligned} S_2 \;=\; \langle &x.read_1 \rightarrow 0, \; y.read_1 \rightarrow 0, \; A_1, \\ &x.write(5)_2, \; y.write(5)_2, \; C_2, \\ &y.read_3(5), \; A_3 \rangle \end{aligned}$$

is equivalent to the completion $H_2 \cdot \langle A_1, A_3 \rangle$ of H_2 and preserves the real-time order of H_2. As every transaction is legal in S_2, history H_2 is final-state opaque. In fact, H_2 is also opaque.

However, at first, it may seem wrong for the *read* operation of transaction T_3 to return the value written to y by the committed transaction T_2, while the following *read* operation, by transaction T_1, returns the old value of y. But if T_1 read value 5 from y, then opacity would be violated. This is because T_1 would observe an inconsistent state of the system: $x = 0$ and $y = 5$. Thus, letting T_1 read 0 from y is the only way to prevent T_1 from being aborted without violating opacity. Multi-version TMs, like JVSTM and LSA-STM, indeed use such optimizations to allow long read-only transactions to commit despite concurrent updates performed by other transactions. In general, it seems that forcing the order between operation executions of different transactions to be preserved, in addition to the real-time order of transactions themselves, would be too strong a requirement.

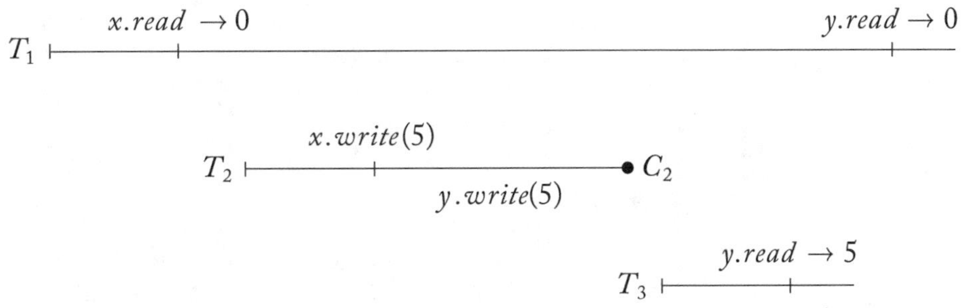

$$x.read \rightarrow 0 \qquad\qquad\qquad\qquad\qquad\qquad\qquad\qquad y.read \rightarrow 0$$
$$T_1 \;\vdash\!\!\!-\!\!\!-\!\!\!+\!\!\!-\!\!\!-\!\!\!-\!\!\!-\!\!\!-\!\!\!-\!\!\!-\!\!\!-\!\!\!-\!\!\!-\!\!\!-\!\!\!-\!\!\!-\!\!\!-\!\!\!-\!\!\!+\!\!\!-\!\!\!-$$

$$x.write(5)$$
$$T_2 \;\vdash\!\!\!-\!\!\!-\!\!\!+\!\!\!-\!\!\!-\!\!\!-\!\!\!-\!\!\!-\!\!\!\bullet\, C_2$$
$$y.write(5)$$

$$y.read \rightarrow 5$$
$$T_3 \;\vdash\!\!\!-\!\!\!-\!\!\!+\!\!\!-\!\!\!-$$

Figure 7.4: An opaque history H_2

7.3 EXAMPLES

To illustrate the definition of (final-state) opacity, we explain here why TM histories H_3 (in Figure 7.5) and H_4 (in Figure 7.6) are opaque, and why TM history H_1 (in Figure 7.3) violates opacity.

Example 7.7 (TM history H_3) In TM history H_3 depicted in Figure 7.5, transaction T_2 precedes transaction T_3, i.e., $T_2 \prec_{H_3} T_3$, while transaction T_1 is concurrent with T_2 and T_3. Transaction T_1 reads the value of t-variable x written by T_2, and not the initial value of x or the value written to x by T_3. Hence, T_1 should appear as if it was executed between T_2 and T_3. Consider then the following sequential history S_3 that is equivalent to H_3 and preserves the real-time order of H_3:

$$S_3 = H_3|T_2 \cdot H_3|T_1 \cdot H_3|T_3.$$

Transactions T_1, T_2, and T_3 are legal in S_3 because:

$$
\begin{aligned}
visible_{S_3}(T_2)|x = \langle write(2) \rangle &\in Seq_{S_3}(x), \\
visible_{S_3}(T_2)|y = \langle write(2) \rangle &\in Seq_{S_3}(y), \\
visible_{S_3}(T_1)|x = \langle write(2),\ read \rightarrow 2 \rangle &\in Seq_{S_3}(x), \\
visible_{S_3}(T_1)|y = \langle write(2),\ write(1) \rangle &\in Seq_{S_3}(y), \\
visible_{S_3}(T_3)|x = \langle write(2),\ write(3) \rangle &\in Seq_{S_3}(x), \text{ and} \\
visible_{S_3}(T_3)|y = \langle write(2),\ read \rightarrow 2 \rangle &\in Seq_{S_3}(y).
\end{aligned}
$$

Therefore, history H_3 is final-state opaque. Analogously, we can prove that every prefix of H_3 is final-state opaque, thus showing that H_3 is opaque.

Example 7.8 (TM history H_4) In TM history H_4 depicted in Figure 7.6, transactions T_1 and T_2 precede transaction T_4, while other pairs of transactions are concurrent, i.e., $\prec_{H_4} = \{(T_1, T_4), (T_2, T_4)\}$. Transaction T_3 reads value 1 from counter t-object c, and so T_3 should appear as if it was executed either just after T_1 and before T_2, or just after T_2 and before T_1, because both T_1 and T_2

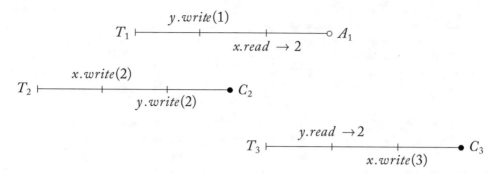

Figure 7.5: An opaque TM history H_3 (x and y are t-variables)

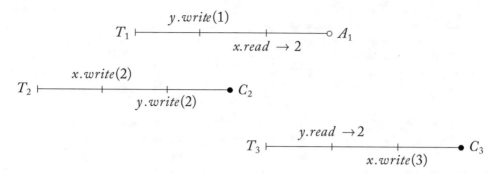

Figure 7.6: An opaque TM history H_4 (x and y are t-variables, c is a counter t-object initialized to 0, and s is a stack t-object that is initially empty; for clarity, operation *init* is omitted)

increment c (initialized to 0). However, T_3 pops from stack t-object s value a, which is pushed to s by T_1. Hence, T_3 must have been logically executed after T_1 and before T_2. Consider the following sequential history S_4 that is equivalent to H_4 and preserves the real-time order of H_4:

$$S_4 = H_4|T_1 \cdot H_4|T_3 \cdot H_4|T_2 \cdot H_4|T_4.$$

It is easy to verify that every transaction is legal in S_4. For example, T_4 is legal in S_4 because of the following:

$$
\begin{aligned}
visibles_{S_4}(T_4)|c &= \langle inc,\ inc,\ read \rightarrow 2 \rangle \in Seq_{S_4}(c), \\
visibles_{S_4}(T_4)|s &= \langle push(a),\ push(b),\ pop \rightarrow b \rangle \in Seq_{S_4}(s),\ \text{and} \\
visibles_{S_4}(T_4)|x &= \langle write(1),\ write(2),\ read \rightarrow 2 \rangle \in Seq_{S_4}(x).
\end{aligned}
$$

Hence, history H_4 is final-state opaque. Analogously, we can prove that every prefix of H_4 is final-state opaque, thus showing that H_4 is opaque.

It is worth noting here that opacity does not preclude transactions T_1 and T_2 from committing concurrently, even though both of them modify the same t-objects c, s, and x. What is important is for transactions T_3 and T_4 to observe consistent states. For example, if T_4 pops value a from stack s, then T_4 must read value 1 from t-variable x. Hence, a TM might allow conflicting transactions to proceed concurrently, thus providing higher parallelism, as long as the TM ensures that updates to all t-objects are applied (logically) in the same global order.

Example 7.9 (TM history H_1)   The only two sequential TM histories that are equivalent to TM history H_1 of Figure 7.3 (and preserve the real-time order of H_1) are histories S_1 and S_1' depicted in Figure 7.2. However, we have already shown, in Section 7.2, that transaction T_1 is not legal in S_1 and in S_1'. Hence, H_1 is not final-state opaque (nor opaque).

CHAPTER 8

Proving Opacity: An Example

In this chapter, we illustrate how one can prove opacity of a given TM implementation. We do so by proving that the two TM algorithms introduced in Chapter 5 indeed ensure opacity. Later, in Chapter 13, we use a similar proof technique to argue the correctness of one of the obstruction-free TM algorithms presented there.

To simplify the proofs, we first introduce a *graph characterization* of opacity. We show how to build a graph G that represents the causal dependencies between transactions in a given TM history H. In such a graph G, transactions are vertices and the causal relations between them are edges. We prove that history H is final-state opaque if, and only if, its corresponding graph G is *acyclic*.

The graph characterization of opacity applies to TM histories that satisfy the following three conditions. First, since the TM algorithms that we present in this book provide only t-variables (they do not support operation *init*), for simplicity, we consider only those TM histories in which all t-objects are t-variables. That is, we focus only on *read* and *write* operations.

Second, the very construction of a dependency graph requires that every time a transaction T_i reads some value v from some t-variable x (in a TM history H), we can uniquely determine the transaction that wrote the version of x read by T_i. This can be a problem if more than one transaction writes the same value v to x, in which case the construction of the dependency graph becomes ambiguous. We thus consider only those TM histories that have *unique writes*, i.e., in which no two transactions write the same value to the same t-variable. Obviously, not all TM histories have unique writes; we explain, however, how to deal with this requirement in the general case.

Third, the theorem stating that a TM history H is final-state opaque if, and only if, its graph is acyclic, requires H to be *consistent*. Consistency captures some very basic requirements that have to be satisfied by every opaque TM history, and that would be difficult to express as graph properties. Intuitively, consistency means that every time a transaction T_i reads a t-variable x, T_i is returned either the latest value that T_i wrote to x before, or any value written to x by any other transaction that is committed or commit-pending. Proving opacity of a TM algorithm first requires showing that all of its histories are indeed consistent.

In the following sections, we first define some terms that are used within this chapter (Section 8.1). Then, we introduce the graph characterization of opacity (Section 8.2). Finally, in Sections 8.3 and 8.4, we prove the opacity of the 2-phase locking TM algorithm $\mathcal{A}_{2PL}$ presented in Section 5.1.2, as well as of the improved TM algorithm $\mathcal{A}_{IR}$ presented in Section 5.2.

8.1   PRELIMINARIES

We assume in this chapter that t-variables are the only t-objects accessed by transactions in any TM history. That is, we consider t-objects that have only *read* and *write* operations.

Let H be any TM history, T_i be any transaction in H, and x be any t-variable. Recall that when T_i invokes operation *read* or *write* on x, then we say that T_i, respectively, reads or writes x. We also say that T_i *reads value* v from x when T_i returns from operation $x.read \rightarrow v$, and we say that T_i *writes value* v to x when T_i invokes operation $x.write(v)$.

Let T_i and T_k be any two different transactions in some TM history H, and let x be any t-variable. We say that transaction T_k *reads t-variable* x *from* transaction T_i in H, if T_i writes some value v to x and T_k reads v from x (in H). We say that T_k *reads from* T_i if T_k reads some t-variable from T_i.

To avoid dealing with the initial values of t-variables separately from the values written to those t-variables by transactions, we introduce a "virtual" committed initializing transaction T_0. We say that T_0 writes value 0 to every t-variable (in every TM history). Also, whenever a transaction T_i reads value 0 from any t-variable x, we say that T_i reads x from T_0.

Let H be any TM history. We say that H has *unique writes* if, for every t-variable x and value v, at most one transaction writes v to x, and no transaction writes v to x twice. That is, intuitively, every *write* operation on x writes a different value. Note that, since T_0 writes value 0 to every t-variable, no other transaction can write 0 to any t-variable.

We divide all operations, executed by any transaction T_i in H, into *local* and *non-local* ones. Intuitively, local *write* operations of T_i are visible only to T_i, even if T_i commits, and local *read* operations of T_i return values that were previously written by T_i. More precisely, an operation $x.read_i \rightarrow v$, executed by a transaction T_i in H, is said to be local if it is preceded in sub-history $H|T_i$ by any *write* operation on x. An operation $x.write(v)_i$, executed by T_i in H, is said to be local if it is followed in $H|T_i$ by an invocation of any *write* operation on x. We denote by $nonlocal(H)$ the history obtained from H by removing all events of operations that are local in H.

For example, consider the following (sequential) TM history H, containing events of only transaction T_1:

$$H \;=\; \langle x.read_1 \rightarrow 0, \; x.write(1)_1, \; x.read_1 \rightarrow 1, \; x.write(2)_1, \; y.write(1)_1 \rangle.$$

In H, operation $x.write(1)$ is local because it is followed, in $H|T_1$, by operation $x.write(2)$. Operation $x.read \rightarrow 1$ is also local because it follows operation $x.write(1)$. The other three operations of T_1 are all non-local. Hence,

$$nonlocal(H) = \langle x.read_1 \rightarrow 0, \; x.write(2)_1, \; y.write(1)_1 \rangle.$$

Let H be any TM history, and e be any operation $x.read \rightarrow v$ in $H|T_i$, where T_i is any transaction, x is any t-variable, and v is any value different than A_i. We say that operation e is *consistent* if the following conditions are satisfied:

1. If e is local, then the latest *write* operation on x preceding e in $H|T_i$ is $x.write(v)$; and

2. If e is non-local, then either (a) $v = 0$, or (b) there is a non-local operation $x.write(v)$ in $H|T_k$, where T_k is some committed or commit-pending transaction different than T_i.

We say that TM history H is *consistent* if every *read* operation in $H|T_i$, for every transaction T_i in H, is consistent. It is straightforward to see that every final-state opaque TM history is consistent.

8.2 A GRAPH CHARACTERIZATION OF OPACITY

We introduce now the graph characterization of opacity that we use for proving the correctness of TM algorithms. We first show how to build a graph representing the dependencies between transactions in a given TM history. Then, we prove (Theorem 8.2) that a consistent TM history H that has unique writes is final-state opaque if, and only if, its corresponding graph is acyclic.

We also introduce here Lemma 8.3 that helps deal with TM histories that do not have unique writes. This result formalizes the intuition that if a control flow of a TM algorithm is independent of the values written to t-variables, and the algorithm ensures opacity when writes are unique, then the algorithm should also ensure opacity when writes are not unique.

Let H be any TM history and x be any t-variable. Every transaction that writes to x in H creates a *version* of x. Because transactions may write to x concurrently, determining the order of those versions in H is not obvious. However, this order can be usually determined in an *implementation* history of a given TM algorithm. When building a graph representing the dependencies between transactions in H, we thus assume that the order of versions of x in H is known.

A *version order* of a t-variable x in a TM history H is thus any total order $\ll_x$ on the set of transactions in H that are the following:

- are committed or commit-pending, and

- write to x,

such that T_0 is the least element according to $\ll_x$. A *version order function* in H is any function that maps every t-variable x to a version order of x in H.

Let H be any TM history (with unique writes). Let $V_\ll$ be any version order function in H. Denote $V_\ll(x)$ by $\ll_x$. We define $OPG(H, V_\ll)$ to be the directed, labelled graph constructed in the following way:

1. For every transaction T_i in H (including T_0) there is a vertex T_i in graph $OPG(H, V_\ll)$. Vertex T_i is labelled as follows: *vis* if T_i is committed in H or if some transaction reads from T_i in H, and *loc*, otherwise.

2. For all vertices T_i and T_k in graph $OPG(H, V_\ll), i \neq k$, there is an edge from T_i to T_k (denoted by $T_i \longrightarrow T_k$) in any of the following cases:

(a) If $T_i \prec_H T_k$ (i.e., T_i precedes T_k in H); then the edge is labelled rt (from "real-time") and denoted $T_i \xrightarrow{rt} T_k$;

(b) If T_k reads from T_i; then the edge is labelled rf and denoted $T_i \xrightarrow{rf} T_k$;

(c) If, for some t-variable x, $T_i \ll_x T_k$; then the edge is labelled ww (from "write before write") and denoted $T_i \xrightarrow{ww} T_k$;

(d) If vertex T_k is labelled vis in G, and there is a transaction T_m in H and a t-variable x, such that: (a) $T_m \ll_x T_k$, and (b) T_i reads x from T_m; then the edge is labelled rw (from "read before write") and denoted $T_i \xrightarrow{rw} T_k$.

Example 8.1   Consider the following TM history H depicted in Figure 8.1a:

$$H = \langle x.write(1)_1, \ x.read_3 \to 0, \ C_1,$$
$$x.read_2 \to 1, \ x.write(3)_3, \ A_3 \rangle.$$

Let $V_\ll$ be any version order function such that $V_\ll(x) = \{(T_0, T_1)\}$. Graph $OPG\left(H, V_\ll\right)$ is shown in Figure 8.1b.

Theorem 8.2   (Graph characterization of opacity).   *A consistent TM history H that has unique writes is final-state opaque if, and only if, there exists a version order function $V_\ll$ in H such that graph $OPG\left(H, V_\ll\right)$ is acyclic.*

Proof. ($\Rightarrow$) Let H be any final-state opaque TM history that has unique writes. By final-state opacity, there exists a sequential history S equivalent to some completion of H, such that S preserves the real-time order of H and every transaction T_i in S is legal in S. For every t-variable x, let $\ll_x$ denote the following version order of x in H: for all transactions T_i and T_k in H that are committed or commit-pending and that write to x, if $T_i \prec_S T_k$ or $i = 0$, then $T_i \ll_x T_k$. Let $V_\ll$ be the version order function in H such that, for every t-variable x, $V_\ll(x) = \ll_x$. We show in the following that graph $G = OPG\left(H, V_\ll\right)$ is acyclic.

Assume, by contradiction, that graph G contains a cycle. Because relation $\prec_S$ is a total order on the set of transactions in H, there must be some transactions T_i and T_k such that there is an edge $T_i \longrightarrow T_k$ in G, and either $k = 0$ or $T_k \prec_S T_i$. Since T_0 is the least element according to total order $\ll_x$, for every t-variable x, it cannot be that $k = 0$. We thus assume that $k \neq 0$ and consider four cases, corresponding to the four possible types of edges, in each case showing a contradiction.

Case 1: $T_i \xrightarrow{rt} T_k$ This means that $T_i \prec_H T_k$. But then, because history S preserves the real-time order of H, $T_i \prec_S T_k$—a contradiction with the assumption that $T_k \prec_S T_i$.

(a)

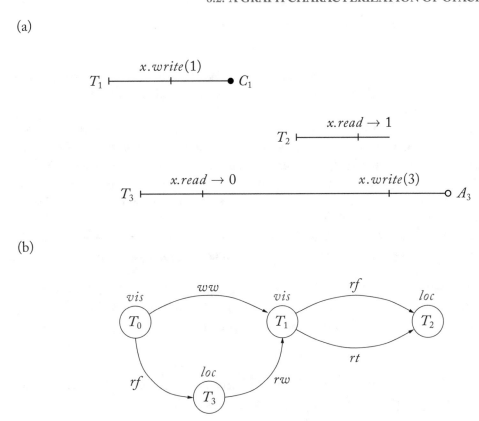

(b)

Figure 8.1: A TM history H and a graph $OPG\left(H, V_{\ll}\right)$, where $V_{\ll}(x) = \{(T_0, T_1)\}$

Case 2: $T_i \xrightarrow{\text{rf}} T_k$ This means that there is a t-variable x, such that T_i writes some value v to x and T_k reads v from x. Because $T_k \prec_S T_i$, and since H has unique writes, $v \neq 0$ and history $S_k = visible_S(T_k)$ does not contain transaction T_i. Hence, since H has unique writes, S_k is not legal. Indeed, in S_k, transaction T_k reads value $v \neq 0$ from t-variable x and no transaction writes value v to x. Therefore, T_i is not legal in S—a contradiction with the assumption that every transaction in S is legal.

Case 3: $T_i \xrightarrow{\text{ww}} T_k$ This means that $T_i \ll_x T_k$ for some t-variable x. But then, by the definition of version order $\ll_x$, $T_i \prec_S T_k$, contradicting the assumption that $T_k \prec_S T_i$.

Case 4: $T_i \xrightarrow{\text{rw}} T_k$ This means that vertex T_k of graph G is labelled vis, and there is a transaction T_m and some t-variable x, such that (a) $T_m \ll_x T_k$, and (b) T_i reads x from T_m. Then, by the definition of version order $\ll_x$ and by our assumption that $T_k \prec_S T_i$, we have:

$$T_m \prec_S T_k \prec_S T_i$$

(or $T_m \ll_x T_k \prec_S T_i$ if $m = 0$), where T_m writes some value v to t-variable x, T_k writes some value v' to x, and T_i reads v from x. Since H has unique writes, $v' \neq v$. Because $T_m \ll_x T_k$, $k \neq 0$.

Consider history $S_i = visible_S(T_i)$. For S_i to be legal, transaction T_k cannot be in S_i, i.e., T_k has to be aborted in S, and so T_k cannot be committed in H. Then, because vertex T_k of graph G is labelled vis, there must be some transaction T_q in H, $q \neq k$, that reads some t-variable y from T_k. Consider history $S_q = visible_S(T_q)$. Because T_k is aborted in S, T_k is not in S_q. In S_q, transaction T_q reads from t-variable y some value different than 0 that is, since H has unique writes, written to y only by T_k (which is not in S_q). Therefore, history S_q is not legal, and so T_q is not legal in S—a contradiction with the assumption that every transaction in S is legal.

($\Leftarrow$) Let H be any consistent TM history that has unique writes. Assume that there is a version order function $V_{\ll}$ such that graph $G = OPG(H, V_{\ll})$ is acyclic. We show that H must be final-state opaque.

Let sequence $T_{s_1}, T_{s_2}, \ldots$ be the result of a topological sort of graph G. Let H_c be any completion of history H, such that every commit-pending transaction T_i in H is (a) committed in H_c if vertex T_i is labelled vis in G, and (b) aborted in H_c, otherwise. Consider the sequential history

$$S = H_c|T_{s_1} \cdot H_c|T_{s_2} \cdot \ldots.$$

Note that history S is equivalent to H_c, and S preserves the real-time order of H (because of the $\xrightarrow{rt}$ edges in graph G and by the properties of a topological sort).

Assume, by contradiction, that there is a transaction $T_i \in S$ that is not legal in S. That is, history $S_i = visible_S(T_i)$ is not legal. Hence, T_i executes an operation $e_{rd} = x.read \to v$ in S_i, where x is some t-variable and v is some value, but either (a) the latest $write$ operation on x preceding e_{rd} in S_i is $e_{wr} = x.write(v')$ where $v' \neq v$, or (b) $v \neq 0$, and there is no $write$ operation on x preceding e_{rd} in S_i.

Observe that operation e_{rd} of T_i must be non-local, as, otherwise, history H would not be consistent. Hence, since H is consistent, there is a committed or commit-pending transaction T_m in H, $m \neq i$, such that T_m writes value v to x. Since H has unique writes, there is exactly one such a transaction. Because T_i reads x from T_m, vertex T_m in G is labelled vis, and there is an edge $T_m \xrightarrow{rf} T_i$ in G.

Since vertex T_m in G is labelled vis, and since transaction T_m is committed or commit-pending in H, T_m is committed in history H_c, and so T_m is also committed in sequential history S. Because $T_m \xrightarrow{rf} T_i$, and by the properties of a topological sort, $T_m \prec_S T_i$. Therefore, T_m is in history S_i. Then, since T_m writes to x, either $v = 0$ (and T_m is the "virtual" transaction T_0) or some $write$ operation on x (e.g., of T_m) precedes e_{rd} of T_i in S_i. We can thus exclude case (b) above.

Let T_k be the transaction that executes operation e_{wr}. Since operation e_{rd} of T_i is non-local, e_{wr} must also be non-local, and T_k must be a different transaction than T_i. Also, since T_k is in history S_i, T_k must be committed in history H_c. Hence, T_k is committed or commit-pending in H and vertex T_k in G is labelled *vis*.

Because e_{wr} is the latest *write* operation on t-variable x that precedes e_{rd} in history S_i, and since T_m writes to x in S_i, it must be that $T_m \prec_S T_k$. Since both T_m and T_k are committed or commit-pending in H, and both transactions write to x, T_m and T_k are ordered by relation $\ll_x = V_\ll(x)$, and so there is an edge labelled ww between vertices T_m and T_k in G. Since $T_m \prec_S T_k$, and by the properties of a topological sort, the edge is $T_m \xrightarrow{ww} T_k$. Therefore, $T_m \ll_x T_k$.

Since vertex T_k is labelled *vis* in G, $T_m \ll_x T_k$, and T_i reads x from T_m, there is an edge $T_i \xrightarrow{rw} T_k$ in G. Hence, by the properties of a topological sort, $T_i \prec_S T_k$. But then, transaction T_k cannot be in history S_i. Hence, contrary to our assumption, operation e_{wr} of T_k cannot precede in S_i operation e_{rd} of T_i. □

Recall from Section 3.1.2 that the domain of the (default) t-variables, i.e., the set of values that can be written to each t-variable, is the set $\mathbb{N}$ of natural numbers. Let F be any function on set $\mathbb{N}$, and let H be any TM history. Intuitively, we denote by $F(H)$ a TM history obtained from H by replacing every value $v \neq 0$ read from or written to any t-variable by value $F(v)$. That is, $F(H)$ is a history obtained from H by replacing every event $inv_i(x.write(v))$ with event $inv_i(x.write(F(v)))$, and every operation $x.read_i \to v$ with operation $x.read_i \to F(v)$, for every t-variable x, transaction T_i, and value $v \neq 0$.

We prove now the following lemma, which helps us, in the following sections, dealing with histories that do not have unique writes.

Lemma 8.3   (Unique writes)   *If H is any final-state opaque TM history, and F is any function on set $\mathbb{N}$, then history $F(H)$ is also final-state opaque.*

Proof. Because history H is final-state opaque, there exists a sequential history S equivalent to some completion H' of H, such that S preserves the real-time order of H and every transaction in S is legal. Let T_i be any transaction in H. Denote by S_i the history $visible_S(T_i)$. By final-state opacity of history H, sequential history S_i must be legal.

Consider sequential history $F(S)$. Clearly, $F(S)$ is equivalent to history $F(H')$ that is a completion of $F(H)$, and $F(S)$ preserves the real-time order of $F(H)$ (which is the same as the real-time order of H). In history $F(S_i)$, every operation $x.read \to v$ of S_i, where $v \neq 0$, becomes $x.read \to F(v)$ if $v \neq 0$, and every operation $x.write(v)$ becomes $x.write(F(v))$. Hence, it is straightforward to see that also $F(S_i)$ must be legal. Therefore, history $F(H)$ is final-state opaque. □

8.3   2-PHASE LOCKING TM

We prove in this section that the 2-phase locking TM algorithm $\mathcal{A}_{2PL}$ presented in Section 5.1.2 and shown in Figure 5.1 indeed ensures opacity. The proof consists of three steps. We consider a shared object M_{2PL} implemented by $\mathcal{A}_{2PL}$ and any finite history H of M_{2PL} that has unique writes. Then:

1. We prove (Lemma 8.7) that H is consistent.

2. We define a version order function $V_{\ll}$ of H and prove (Lemma 8.8) that graph $OPG\,(H, V_{\ll})$ is acyclic, thus showing that H ensures final-state opacity.

3. Finally, we show (Lemma 8.9) that, roughly speaking, every finite history H' of M_{2PL} (not necessarily having unique writes) can be transformed into a history H of M_{2PL}, such that (a) H has unique writes, and (b) H is final-state opaque only if H' is final-state opaque.

Therefore, we first show that every finite history of M_{2PL} that has unique writes is final-state opaque (points 1 and 2 above, and by Theorem 8.2), and then we show that every finite history of M_{2PL} is final-state opaque (point 3 above, and by Theorem 8.10). Hence, by Observation 7.4, we prove that M_{2PL} is opaque, i.e., that every history of M_{2PL} is opaque.

Let M_{2PL} be any shared object implemented by $\mathcal{A}_{2PL}$. Let E be any finite implementation history of M_{2PL}, and denote by H the history $E|M_{2PL}$. Assume that H has unique writes. We make the following observations about every transaction T_i in H accessing any t-variable x_m, which follow directly from algorithm $\mathcal{A}_{2PL}$:

Observation 8.4   If T_i reads from register $TVar[m]$, then T_i holds try-lock $L[m]$ (in shared or exclusive mode) continuously throughout all steps executed by T_i on $TVar[m]$, and all subsequent steps executed by T_i on any register in array $TVar$.

Observation 8.5   If T_i writes to register $TVar[m]$, then T_i holds try-lock $L[m]$ in exclusive mode continuously throughout step $TVar[m].read$ executed by T_i in line 12 and all subsequent steps executed by T_i on any register in array $TVar$.

We prove that history H of M_{2PL} is opaque. Before doing that, however, we prove the following auxiliary lemma that we refer to throughout this section.

Lemma 8.6   *For every transaction T_i in H, time t, t-variable x_m, and value $v \neq A_i$, if T_i reads v from register $TVar[m]$ at t within a non-local operation read on x_m (in line 6), then:*

1. *If $v \neq 0$ then there exists exactly one committed or commit-pending transaction T_k in H, $k \neq i$, such that (a) T_k writes v to $TVar[m]$ in line 13 at some time $t' < t$ within a non-local operation write(v) on x_m, and (b) no committed or commit-pending transaction writes to $TVar[m]$ between t' and t; and*

2. *If $v = 0$ then no committed or commit-pending transaction writes to $TVar[m]$ before t.*

Proof. Observe first that every transaction T_q that modifies the state of register $TVar[m]$ executes the following steps:

1. T_q acquires try-lock $L[m]$ in exclusive mode (line 9).

2. T_q reads the current state of $TVar[m]$ and saves it in local variable $oldval[m]$ (line 12).

3. T_q changes the state of $TVar[m]$, possibly multiple times (line 13).

4. If T_q invokes function *abort*, T_q reverts the state of $TVar[m]$ to the value in $oldval[m]$.

5. T_q unlocks $L[m]$.

By the mutual exclusion property of $L[m]$, when T_q executes any of the above steps, no other transaction can access register $TVar[m]$ (Observations 8.4 and 8.5). Hence, the value of $TVar[m]$ just after T_q releases $L[m]$ is equal to either (a) the value of $TVar[m]$ just before T_q acquires $L[m]$, if T_q invokes function $abort(T_k)$, or (b) the last value written to t-variable x_m by T_q, if T_q is committed or commit-pending in H. Then, since H has unique writes, if the value of $TVar[m]$ is v at some time t, and then a committed or commit-pending transaction T_q writes a value v' to $TVar[m]$ (in line 13) at some time $t' > t$, then $v' \neq v$ and the value of $TVar[m]$ is different than v after t' forever. Therefore, it is straightforward to see that the lemma holds.   □

Lemma 8.7   *History H of M_{2PL} is consistent.*

Proof. Consider any operation $e_{rd} = x_m.read_i \to v$ of any transaction T_i in H, where x_m is any t-variable and v is any value. Within operation e_{rd}, transaction T_i executes step $s_{rd} = TVar[m].read \to v$ in line 6.

Assume first that e_{rd} is local. Then, T_i writes to x_m before e_{rd}, and so T_i executes a *write* step s_{wr} on $TVar[m]$ before step s_{rd}. Since T_i holds try-lock $L[m]$ in exclusive mode continuously throughout steps s_{wr} and s_{rd} (Observation 8.5), and since $L[m]$ ensures mutual exclusion, no transaction other than T_i can write to $TVar[m]$ between s_{wr} and s_{rd}. Hence, the latest *write* step on $TVar[m]$ that precedes s_{rd} in H must be $TVar[m].write(v)$ executed by T_i in line 13, and so operation $x_m.write(v)$ is the latest *write* operation executed by T_i before operation e_{rd}. Therefore, e_{rd} is consistent.

Assume then that operation e_{rd} is non-local and that $v \neq 0$. Hence, by Lemma 8.6, there exists a committed or commit-pending transaction T_k in H, $k \neq i$, that writes value v in history $nonlocal(H)$. Therefore, e_{rd} is consistent.   □

Let τ denote the function that maps every transaction T_i in history H to a time $\tau(T_i)$ that is the execution time of the latest of the following events in E:

- step $TVar[m].read$ executed by T_i in line 6, for any t-variable x_m,

- step $TVar[m].write$ executed by T_i in line 13, for any t-variable x_m, or

- the first event of T_i.

Note that, by Observations 8.4 and 8.5, $\tau(T_i)$ is a time at which transaction T_i holds all try-locks that T_i ever acquires in E (except, possibly, for a single try-lock $L[w]$, if T_i acquires $L[w]$ and then stops before writing to $TVar[w]$ in line 13).

Let $\ll$ denote the total order on the set of transactions in history H, such that, for all transactions T_i and T_k in H, $i \neq k$, if $i = 0$ or $\tau(T_i) < \tau(T_k)$ then $T_i \ll T_k$. For every t-variable x_m, let $\ll_m$ denote the version order of x_m that is a subset of total order $\ll$. Let $V_\ll$ denote the version order function that maps every t-variable x_m to version order $\ll_m$.

Lemma 8.8   *Graph $G = OPG\left(H, V_\ll\right)$ is acyclic.*

Proof. By contradiction, assume that graph G has a cycle. Because $\ll$ is a total order on the set of transactions in history H, there must be some transactions T_i and T_k, such that $T_k \ll T_i$ and there is an edge $T_i \longrightarrow T_k$ in G. There can be four kinds of edges in graph G—we thus consider four cases, in each showing a contradiction. (Cases 2 and 4 are illustrated in Figure 8.2.)

Case 1: edge $T_i \xrightarrow{\text{rt}} T_k$ Then, T_i is completed and the last event of T_i precedes the first event of T_k in H. It is thus impossible that $T_k \ll T_i$.

Case 2: edge $T_i \xrightarrow{\text{rf}} T_k$ Then, T_i executes an operation $e_{\text{wr}} = x_m.write(v)$, and T_k executes an operation $e_{\text{rd}} = x_m.read \to v$, for some t-variable x_m and value v. Note that, since $T_k \ll T_i$, $i \neq 0$, and so, because H has unique writes, $v \neq 0$. Within operation e_{wr}, T_i executes step $s_{\text{wr}} = TVar[m].write(v)$ in line 13. Within operation e_{rd}, T_k executes step $s_{\text{rd}} = TVar[m].read \to v$ in line 6.

Since T_i writes v to x_m and because H has unique writes, T_k cannot write v to x_m. Hence, since H is consistent (by Lemma 8.7), operation e_{rd} is non-local. Hence, by Lemma 8.6, step s_{wr} of T_i precedes step s_{rd} of T_k. Since T_i holds try-lock $L[m]$ in exclusive mode during s_{wr} and all subsequent steps executed by T_i on registers in array $TVar$ (Observation 8.5), and T_k holds $L[m]$ during s_{rd} and all subsequent steps executed by T_k on registers in $TVar$ (Observation 8.4), and because $L[m]$ ensures mutual exclusion, it must be that $\tau(T_i) < \tau(T_k)$. Hence, we reach a contradiction with the assumption that $T_k \ll T_i$.

Case 3: edge $T_i \xrightarrow{\text{ww}} T_k$ Then, $T_i \ll_m T_k$ for some t-variable x_m. Hence, it is impossible that $T_k \ll T_i$.

Case 4: edge $T_i \xrightarrow{\text{rw}} T_k$ Then, vertex T_k in graph G is labelled *vis*, and there exists a transaction T_q and a t-variable x_m, such that $T_q \ll_m T_k$, and T_i reads x_m from T_q. Hence, in history *nonlocal*(H), T_q writes some value v to x_m (operation e_{wr}^q), T_i reads v from x_m (operation e_{rd}^i), and, since $T_q \ll_m T_k$, transaction T_k writes some value $v' \neq v$ to x_m (operation e_{wr}^k). Because $T_q \ll_m T_k \ll T_i$, only q can be 0 (in which case $v = 0$).

Case 2: $T_i \xrightarrow{\text{rf}} T_k$ (but $T_k \ll T_i$, and so $\tau(T_k) < \tau(T_i)$)

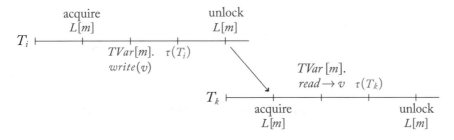

Case 4: $T_i \xrightarrow{\text{rw}} T_k$ (but $T_q \ll_m T_k \ll T_i$, and so $\tau(T_q) < \tau(T_k) < \tau(T_i)$)

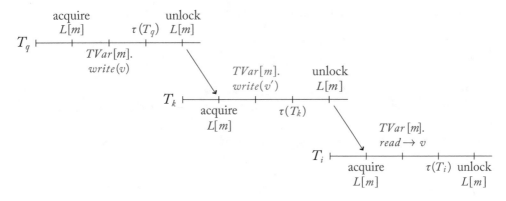

Figure 8.2: Illustration of the proof of Lemma 8.8

Within its (non-local) operation e^i_{rd}, transaction T_i reads value v from register $TVar[m]$ (in line 6) at some time $t^i_{\text{rd}} \leq \tau(T_i)$. Within its (non-local) operation e^k_{wr}, transaction T_k writes v to $TVar[m]$ (in line 13) at some time $t^k_{\text{wr}} \leq \tau(T_k)$. Transaction T_k holds try-lock $L[m]$ in exclusive mode continuously from time t^k_{wr} until time $\tau(T_k)$ (Observation 8.5), and transaction T_i holds $L[m]$ from time t^i_{rd} until $\tau(T_i)$ (Observation 8.4). Hence, since $\tau(T_k) < \tau(T_i)$ (because $T_k \ll T_i$), and by the mutual exclusion property of $L[m]$, $t^k_{\text{wr}} < t^i_{\text{rd}}$.

Since $T_q \ll_m T_k$, transaction T_k is committed or commit-pending. Hence, if $v = 0$, then we reach a contradiction with Lemma 8.6 because T_k executes a *write* operation on $TVar[m]$ before time t^i_{rd}. Therefore, $v \neq 0$, which means that T_q is a transaction different than T_0.

Within its (non-local) operation e^q_{wr}, transaction T_q writes value v to register $TVar[m]$ in line 13 at some time $t^q_{\text{wr}} \leq \tau(T_q)$. Hence, T_q holds try-lock $L[m]$ in exclusive mode between t^q_{wr} and $\tau(T_q)$ (Observation 8.5). Since $\tau(T_q) < \tau(T_k)$ (as $T_q \ll_m T_k$), and because T_k holds $L[m]$

between t_{wr}^k and $\tau(T_k)$, and by the mutual exclusion property of $L[m]$, it must be that $t_{\mathrm{wr}}^q < t_{\mathrm{wr}}^k$. But this contradicts Lemma 8.6 because T_k writes to $TVar[m]$ at time t_{wr}^k that is between t_{wr}^q and t_{rd}^i.   □

Lemma 8.9   *If H is a history of $M_{2\mathrm{PL}}$, then there exists a history H' of $M_{2\mathrm{PL}}$, such that H' has unique writes, and $F(H') = H$ for some function F on set $\mathbb{N}$.*

Proof.   Let E be any implementation history of $M_{2\mathrm{PL}}$. Consider an implementation history E' of M that satisfies the following conditions:

1. Transactions in $E'|M_{2\mathrm{PL}}$ invoke the same operations on $M_{2\mathrm{PL}}$ as in $E|M_{2\mathrm{PL}}$, except that every invocation of operation $write(v)$, $v \neq 0$, on any t-variable, becomes $write(v')$, where v' is some unique value different than 0 (e.g., the time of this invocation event).

2. Processes execute steps in E' in the same order as in E. That is, the schedule is the same in E' as in E.

The control flow of the algorithm $\mathcal{A}_{2\mathrm{PL}}$ of $M_{2\mathrm{PL}}$ does not depend on the values written to any t-variable, or on the values read from or written to any register in array $TVar$. Hence, implementation history E' that ensures conditions 1 and 2 above exists, and there is a function F on set $\mathbb{N}$ such that $F(E'|M) = E|M$. Therefore, since history $E'|M_{2\mathrm{PL}}$ of $M_{2\mathrm{PL}}$ has unique writes, the lemma holds.
□

Theorem 8.10   *Shared TM object $M_{2\mathrm{PL}}$ implemented by algorithm $\mathcal{A}_{2\mathrm{PL}}$ is opaque.*

Proof.   Let H be any history of $M_{2\mathrm{PL}}$. By Lemma 8.9, there exists a history H' of $M_{2\mathrm{PL}}$, such that H' has unique writes and $F(H') = H$ for some function F on set $\mathbb{N}$. By Lemma 8.7, Lemma 8.8, and Theorem 8.2, history H' is final-state opaque. Therefore, by Lemma 8.3, $H = F(H')$ is final-state opaque. Hence, by Observation 7.4, $M_{2\mathrm{PL}}$ is opaque.   □

8.4   TM WITH INVISIBLE READS

We prove in this section that the TM algorithm $\mathcal{A}_{\mathrm{IR}}$ presented in Section 5.2 and depicted in Figures 5.3 and 5.4 indeed ensures opacity. The proof consists of three steps, analogous to those in the proof given in the previous section. We consider a shared object M_{IR} implemented by $\mathcal{A}_{\mathrm{IR}}$ and any history H of M_{IR} that has unique writes. First, we prove (Lemma 8.15) that H is consistent. Second, we define a version order function $V_{\ll}$ on H and prove (Lemma 8.16) that graph $OPG\,(H, V_{\ll})$ is acyclic. Finally, we show (Lemma 8.17) that, roughly speaking, every history H' of M_{IR} can be transformed into a history H of M_{IR}, such that (a) H has unique writes, and (b) H is final-state opaque only if H' is final-state opaque. Therefore, since we show that every history of M_{IR} that has unique writes is final-state opaque, we also show that every history of M_{IR} is final-state opaque, thus showing, by Observation 7.4, that M_{IR} is opaque (Theorem 8.18).

In the following proofs, when considering a tuple $(v, ts, locked)$, if some element of the tuple can have an arbitrary value, we denote it by "$-$". For example, $(v, -, -)$ denotes a 3-tuple in which the first element equals v and the two other elements can be arbitrary.

Let M_{IR} be any shared object implemented by algorithm $\mathcal{A}_{IR}$. Consider any implementation history E of M_{IR}, and denote by H the history $E|M_{IR}$. Assume that H has unique writes.

Consider any transaction T_i in H that executes a step s_{rd} in line 2 in which T_i reads some value $(v, ts, false)$ from some register $TVar[m]$. We say that step s_{rd} is *validated* if T_i, after executing s_{rd}, executes a response event $ret(v)$ (from the operation *read* on x_m that contains s_{rd}).

Consider any transaction T_i in H that executes a step s_{wr} in line 17 in which T_i writes some value $(v, ts, true)$ to some register $TVar[m]$. We say that T_i *commits* step s_{wr} if T_i writes value $(v, ts + 1, false)$ to $TVar[m]$ in line 23. Then, we also say that step s_{wr} is *committed*.

The following observations about any transaction T_i in H, accessing any t-variable x_m, follow directly from algorithm $\mathcal{A}_{IR}$:

Observation 8.11 If T_i writes to register $TVar[m]$, then T_i holds try-lock $L[m]$ continuously throughout step $TVar[m].read$ executed by T_i in line 13 and all subsequent steps executed by T_i on $TVar[m]$.

Observation 8.12 If T_i commits any *write* step executed in line 17, then T_i is either committed or commit-pending.

Lemma 8.13 *For every transaction T_i in H, time t_{rd}, t-variable x_m, and values v and ts, if T_i reads value $(v, -, false)$ from register $TVar[m]$ at t_{rd}, then:*

1. *If $v \neq 0$ then there exists exactly one transaction T_k in H, $k \neq i$, such that (a) T_k executes a step $write((v, -, true))$ on $TVar[m]$ in line 17, within a non-local operation $write(v)$ on x_m, and then commits this step (in line 23) at some time $t_c < t_{rd}$, and (b) no transaction executes any committed write step on $TVar[m]$ between t_c and t_{rd}; and*

2. *If $v = 0$ then no transaction executes any committed write step on $TVar[m]$ before t_{rd}.*

Proof. Observe first that every transaction T_q that modifies the state of register $TVar[m]$ goes through the following sequence of steps:

1. T_q acquires try-lock $L[m]$ (line 11).

2. T_q reads the current state of $TVar[m]$ and saves it in local variables $oldval[m]$ and $oldts[m]$ (lines 14 and 15).

3. T_q writes to $TVar[m]$ a value $(-, oldts[m], true)$, possibly multiple times (line 17).

4. If T_q invokes function $abort(T_k)$, T_q reverts the state of $TVar[m]$ to value $(oldval[m], oldts[m], false)$ (line 31).

5. If T_q reaches line 22, T_q first reads a value $(v, ts, -)$ from $TVar[m]$ and then writes value $(v, ts + 1, false)$ to $TVar[m]$ (line 23).

6. T_q unlocks $L[m]$.

By the mutual exclusion property of $L[m]$, when T_q executes any of the above steps, no other transaction can write to register $TVar[m]$. Hence, once T_q executes its first *write* step on $TVar[m]$, and until T_q writes to $TVar[m]$ in line 23 or line 31, the value of $TVar[m]$ is always $(-, -, true)$. Moreover, if the value of $TVar[m]$ just before T_q executes its first *write* step on $TVar[m]$ is $(v, ts, false)$, then the value of $TVar[m]$ just after T_q executes its last *write* on $TVar[m]$ is: (a) $(v, ts, false)$ if T_q writes to $TVar[m]$ in line 31, and so T_q does not commit any *write* step; (b) $(v', ts + 1, false)$ if T_q writes to $TVar[m]$ in line 23, and so T_q commits its step $TVar[m].write((v', ts, true))$ executed in line 17; or (c) $(-, ts, true)$ if T_q is live and its last *write* operation on $TVar[m]$ is executed in line 17, in which case, the value of $TVar[m]$ remains $(-, ts, true)$ forever.

Therefore, since H has unique writes, if the value of $TVar[m]$ is $(v, -, false)$ at some time t, and then some transaction T_q executes a committed step $write((v', -, true))$ (in line 17) at some time $t_{wr} > t$, then $v' \neq v$ and the value of $TVar[m]$ is different than $(v, -, false)$ after t_{wr} forever. Therefore, it is straightforward to see that the lemma holds.   □

Lemma 8.14   *For every transaction T_i in H and t-variable x_m, if T_i reads from register $TVar[m]$ some value $(v, ts, false)$, and then reads again from $TVar[m]$ some value $(v', ts', false)$, and if $ts' = ts$, then $v' = v$.*

Proof. Consider a situation in which T_i reads some value $(v, ts, false)$ from $TVar[m]$ at some time t, and then reads some value $(v', ts', false)$, where $v' \neq v$, at some time $t' > t$. Let T_k be any transaction that writes to $TVar[m]$ between t and t'. As we showed in the proof of Lemma 8.13, if the value of $TVar[m]$ just before T_k writes to $TVar[m]$ for the first time (in line 17) is $(v, ts, false)$, and the value just after T_k writes to $TVar[m]$ for the last time is $(v', ts', false)$, then $ts' = ts + 1$.   □

Lemma 8.15   *History H of M_{IR} is consistent.*

Proof. Consider any operation $e_{rd} = x_m.read \rightarrow v$ in $H|T_i$, where x_m is any t-variable, T_i is any transaction, and v is any value. Within operation e_{rd}, transaction T_i must execute a step $s_{rd} = TVar[m].read \rightarrow (v, -, -)$ (in line 2).

Assume first that e_{rd} is local. Then, T_i writes to x_m before e_{rd}, and so T_i writes to $TVar[m]$ before step s_{rd}. Since T_i holds try-lock $L[m]$ continuously throughout its all *write* steps on $TVar[m]$, and until step s_{rd} (Observation 8.11), and since $L[m]$ ensures mutual exclusion, no other transaction can write to $TVar[m]$ between the first *write* step of T_i on $TVar[m]$ and step s_{rd}. Hence, the latest *write* operation on $TVar[m]$ that precedes step s_{rd} must be an operation $write((v, -, true))$ executed by T_i in line 17 within operation $e_{\mathrm{wr}} = x_m.write(v)$. Since T_i writes to $TVar[m]$ in every *write* operation preceding e_{rd}, e_{wr} is the latest *write* operation on x_m preceding e_{rd}, and so e_{rd} is consistent.

Assume then that operation e_{rd} is not local, and $v \neq 0$. Then, T_i reads in step s_{rd} a value $(v, -, false)$ from $TVar[m]$. Hence, by Lemma 8.13, there is a transaction T_k in H that executes a committed operation $write((v, -, -))$ on register $TVar[m]$. Hence, T_k writes value v to x_m in history $nonlocal(H)$, and T_k is either committed or commit-pending (Observation 8.12). Therefore, e_{rd} is consistent. □

Let τ be the function that maps every transaction T_i in history H to a time $\tau(T_i)$ that is the execution time of the latest of the following steps:

- committed step $TVar[m].write$, for any t-variable x_m, executed by T_i in line 17;

- validated step $TVar[m].read$, for any t-variable x_m, executed by T_i within a non-local operation $x_m.read$ (in line 2); and

- first event of T_i.

Let $\ll$ denote the total order on the transactions in H, such that $T_i \ll T_k$ if $i = 0$ or $\tau(T_i) < \tau(T_k)$. For every t-variable x_m, we denote by $\ll_m$ the version order of x_m that is a subset of total order $\ll$. Let $V_\ll$ be the version order function that maps every t-variable x_m to $\ll_m$.

Lemma 8.16 *Graph $G = OPG\left(H, V_\ll\right)$ is acyclic.*

Proof. By contradiction, assume that there is a cycle in graph G. Because $\ll$ is a total order on the set of all transactions in H, there must be some two transactions T_i and T_k, such that (1) there is an edge $T_i \longrightarrow T_k$ in G, but (2) $T_k \ll T_i$. Note that $T_i \neq T_0$ since $T_0 \ll T_q$ for every transaction T_q in H. We consider four cases, for each possible type of edge $T_i \longrightarrow T_k$, showing a contradiction in each case. (Cases 2 and 4 are illustrated in Figure 8.3.)

Case 1: $T_i \xrightarrow{\mathrm{rt}} T_k$ Then, T_i is completed in H and the last event of T_i precedes the first event of T_k. Hence, it is impossible that $T_k \ll T_i$.

Case 2: $T_i \xrightarrow{\mathrm{rf}} T_k$ Then, T_i writes some value v to some t-variable x_m (operation e_{wr}^i), and T_k reads v from x_m (operation e_{rd}^k). Since T_i and T_k are different transactions, and because history H is consistent and has unique writes, operation e_{rd}^k is non-local. Hence, within e_{rd}^k, transaction T_k executes a validated operation $read \rightarrow (v, -, false)$ on register $TVar[m]$ at some time $t_{\mathrm{rd}}^k \leq \tau(T_k)$.

Case 2: $T_i \xrightarrow{\text{rf}} T_k$ (but $T_k \ll T_i$, and so $\tau(T_k) < \tau(T_i)$)

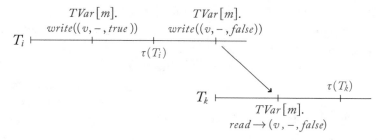

Case 4: $T_i \xrightarrow{\text{rw}} T_k$ (but $T_q \ll_m T_k \ll T_i$, and so $\tau(T_q) < \tau(T_k) < \tau(T_i)$)

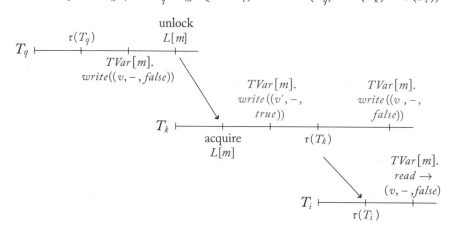

Figure 8.3: Illustration of the proof of Lemma 8.16

By Lemma 8.13, T_k must execute an operation $write((v, -, -))$ on $TVar[m]$ and commit this operation at some time $t_c^i < t_{rd}^k$. But then, since $t_c^i \geq \tau(T_i)$, $\tau(T_i) < \tau(T_k)$—a contradiction with the assumption that $T_k \ll T_i$.

Case 3: $T_i \xrightarrow{\text{ww}} T_k$ Then, $T_i \ll_m T_k$ for some t-variable x_m, and so it cannot be that $T_k \ll T_i$.

Case 4: $T_i \xrightarrow{\text{rw}} T_k$ Then, vertex T_k in graph G is labelled vis, and there exists a transaction T_q and a t-variable x_m, such that $T_q \ll_m T_k$, and T_i reads x_m from T_q. Hence, T_q writes some value v to x_m (operation e_{wr}^q), T_i reads v from x_m (operation e_{rd}^i), and, since $T_q \ll_m T_k$, transaction T_k writes some value v' to x_m (operation e_{wr}^k; if T_k writes to x_m several times, e_{wr}^k is the last (non-local) *write* operation of T_k on x_m). Because T_i and T_k are different transactions, and because history H is consistent (by Lemma 8.15) and has unique writes, operations e_{wr}^q and e_{rd}^i are both non-local. Since H has unique writes, $v' \neq v$. Because $T_q \ll_m T_k \ll T_i$, only q can be 0 (in which case $v = 0$).

Within its (non-local) operation e_{rd}^i, transaction T_i reads from register $TVar[m]$ some value $(v, ts, false)$ (in line 2) at some time $t_{rd}^i \leq \tau(T_i)$. If T_i does not execute, within a non-local operation, any validated *read* or committed *write* step on any register in array $TVar$ after t_{rd}^i, then $t_{rd}^i = \tau(T_i)$. Otherwise, T_i returns *true* from some function *validate* invoked (in line 4 or line 20) after T_i returns from operation e_{rd}^i, with variable *rset* containing value m. Then, T_i reads some value $(v'', ts, false)$ (in line 37) at some time $t_v^i > \tau(T_i)$. By Lemma 8.14, $v'' = v$. Hence, T_i reads a value $(v, -, false)$ at time $\tau(T_i)$ or later.

Within its (non-local) operation e_{wr}^k, transaction T_k writes to register $TVar[m]$ a value $(v', -, true)$ (in line 17) at some time $t_{wr}^k \leq \tau(T_k)$.

Assume first that T_k does not commit its *write* operation executed at time t_{wr}^k, i.e., T_k does not write a value $(v', -, false)$ to $TVar[m]$ in line 23. Because vertex T_k in G is labelled *vis*, and T_k cannot be committed, T_k is commit-pending and some transaction T_s reads from T_k. Hence, by Lemma 8.13, T_k must commit some *write* operation in line 23, and so T_k does not write a value $(-, -, false)$ to $TVar[m]$ in line 31. Therefore, T_k never writes a value $(-, -, false)$ to $TVar[m]$ after time t_{wr}^k, and since T_k holds try-lock $L[m]$ from time t_{wr}^k forever, no other transaction writes any value to $TVar[m]$ after t_{wr}^k. But then, since $t_{wr}^k \leq \tau(T_k) < \tau(T_i)$, transaction T_i cannot read at time $\tau(T_i)$ or later a value $(-, -, false)$ from $TVar[m]$—a contradiction.

Assume then that T_k commits its *write* operation executed at time t_{wr}^k. If $v = 0$, then we reach a contradiction with Lemma 8.13 because T_k executes a committed *write* operation on $TVar[m]$ before time t_{rd}^i or t_v^i.

Assume then that $v \neq 0$. Hence, T_q is a transaction different than T_0. Since $\tau(T_q) < \tau(T_k)$, and since both T_q and T_k write to x_m, transaction T_q must release try-lock $L[m]$ at some time t_{rel}^q that is before the time t_{acq}^k at which T_k acquires $L[m]$. By Lemma 8.13, T_q commits a *write* operation on $TVar[m]$ at some time before t_{rel}^q, and no transaction executes any committed *write* operation on $TVar[m]$ between t_{rel}^q and $\tau(T_i)$. But then, T_k cannot execute a committed *write* operation on $TVar[m]$ at time t_{wr}^k, $t_{rel}^q < t_{acq}^k < t_{wr}^k < \tau(T_i)$—a contradiction. □

Lemma 8.17   *If H is a history of M_{IR}, then there exists a history H' of M_{IR}, such that H' has unique writes, and $F(H') = H$ for some function F on set $\mathbb{N}$.*

Proof. The proof is analogous to the proof of Lemma 8.9 in Section 8.3.   □

Theorem 8.18   *Shared TM object M_{IR} implemented by algorithm $\mathcal{A}_{IR}$ is opaque.*

Proof. Let H be any history of M_{IR}. By Lemma 8.17, there exists a history H' of M_{IR}, such that H' has unique writes and $F(H') = H$ for some function F on set $\mathbb{N}$. By Lemma 8.15, Lemma 8.16, and Theorem 8.2, history H' is final-state opaque. Therefore, by Lemma 8.17, $H = F(H')$ is also final-state opaque. Hence, by Observation 7.4, M_{IR} is opaque. □

CHAPTER 9

Opacity vs. Atomicity

The correctness of database transactions has been traditionally described formally using the notion of *atomicity*.[1] In our model, we can define atomicity using the notion of opacity. A TM history H is *final-state atomic*, if there exists a subset C of the set of commit-pending transactions in H, such that the restriction of H to events of only transactions that are committed or in set C is final-state opaque. TM history H is *atomic*, if every prefix of H (including H itself) is final-state atomic. The difference between so-defined atomicity and opacity is then clear: atomicity does not guarantee anything for live and aborted transactions. That is, a transaction T_i can be returned any values from its operations as long as T_i never commits.

Atomicity might be a good alternative to opacity when it is possible to ensure that all operations executed by an application inside an **atomic** block (on t-objects, shared objects, local data, and external devices) have no effect when the transaction executing the **atomic** block aborts. By sandboxing the application and buffering operations that cannot be undone, it is indeed possible to make aborted transactions invisible to the application. Then, a TM implementation that only ensures atomicity will be indistinguishable for the application from a TM that ensures opacity.

An important question, however, is whether there is any additional cost of ensuring opacity as compared to ensuring atomicity. In this chapter, we prove that yes, opacity can be indeed inherently more expensive to implement than atomicity. We do so by proving a *complexity lower bound* that holds only for opacity, and not atomicity.

Namely, we prove that, roughly speaking, the worst-case time complexity of a *single read* operation executed by a transaction T_k (and returning a non-A_k value) is proportional to the size of the read set of T_k, for every TM implementation that (1) ensures opacity, (2) uses invisible reads, (3) ensures *minimal progressiveness*, and (4) uses *strict data partitioning*. Recall from Section 5.2 that, intuitively, in a TM that uses invisible reads, read-only operations of a transaction are not visible to other transactions. Minimal progressiveness is a basic *progress* property. It requires that a transaction T_k can be forceably aborted only if T_k is concurrent to another transaction. (We talk more about progress properties of TMs in Part III of this manuscript.) Most, if not all, TM implementations are minimally progressive, e.g., DSTM, TL2, TinySTM, SwissTM, and our TM algorithms $\mathcal{A}_{2PL}$ and $\mathcal{A}_{IR}$ presented in Chapter 5. Strict data partitioning requires, roughly speaking, that the set of base objects used by a TM implementation is divided into disjoint subsets, each corresponding to exactly one t-object, and a process that executes a transaction T_k can access a base object corresponding to a t-object x only if x is in the read-set or the write-set of T_k. Hence,

---

[1] We use here the term "atomicity" as originally defined by Weihl [1989], which is a generalization of the concept of "serializability" defined by Papadimitriou [1979].

strict data partitioning means, in particular, that transactions accessing disjoint sets of t-objects (e.g., transactions implementing operations on different data structures) can be executed completely independently, i.e., without delaying each other. (This property is related to strict disjoint-access-parallelism, which we introduce in Section 13.4.)

Our complexity lower bound is tight: TM algorithm $\mathcal{A}_{IR}$, which we presented in Section 5.2, satisfies the above requirements (1)–(4), and its function *validate*, which is invoked by *read* operations, has time complexity proportional to the size of the current read set of a transaction.

While the main purpose of the lower bound we present here is to show that there is a fundamental difference between opacity and atomicity, the result has some practical consequences. Namely, it shows that non-trivial TMs that use invisible reads need to either use incremental validation (as in algorithm $\mathcal{A}_{IR}$), which is expensive for transactions with large read sets, or make unrelated transactions access some common base objects, e.g., to assign them increasing timestamps (as in, e.g., TL2, TinySTM, and SwissTM). (By "non-trivial TMs" we mean here TMs that ensure minimal progressiveness, which is indeed a very basic property.)

In the following sections, we first define the properties (2)–(4) outlined above (for the definition of opacity, refer to Chapter 7). Then, we prove our complexity lower bound. Finally, we discuss how the lower bound can be overcome by relaxing requirements (1)–(4). In particular, we show that ensuring atomicity instead of opacity allows for implementing a TM that has constant worst-case time complexity of its *texec* operation.

9.1   PROPERTIES OF TM IMPLEMENTATIONS

Intuitively, a TM shared object M uses *invisible reads* if no transaction T_i modifies the state of any base object within any *read-only* and *successful* operation on any t-object. By "successful," we mean an operation that does not return value A_i, i.e., an operation after which T_i is still live. (Recall from Chapter 3 that when we say that a transaction T_i executes a step, we mean that some process executes this step, within some TM operation, while executing T_i.) For instance, algorithm $\mathcal{A}_{IR}$ described in Section 5.2 indeed implements a TM that uses invisible reads: a transaction T_i that executes a successful operation *read* on a t-variable x_m only reads from register $TVar[m]$. More formally:

Definition 9.1 (Invisible reads).   A TM shared object M is said to use *invisible reads* if, in every implementation history E of M, and for every operation $e = x.op_i \rightarrow v$ in $(E|M)|T_i$, where T_i is any transaction, x is any t-object, op is any read-only operation, and v is any value different than A_i, no step executed by T_i in E within e changes the state of any base object.

Intuitively, a TM object M is *minimally progressive* if M forceably aborts a transaction T_i only if T_i is concurrent to some other transaction. More formally:

Definition 9.2 (Minimal progressiveness).   A TM object M is *minimally progressive* if, for every history H of M, and every transaction T_i in H, if T_i is forceably aborted, then T_i is concurrent to some other transaction in H.

Intuitively, a TM shared object M uses *strict data partitioning* if the set of objects used by M is split into *disjoint* sets, each storing information of only a single t-object. That is, every t-object x corresponds to a set $Base_M(x)$ of base objects, and all the information about x, e.g., the value of x, the state of locks protecting x, the current version number of x, is stored only in base objects from set $Base_M(x)$. Moreover, a transaction T_i can access a base object from set $Base_M(x)$ only if T_i accesses t-object x.

More precisely, let H be any TM history and x be any t-object. We denote by $H|-x$ the TM history obtained from H by removing all events of operations on x. Then:

Definition 9.3 (Strict data partitioning). A TM shared object M is said to use *strict data partitioning* if, for every t-object x, there exists a set of base objects, which we denote by $Base_M(x)$, such that the following requirements are satisfied:

1. Sets $Base_M(x_1)$, $Base_M(x_2)$, ... are disjoint;

2. For every implementation history E of M and every transaction T_i in E, every base object accessed by T_i in E is in set $Base_M(x)$ for some t-object $x \in RWSet_E(T_i)$; and

3. For all finite implementation histories E and E' of M, if $(E|M)|-x = (E'|M)|-x$ for some t-object x, then the configurations after E and E' can differ only in the states of base objects in set $Base_M(x)$.

We define the *time complexity* of an operation op of a shared object X, in a given implementation history of X, in a straightforward way:

Definition 9.4 (Time complexity). We say that an operation op of a shared object X in an implementation history E of X has *time complexity* k, if the maximum number of steps within any execution of op in $E|p_i$, for any process p_i, is k.

9.2   COMPLEXITY LOWER BOUND

Consider any minimally progressive TM shared object M that uses invisible reads and strict data partitioning (and that ensures opacity and wait-freedom). We prove in this section that there is an implementation history E of M in which an operation $texec(T_1, x.read) \to v$, where x is some t-variable and $v \neq A_1$, takes at least $|RSet_E(T_1)| - 1$ steps to complete. Hence, we prove (Theorem 9.8) that the time complexity of a (single) successful *read* operation of a transaction executed by M is, in the worst case, proportional to the size of the read set of this transaction.

The proof is structured as follows. Let m be any natural number. We consider TM histories H_0, H_1^A, ..., H_{m-1}^A, and H_1^0, ..., H_{m-1}^0 depicted in Figure 9.1. Note that the size of the read set of transaction T_1 in all those histories is m. We then prove that H_0 is a history of M (Lemma 9.5), and,

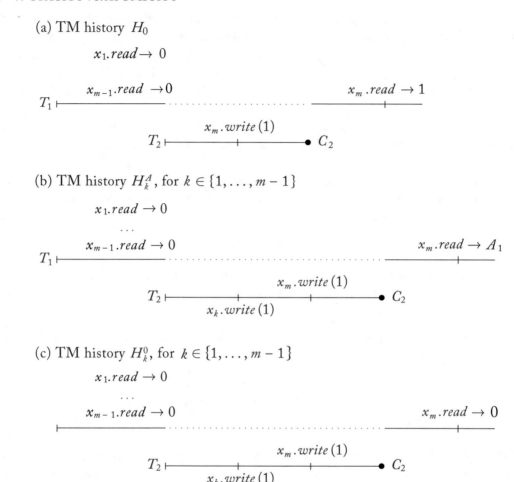

(a) TM history H_0

$x_1.read \to 0$

$x_{m-1}.read \to 0$ ⋯⋯⋯⋯⋯⋯ $x_m.read \to 1$
T_1

$x_m.write(1)$
T_2 • C_2

(b) TM history H_k^A, for $k \in \{1, \ldots, m-1\}$

$x_1.read \to 0$
$\cdots$
$x_{m-1}.read \to 0$ ⋯⋯⋯⋯⋯⋯ $x_m.read \to A_1$
T_1

$x_m.write(1)$
T_2 • C_2
$x_k.write(1)$

(c) TM history H_k^0, for $k \in \{1, \ldots, m-1\}$

$x_1.read \to 0$
$\cdots$
$x_{m-1}.read \to 0$ ⋯⋯⋯⋯⋯⋯ $x_m.read \to 0$

$x_m.write(1)$
T_2 • C_2
$x_k.write(1)$

Figure 9.1: TM histories used in the proof of the complexity lower bound

for every $k = 1, \ldots, m-1$, either H_k^A or H_k^0 is a history of M (Lemma 9.6). Finally, we argue that the process executing transaction T_1 in an implementation history E_0 of M, such that $E_0|M = H_0$, needs to execute at least $m-1$ steps in the last operation of T_1 in E_0 (Theorem 9.8).

Consider the following TM history H_0 (depicted in Figure 9.1a), in which all t-objects are t-variables with the initial value 0:

$$
\begin{aligned}
H_0 \;=\; & \langle x_1.read_1 \to 0, \; x_2.read_1 \to 0, \; \ldots, \; x_{m-1}.read_1 \to 0, \\
& x_m.write(1)_2, \; C_2, \\
& x_m.read \to 1 \rangle.
\end{aligned}
$$

We prove first that H_0 is indeed a history of M:

Lemma 9.5   *There exists an implementation history E_0 of M such that $E_0|M = H_0$.*

Proof. Assume otherwise—that such an implementation history E of M does not exist. Let E be the longest implementation history of M such that $E|M$ differs from some prefix of H_0 only by the last (response) event, and in which processes p_1 and p_2 execute transactions T_1 and T_2, respectively. Then, one of the following cases must apply:

1. Transaction T_1 is forceably aborted in E and T_2 is not in E, i.e., T_1 is returned A_1 from a *read* operation on a t-variable x_k, where $k \in \{1, \ldots, m-1\}$. But then, T_1 is the only transaction in E, and so we reach a contradiction with the assumption that M is minimally progressive.

2. Transaction T_1 reads a value different than 0 from some t-variable x_k, $k \in \{1, \ldots, m-1\}$ in E. But then, since the initial value of x_k is 0 and no transaction writes to x_k in E, TM history $E|M$ violates opacity—a contradiction with the assumption that M is opaque.

3. Transaction T_2 is forceably aborted in E. Since M uses invisible reads and because transaction T_1 executes only *read* operations in E, implementation history E is indistinguishable for process p_2 from $E|p_2$. Hence, $E|p_2$ must also be an implementation history of M. But in $E|p_2$ transaction T_2 executes alone and is forceably aborted—a contradiction with the assumption that M is minimally progressive.

4. Transaction T_1 is returned a value $v \neq 1$ from its *read* operation on t-variable x_m in E. Since M uses strict data partitioning and because T_1 does not access t-variable x_m before T_2 commits, p_1 does not access any base object from set $Base_M(x_m)$ until T_2 commits, and p_2 accesses base objects only from set $Base_M(x_m)$. Hence, sequence $E' = E|p_2 \cdot E|p_1$ is indistinguishable to both p_1 and p_2 from E, and so E' is also an implementation history of M. But then, if $v = A_1$ (i.e., T_1 is forceably aborted in E), then E' violates minimal progressiveness because transactions T_1 and T_2 are not concurrent in E'. However, if $v \neq A_1$ and $v \neq 1$ (e.g., $v = 0$), then E' violates opacity. This is because T_2 precedes T_1 in E', and so T_1 must read from x_m value 1—the value written to x_m by T_2. Therefore, we reach a contradiction with the assumption that M is a minimally progressive and opaque TM.

Hence, in each case we reach a contradiction.   □

Consider TM histories $H_1^A, \ldots, H_{m-1}^A$ (depicted in Figure 9.1b), where each TM history H_k^A, $k = 1, \ldots, m-1$, is the following (as in H_0, all t-objects are t-variables initialized to 0):

$$H_k = \langle x_1.read_1 \to 0, \ x_2.read_1 \to 0, \ \ldots, \ x_{m-1}.read_1 \to 0,$$
$$x_k.write(1)_2, \ x_m.write(1)_2, \ C_2,$$
$$x_m.read \to A_1 \rangle.$$

Consider also TM histories $H_1^0, \ldots, H_{m-1}^0$ (depicted in Figure 9.1c), where each TM history H_k^0, $k = 1, \ldots, m - 1$, is the same as H_k^A, except that the last operation in H_k^0 returns value 0 instead of A_1. We prove now that, for every $k = 1, \ldots, m - 1$, either H_k^A or H_k^0 is a history of M:

Lemma 9.6   *For every $k = 1, \ldots, m - 1$, there exists an implementation history E_k of M such that either $E_k|M = H_k^A$ or $E_k|M = H_k^0$.*

Proof. By contradiction, assume that, for some $k \in \{1, \ldots, m - 1\}$, neither H_k^A nor H_k^0 is a history of M. Let E be the longest implementation history of M such that $E|M$ differs from some prefix of H_k^A or H_k^0 only by the last (response) event, and in which processes p_1 and p_2 execute transactions T_1 and T_2, respectively. Then, one of the following cases must apply (note that cases 1–3 are analogous to the ones in the proof of Lemma 9.5):

1. Transaction T_1 is forceably aborted in E, and T_2 is not in E, i.e., T_1 is returned A_1 from a *read* operation on a t-variable x_l, where $l \in \{1, \ldots, m - 1\}$. But then, T_1 is the only transaction in E, and so we reach a contradiction with the assumption that M is minimally progressive.

2. Transaction T_1 reads a value different than 0 from some t-variable $x_l, l \in \{1, \ldots, m - 1\}$ in E. But then, since the initial value of x_k is 0 and no transaction writes to x_k in E, TM history $E|M$ violates opacity—a contradiction with the assumption that M is opaque.

3. Transaction T_2 is forceably aborted in E. Since M uses invisible reads, and T_1 executes only *read* operations in E, E is indistinguishable for process p_2 from sequence $E|p_2$. Therefore, $E|p_2$ must be an implementation history of M. But in $E|p_2$ transaction T_2 executes alone and is forceably aborted—a contradiction with the assumption that M is minimally progressive.

4. Transaction T_1 is returned a value $v \notin \{A_1, 0\}$ from its *read* operation on t-variable x_m in E. But then E violates (final-state) opacity: since T_1 reads value 0 from t-variable x_k, and since T_2, which is committed in E, writes value 1 to x_k in E, T_1 must be ordered before T_2 in any witness (sequential) history of $E|M$. However, then T_1 can only be returned value 0 or A_1 from its *read* operation on t-variable x_m. Hence, we reach a contradiction with the assumption that M is opaque.

Therefore, in each case, we reach a contradiction.   □

Let then $E_0, E_1, \ldots, E_{m-1}$ be the implementation histories of M whose existence we proved in Lemmas 9.5 and 9.6. Assume that transaction T_1 is executed by process p_1 in all of those implementation histories. We prove now the following key lemma:

Lemma 9.7   *There are at least $m - 1$ steps executed within operation texec$(T_1, x_m.read) \to 1$ in $E_0|p_1$.*

Proof. Denote by e the execution of operation $texec(T_1, x_m.read) \to 1$ in $E_0|M$. Until process p_1 executes its first step within e, implementation history E_0 is indistinguishable for p_1 from every implementation history $E_k, k = 1, ..., m - 1$. Since process p_1 is returned value 1 from e in E_0, and either value A_1 or value 0 from operation $texec(T_1, x_m.read)$ in $E_1, ..., E_{m-1}$, process p_1 must execute sufficiently many steps to distinguish E_0 from all implementation histories $E_1, ..., E_{m-1}$.

Since M uses strict data partitioning, the configuration c_k after every implementation history $E_k, k = 1, ..., m - 1$, differs from the configuration c_0 after E_0 only by the states of base objects in set $Base_M(x_k)$. That is, $c_k(X) = c_0(X)$ for every base object X that is not in set $Base_M(x_k)$. Hence, since sets $Base_M(x_1), ..., Base_M(x_{m-1})$ are disjoint, process p_1 has to access at least $m - 1$ base objects to distinguish configuration c_0 from every configuration $c_k, k = 1, ..., m - 1$. That is, p_1 executes at least $m - 1$ steps in operation e. □

By Lemma 9.7, and since M is an arbitrary minimally progressive TM that uses invisible reads and strict data partitioning, we directly obtain the following theorem:

Theorem 9.8   *For every minimally progressive, opaque TM implementation M that uses invisible reads and strict data partitioning there exists an implementation history E of M and a transaction T_k in E, such that the time complexity of some read operation of T_k in E, which returns a value different than A_k, is at least $|RSet_E(T_k)| - 1$ steps.*

9.3   CIRCUMVENTING THE LOWER BOUND

Requirements (1)–(4) are all crucial for the lower bound to hold. For instance, TM algorithm $\mathcal{A}_{2PL}$, presented in Section 5.1.2, which ensures opacity, is minimally progressive, and uses strict data partitioning, but which uses visible reads, has time complexity of its successful *texec* operation independent of the read sets of transactions. A trivial TM that forceably aborts every transaction T_k immediately upon the first invocation event of T_k ensures opacity, uses invisible reads and strict data partitioning (since it does not use any base objects), but clearly violates minimal progressiveness; every operation of such a TM has time complexity equal to 0. Finally, e.g., TL2 [Dice et al., 2006] (which we present in more detail in Section 12.2.3) ensures opacity, uses invisible reads, and is minimally progressive; however, since TL2 uses time-based validation, which violates strict data partitioning, it has a constant time complexity of its every successful *texec* operation. (Note, however, that TinySTM has the worst-case time complexity proportional to the size of the read set of a transaction, even though it uses time-based validation.)

We need to show, however, that the complexity lower bound does not hold for minimally progressive TMs that use invisible reads and strict data partitioning, but that ensure atomicity instead of opacity. Consider a TM algorithm $\mathcal{A}_{IR}^A$ that is the same as $\mathcal{A}_{IR}$ (presented in Section 5.2), except that the call to function *validate* in line 4 is replaced by constant *true*. It is straightforward to see that $\mathcal{A}_{IR}^A$ is minimally progressive, and that it uses invisible reads and strict data partitioning. Also, every operation $texec(T_k, x_m.read) \to v$ of $\mathcal{A}_{IR}^A$, where T_k is any transaction, x_m is any t-variable, and $v \neq A_k$, has the time complexity of exactly one step (executed in line 2). We need to show only that $\mathcal{A}_{\text{IR}}^{\text{A}}$ indeed ensures atomicity.

Consider any implementation history E of a shared object M implemented by algorithm $\mathcal{A}_{\text{IR}}^{\text{A}}$. Let C denote the set of those commit-pending transactions in E that have reached line 22 of $\mathcal{A}_{\text{IR}}^{\text{A}}$. Denote by H the restriction of history $E|M$ to events of only transactions that are either committed or in set C. One can now follow exactly the proofs given in Section 8.4 for algorithm $\mathcal{A}_{\text{IR}}$, taking implementation history E and history H defined above, thus showing that H ensures final-state opacity. Hence, we obtain the following theorem:

Theorem 9.9   *There exists a minimally progressive TM shared object M that ensures atomicity instead of opacity, and that uses invisible reads and strict data partitioning, such that, for every implementation history E of M, every transaction T_k, and every t–variable x, the time complexity of every read operation executed by T_k in E, and returning a value different than A_k, is exactly one step.*

CHAPTER 10

Further Reading

10.1 THE ROOTS OF OPACITY

Database systems   Opacity has its roots in the theories of databases and shared memory systems. The atomicity of database transactions was first captured formally by Eswaran et al. [1976] under the notion of *consistency*. Papadimitriou [1979] defined the notion of *serializability*, and he distinguished between three kinds of serializability: conflict serializability, view serializability, and final-state serializability. Final-state opacity, and opacity, are close to view serializability. The original definition of serializability was assuming a model with only *read* and *write* operations, and with each t-variable having only a single version. Bernstein and Goodman [1983] introduced *1-copy serializability* to capture multi-version database systems. Weihl [1989] defined a general version of serializability that allows arbitrary data types, and also multi-version protocols, under the notion of *global atomicity*. The definition of opacity shares much of its theoretical framework with the definition of global atomicity. The main difference between opacity and global atomicity (or serializability) is the fact that the latter does not put any restrictions on the state observed by live or aborted transactions (cf. Chapter 9).

Hadzilacos [1988] described certain issues that can arise when live transactions observe inconsistent states of the system (e.g., cascading aborts). He defined three *recoverability* properties, each preventing some of those issues. In its strongest form, recoverability says that, intuitively, if a transaction T_i updates a t-object x, then no other transaction can access x until T_i commits or aborts. This, however, does not entirely prevent transactions from observing inconsistent states. For instance, TM history H_1 depicted in Figure 7.3 in Section 7.2, which violates opacity, ensures both serializability and recoverability. Also, recoverability was defined in a model with only *read* and *write* operations, and assuming a single-version protocol; it would be difficult to express it in our more general model.

Breitbart et al. [1991] defined the notion of *rigorous scheduling*, which captures the safety property of database systems that use, e.g., the strict 2-phase locking protocol [Eswaran et al., 1976]. Rigorous scheduling is stronger than opacity, in that it is not ensured by some opaque TM implementations (e.g., those using invisible reads, such as DSTM [Herlihy et al., 2003a] or TL2 [Dice et al., 2006]).

Our graph characterization of opacity (Chapter 8) is inspired by the graph characterizations of serializability [Papadimitriou, 1979] and 1-copy serializability [Bernstein and Goodman, 1983].

Distributed transactional systems   Lynch et al. [1994] introduced a very general model of a transactional system and defined the notion of atomicity in that model. Their atomicity can be applied to only committed transactions, or to all transactions. In the latter case, atomicity becomes very close to opacity. However, the model underlying atomicity is different than our model. In particular, instead of considering transactions and their operations separately, Lynch et al. consider each operation to be a separate transaction and allow transactions to be arbitrarily nested. The difference is not only conceptual: if the operations of a transaction are treated as nested transactions, the ordering requirements (called *external consistency* by Lynch et al.) become stronger than the real-time ordering required by opacity. Note that we could also define opacity in the very general model of Lynch et al. However, the goal of opacity is to capture the correctness of TMs, not of all transactional systems, and so we could trade generality for simplicity. Indeed, we wanted our model to correspond closely to the interfaces of existing TM implementations.

Also, the atomicity of Lynch et al. applied to all transactions allows different transactions (including committed ones) in a TM history H to observe different witness sequential histories of H, which is to weak a requirement for a TM.

Shared memory systems   Linearizability [Herlihy and Wing, 1990] is a correctness condition that is commonly used to describe implementations of shared objects. It captures the notion of atomicity of individual operations. Although referring to linearizability as a correctness condition for TM is a common trend in the TM literature, this can be done only in an informal context, or when describing the semantics of a shared object that is implemented using a TM (i.e., that internally uses transactions). Indeed, linearizability says that every operation should appear atomic, but TMs guarantee that all operations of every transaction appear atomic. It makes sense to talk about linearizability when we treat the entire transaction as a single operation. Then, however, we have to assume that the operations of a transaction, and their return values, are hidden from the application, since linearizability does not say anything about those operations. This is true only in a few TM systems.

Scott [2006] proposed to describe the semantics of a TM by assuming that individual operations of a TM are linearizable, and then specifying the sequential behavior of the TM. Note, however, that here "sequential" refers to operations, not to transactions. Hence, assuming linearizability of TM operations still requires reasoning about almost arbitrary TM histories. Scott indeed proposes a sequential specification of a TM, but it captures only strict serializability and assumes a single-version TM supporting only *read* and *write* operations.

10.2   ALTERNATIVES AND EXTENSIONS OF OPACITY

Weaker conditions   Recently, two correctness conditions have been proposed as an alternative to opacity: virtual world consistency [Imbs et al., 2009] and weakest reasonable condition (WRC) [Doherty et al., 2009]. Both of those conditions are stronger than serializability in that they require all transactions to observe consistent states of the system. Indeed, both conditions were inspired by opacity. However, unlike opacity, they allow different aborted transactions in the same TM history to observe different order of committed transactions. That is, roughly speaking, the witness sequential history can be different for each aborted transaction. While those correctness conditions are interesting, there has been so far no evidence that there is any practical or fundamental difference between each of them and opacity. That is, it is not clear that ensuring virtual world consistency or WRC instead of opacity can result in a more efficient TM implementation, or allow for overcoming some inherent complexity lower bound that holds for opacity. In particular, Theorem 9.8 that we proved in Chapter 9 holds also for WRC.

Extensions of opacity   As we pointed out in Chapter 3, we do not discuss in this manuscript the semantics of executions in which the same shared data is accessed both inside and outside of transactions. Blundell et al. [2005, 2006] were first to point out the semantic issues that can arise in such executions. Grossman et al. [2006] show that the situation becomes even more involved when operations on shared variables (base objects) cannot be assumed to be atomic. Indeed, even defining a *memory model*, which specifies the semantics of concurrent non-transactional accesses to shared memory, is already a complex task. Extending a memory model with transactions complicates the matter further. Menon et al. [2008] discuss how this could be done for the Java memory model [Manson et al., 2005], while Dalessandro and Scott [2009]; Spear et al. [2008a] describe a more general approach. Guerraoui et al. [2009] define a property called *parametrized opacity* that combines opacity with an arbitrary memory model (given as a parameter). Roughly speaking, parametrized opacity requires opacity for transactions, preserves the constraints of the given memory model for non-transactional operations, and enforces strong isolation between transactions and non-transactional code.

The graph interpretation of opacity that we present in Chapter 8 helps in manual proofs of correctness of TM algorithms. Guerraoui et al. [2008a,b] propose an approach to computer-aided verification of opacity of TMs. Using this technique, they verify correctness of existing TM protocols such as DSTM [Herlihy et al., 2003a] and TL2 [Dice et al., 2006].

Programming language perspective   Abadi et al. [2008]; Jagannathan et al. [2005]; Moore and Grossman [2008] considered simple programming languages with embedded support for transactions, and then they defined the semantics of those languages. This approach to specifying the correctness of a TM is orthogonal to ours. On the one hand, it allows defining precisely the interaction between transactional constructs (such as **atomic** blocks) and other elements of a programming language. On the other hand, the three above papers make assumptions about how the TM is implemented—they focus on some specific TM protocol, or class of protocols. Opacity is thus a more general correctness condition.

A similar approach is taken, e.g., by Menon et al. [2008]. They, however, take an existing programming language, namely Java, and extend its memory model to account for **atomic** blocks. Their focus is on defining the interaction between transactional and non-transactional accesses to the same shared data, and the transactional semantics they define is not precise enough for formal reasoning.

PART III

Progress

CHAPTER 11

The Liveness of a TM

In the previous chapters, we introduced and discussed opacity—a correctness condition for TM implementations. Opacity guarantees *safety*: that nothing bad will ever happen—that no transaction will ever observe concurrency from other transactions. If an application expects a TM to be opaque, and the TM violates opacity, the result may be fatal—even a single incorrect value received from the TM can cause the application to enter an illegal state and then crash or misbehave.

But guaranteeing opacity is not enough, for this correctness condition does not say when transactions should make *progress*. A TM implementation that (forceably) aborts every transaction, or that blocks every transaction infinitely long inside some operation, might indeed be opaque, but is clearly useless. A TM has to ensure some *liveness*: that some processes eventually commit their transactions.

There are two orthogonal dimensions of the liveness of TMs. The first dimension concerns individual operations executed by transactions, i.e., the question of when a transaction T_i that invokes some operation on a TM shared object returns from this operation. The second dimension concerns the progress of entire transactions, i.e., when a transaction is guaranteed to commit.

In the following chapters, we first look at the liveness of two dominating classes of TM implementations: lock-based TMs (Chapter 12) and obstruction-free TMs (Chapter 13). Those TMs usually ensure wait-freedom of individual operations of every transaction. There are some optional modules that can compromise wait-freedom, e.g., contention managers that block transactions indefinitely, or mechanisms for handling overflows (e.g., of timestamps). However, most contention managers block transactions only for a specified (and usually short) time, and overflows happen very rarely. We can thus assume wait-freedom of individual TM operations, and then focus only on specifying when transactions are guaranteed to commit (the second dimension of the liveness of a TM). Then, we describe the liveness of a lock-based or obstruction-free TM by giving its *progress property*. A progress property specifies when a TM is allowed to forceably abort a given transaction. (Note that, strictly speaking, our progress properties are not liveness properties [Alpern and Schneider, 1985], unlike, e.g., wait-freedom, since they can be violated in finite TM histories. We talk about liveness properties of TMs in Chapter 14.)

We also ask, in Chapter 14, a fundamental question about how much liveness a TM can guarantee, both at the level of individual operations and at the level of entire transactions. To answer this question, we first define a theoretical framework that helps reason about the general liveness of a TM at those two levels. Then, we determine a liveness property that is, in a precise sense, the strongest a TM can implement in an asynchronous system.

CHAPTER 12

Lock-Based TMs

We focus in this chapter on the liveness of lock-based TMs. A lock-based TM is one that internally uses some form of mutual exclusion, usually (often implicit) try-locks. Algorithms implementing such TMs were presented in Chapter 5.

From a user's perspective, the choice of the mechanisms used by a TM is not very important. What is important is how those mechanisms manifest themselves on the public interface of the TM, i.e., what properties are guaranteed by the TM, and what are the time and space complexities of the operations implemented by the TM.

We define a class of lock-based TMs by stating three properties that each TM in this class must ensure. Those are: opacity, wait-freedom of individual operations of a TM, and a progress property that we call *strong progressiveness* and which we define in Section 12.1. Indeed, many existing lock-based TMs ensure those properties, e.g., TL2 [Dice et al., 2006], TinySTM [Felber et al., 2008], the lock-based versions of RSTM [Spear et al., 2006], and SwissTM [Dragojević et al., 2009].[1]

It is worth highlighting that wait-freedom of individual operations is indeed a commonly ensured property among lock-based TMs. To understand why it is so, note that those TMs use try-locks, or similar mutual exclusion mechanisms that do not cause processes to get blocked indefinitely. When a transaction T_k invokes an operation of a TM and, within this operation, tries to acquire some try-lock that is held by another transaction, T_k is either blocked for some specified (and usually short) time or aborts immediately. That is, T_k does not wait for other transactions to release their try-locks. Wait-freedom of individual TM operations can be violated, however, if the TM uses some blocking contention manager. Such contention managers are available as an option in some lock-based TMs, e.g., SwissTM.

Once we define strong progressiveness in Section 12.1, we prove that certain TM implementations indeed ensure this property. To make this easier, we give, in Section 12.2, a theorem that reduces the problem of proving strong progressiveness of a TM to the problem of proving a simple property of each try-lock (or a similar mutual exclusion object) that this TM uses. Using this theorem, we show that our TM algorithm $\mathcal{A}_{IR}$ presented in Chapter 5, as well as the TL2 algorithm, which we outline in this chapter, are both strongly progressive. Similar proofs can be carried out for other lock-based TMs such as TinySTM and SwissTM.

We also ask what objects are necessary and sufficient to implement a TM that is strongly progressive. More specifically, we prove, in Section 12.3, that such a TM cannot be implemented using only read-write shared memory, i.e., registers; however, very strong objects such as compare-

---

[1]This is assuming no false conflicts. We explained the problem of false conflicts, and a way of extending our theoretical framework so that it allows dealing with those, in Section 3.4.3.

and-swap are not strictly necessary. The proof goes through a result that is interesting on its own: we show that every strongly progressive TM is equivalent to a particular kind of a try-lock that we call a *strong try-lock*. That is, it is possible to implement a strongly progressive TM using only strong try-locks and registers, and to implement a strong try-lock using strongly progressive TM objects and registers. Since, as we show, a strong try-lock cannot be implemented from only registers, but can be implemented using a base object such as test-and-set, the same is true for a strongly progressive TM. (Recall from Section 2.1.8 that test-and-set is a relatively weak object as it can implement consensus for at most 2 processes; compare-and-swap, for instance, can implement consensus for any number of processes.)

Nailing down precisely the progress property of a lock-based TM also helps consider alternative semantics and their impacts. For instance, we discuss, in Section 12.4, how one has to weaken the progress property of a lock-based TM so that it could be implemented with registers only.

12.1   STRONG PROGRESSIVENESS

Intuitively, strong progressiveness stipulates that (1) if a transaction has no *conflict* then it cannot be forceably aborted and (2) if a group of transactions conflict on a single t-object, then not all of those transactions can be forceably aborted. Roughly speaking, two concurrent transactions conflict if they both invoke some operations on a common t-object and at least one of those operations is not read-only (refer to Section 3.2.3 for a precise definition of a conflict).

Strong progressiveness gives the programmer the following important advantages. First, it guarantees that if two independent subsystems of an application do not share any memory locations (or t-objects), then their transactions are completely independent of each other (i.e., a transaction executed by a subsystem A does not cause a transaction in a subsystem B to be forceably aborted). Second, it avoids "spurious" aborts: the cases when a transaction can abort are strictly restricted. Third, it ensures global progress for transactions that access only a single t-object, which might be important for some applications. (Note that such transactions, albeit very simple, already provide processes with some means of communication.)

Let H be any TM history, and T_i be any transaction in H. We denote by $CObj_H(T_i)$ the set of t-objects on which T_i conflicts with any other transaction in history H. That is, a t-object x is in $CObj_H(T_i)$ if there exists a transaction T_k in H, $k \neq i$, such that T_i conflicts with T_k on t-object x.

Let $Q \subseteq Trans$ be any subset of the set of transactions in a history H. We denote by $CObj_H(Q)$ the union of sets $CObj_H(T_i)$ for all $T_i \in Q$.

Let W be the set of all transactions in a TM history H. We denote by $CTrans(H)$ the set of nonempty subsets of set W, such that a set Q is in $CTrans(H)$ if no transaction in Q conflicts with a transaction *not* in Q. In particular, if T_i is a transaction in history H and T_i does not conflict with any other transaction in H, then $\{T_i\} \in CTrans(H)$.

For example, consider the TM history H illustrated in Figure 12.1. In H, transactions T_1 and T_2 conflict on t-object x, while transaction T_3 has no conflicts. Then, we have, for instance:

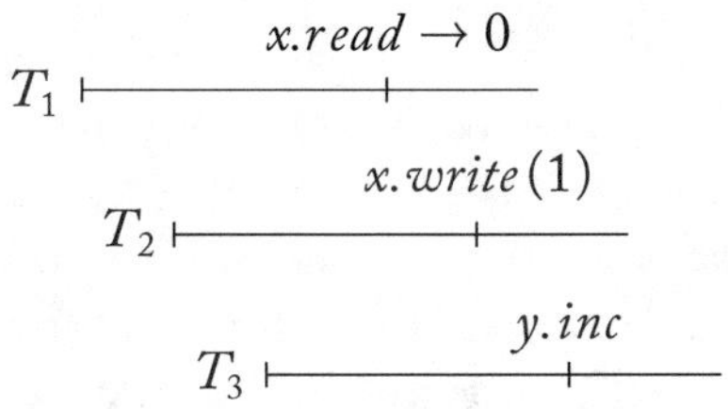

$$T_1 \;\vdash\!\!\!-\!\!\!-\!\!\!\underset{\displaystyle x.read \to 0}{\mid}\!\!\!-\!\!\!-\!\!\!-\!\!\!-$$

$$T_2 \;\vdash\!\!\!-\!\!\!-\!\!\!\underset{\displaystyle x.write\,(1)}{\mid}\!\!\!-\!\!\!-\!\!\!-$$

$$T_3 \;\vdash\!\!\!-\!\!\!-\!\!\!-\!\!\!\underset{\displaystyle y.inc}{\mid}\!\!\!-\!\!\!-\!\!\!-$$

Figure 12.1: A TM history H in which transactions T_1 and T_2 conflict on t-object x

$$
\begin{aligned}
CObj_H(T_1) &= \{x\}, \\
CObj_H(T_3) &= \varnothing, \\
CObj_H(\{T_1,\ T_2,\ T_3\}) &= \{x\}, \text{ and} \\
CTrans(H) &= \{\{T_1,\ T_2\},\ \{T_3\},\ \{T_1,\ T_2,\ T_3\}\}.
\end{aligned}
$$

Definition 12.1 (Strong progressiveness). A TM history H is *strongly progressive* if, for every set $Q \in CTrans(H)$ such that $|CObj_H(Q)| \leq 1$, some transaction in Q is not forceably aborted in H.

Definition 12.2 (Strongly progressive TM). A TM object M is *strongly progressive* if every history of M is strongly progressive.

For example, in the TM history H depicted in Figure 12.1, transaction T_3 cannot be forceably aborted, since T_3 does not have any conflicts. Moreover, at most one of transactions T_1 and T_2 can be forceably aborted because those transactions conflict on exactly one t-object.

Note that strong progressiveness is a property that is strictly stronger than minimal progressiveness defined in Section 9.1. That is, every strongly progressive TM is also minimally progressive, while the opposite is generally not true.

12.2 VERIFYING STRONG PROGRESSIVENESS

In this section, we show how to reduce the problem of proving strong progressiveness of TM histories with arbitrary numbers of transactions and t-objects to proving a simple property of each individual (logical) try-lock used in those histories. Basically, we show that if a TM implementation M uses try-locks, or if one can assign "logical" try-locks to some parts of the algorithm of M, and if each of those try-locks is *strong*, then M ensures strong progressiveness (in every history of M). We define what it means for a try-lock to be strong in the following section.

12.2.1 STRONG TRY-LOCKS

As we said in Section 5.1.1, a try-lock is an object that has two operations: *trylock* and *unlock*. (We focus here only on non-read-write try-locks, i.e., on those try-locks that can be acquired only in exclusive mode.) When a process p_i is returned value *true* from operation *trylock* invoked on a try-lock object L, we say that p_i *acquires* L, and then *holds* L until p_i invokes *unlock* on L. We also say then that L is *locked* (by p_i) until p_i returns from operation *unlock* on L. (Hence, whenever some process holds L, L is locked; the converse, however, is not always true.) The mutual exclusion property ensures that at most one process can hold L at any time.

Try-locks are wait-free objects. This means that whenever a correct process p_i invokes operation *trylock* on a try-lock L, p_i must eventually return from this operation, even if L still being held by another process. In this situation, p_i is returned value *false*, meaning that p_i has not acquired L.

So far we were not very precise about when operation *trylock* can return *false*. We just assumed that a typical try-lock will do something sensible here and, e.g., try not to return *false* too often. This is sufficient when talking about correctness (i.e., opacity) of TMs that use try-locks. Indeed, reasoning about the correctness of the TM implementations that we showed in Chapter 5 requires only the assumption of the mutual exclusion of try-locks. However, when reasoning about progress properties of those TMs, we need some restrictions on when *trylock* can return *false*. For instance, if the TMs from Chapter 5 use try-locks that always return *false* from their *trylock* operation, those TMs still ensure opacity, but provide no progress whatsoever—every transaction that tries to update some t-variable gets forceably aborted.

We introduce thus a class of try-locks that we call *strong*. Intuitively, we say that a try-lock L is strong if whenever several processes compete for unlocked L, then one should be able to acquire L. More precisely:

Definition 12.3   (Strong try-lock).   We say that a try-lock L is *strong*, if L ensures the following property, in its every history H: if L is not locked at some time t in H, and if some process invokes operation *trylock* on L at t, then some process acquires L after t or some *trylock* operation is pending in H.

Hence, if a strong try-lock L is unlocked at some time t, and then one or more processes invoke operation *trylock* on L, there must be some process p_i that is *not* returned *false* from this operation. That is, either p_i is returned *true* from operation *trylock* on L after time t, i.e., p_i acquires L, or p_i crashes while executing operation *trylock* on L, in which case p_i never returns from this operation.

Example 12.4   An example algorithm that implements a strong try-lock, using a single test-and-set base object, is given in Figure 12.2. The properties of a try-lock L implemented by this algorithm are almost trivial to verify. First, a process p_i that acquires L must have changed the state of test-and-set object S to *true*. Then, no other process can be returned *false* from the *test-and-set* operation on S until p_i releases L, i.e., invokes operation *unlock* on L. Hence, L ensures mutual exclusion. Second, when L is not locked, then the state of base object S is *false*. Hence, the first process p_i that executes

uses: S—test-and-set object
initially: $S = false$

1 **operation** *trylock*
2   *locked* $\leftarrow$ S.*test-and-set*;
3   **return** $\neg$ *locked*;

4 **operation** *unlock*
5   S.*reset*;

Figure 12.2: An implementation of a strong try-lock from a test-and-set base object

the *test-and-set* operation on base object S, after invoking operation *trylock*, is returned *true* from *test-and-set*. That is, p_i will either eventually acquire L or its operation will be pending forever (if p_i crashes). Therefore, L is a strong try-lock.

12.2.2 REDUCTION THEOREM

Let M be any TM shared object, and E be any implementation history of M. We say that a process p_i executes a transaction T_k at a time t in E, if T_k is in $E|p_i$ and T_k is live in the prefix of history $E|M$ containing all events executed before t.

Let E' be any implementation history that is obtained from E by inserting into E any number of invocations and responses of operations of a try-lock L_x for every t-object x. We say that E' is a *strong try-lock extension* of E, if the following conditions are satisfied in E':

STLE1. For every t-object x, $E'|L_x$ is a (well-formed) history of a strong try-lock object (note that $E'|L_x$ must also satisfy the assumptions that we listed in Section 5.1.1 where we introduced try-locks);

STLE2. For every process p_i and every t-object x, if, at some time t, p_i invokes operation *trylock* on L_x, or if L_x is locked by p_i at t, then p_i executes at t in E' a transaction T_k such that $x \in WSet_{E'}(T_k)$;

STLE3. For every process p_i and every transaction T_k in $E'|p_i$, if T_k is forceably aborted in E', then either (1) p_i, while executing T_k, is returned *false* from every operation *trylock* on some try-lock L_x, or (2) there is a t-object $x \in RSet_{E'}(T_k)$, such that some process other than p_i holds L_x at some point while p_i executes T_k but before T_k acquires L_x (if at all).

Theorem 12.5 (Reduction). *For every implementation history E of every TM shared object M, if there exists a strong try-lock extension of E, then TM history $E|M$ is strongly progressive.*

Proof. Assume, by contradiction, that there exists a TM shared object M, such that some implementation history E of M has a strong try-lock extension E', but TM history $H = E|M$ violates strong progressiveness. This means that there is a set Q in $CTrans(H)$, such that $|CObj_H(Q)| \leq 1$ and every transaction in Q is forceably aborted in H. (Recall that Q is a subset of the set of transactions in H, such that no transaction in Q has a conflict with a transaction outside of Q.) Note that $E'|M = H$, and so every transaction in Q is forceably aborted also in E'. In the following paragraphs, we focus on events and steps executed in E'.

Assume first that $CObj_H(Q) = \emptyset$. Then no transaction in set Q has a conflict, and so, by STLE1–2, no transaction in Q can fail to acquire a try-lock L_x, or read a t-object x such that try-lock L_x is held by a concurrent transaction. Hence, by STLE3, no transaction in Q can be forceably aborted—a contradiction.

Therefore, $|CObj_H(Q)| = 1$. Let x be the t-object that is the only element of set $CObj_H(Q)$. Note first that if a transaction $T_k \in Q$ invokes operation *trylock* on some try-lock L_y (where y is any t-object different than x) then, by STLE2, y is in the write set of T_k. Hence, since no transaction in Q conflicts on a t-object different than x, no transaction concurrent to T_k reads t-object y or, by STLE2, invokes *trylock* on L_y. This means that since, by STLE1, $H|L_y$ is a history of a strong try-lock, T_k cannot be returned *false* from any operation *trylock* on L_y.

Assume first that no transaction in set Q acquires try-lock L_x. Then, since no transaction that is not in set Q conflicts with a transaction in Q, and by STLE2, try-lock L_x is not locked by any process while any transaction in Q is executed. Hence, since $H|L_x$ is a history of a strong try-lock, no transaction in set Q that invokes operation *trylock* on L_x can be returned *false* from this operation. But then, property STLE3 is violated—a contradiction.

Therefore, some transaction in Q acquires try-lock L_x. Let T_k be the first transaction from set Q to acquire L_x. Consider any t-object $y \in RWSet_H(T_k)$ different than x, and let t be any time at which T_k is executed in H. Since T_k does not conflict with any transaction on y, and by STLE2, try-lock L_y cannot be locked by any transaction other than T_k at t, and no transaction other than T_k invokes *trylock* on L_y at t. Therefore, by STLE3, and because T_k is forceably aborted, there is a transaction T_i that holds L_x after T_k starts and before T_k acquires L_x. Then, by STLE2, x must be in $WSet_H(T_i)$, and so T_i is in set Q. But then T_i acquires L_x before T_k—a contradiction with the assumption that T_k is the first transaction from set Q to acquire L_x. $\square$

Corollary 12.6   *For every TM shared object M, if there exists a strong try-lock extension of every implementation history of M, then M is strongly progressive.*

12.2.3   EXAMPLES

We show now how the reduction theorem can be used to prove strong progressiveness of our TM algorithm $\mathcal{A}_{\text{IR}}$ (introduced in Section 5.2), and of the TL2 implementation. We then show why our

TM algorithm $\mathcal{A}_{2PL}$ (presented in Section 5.1.2), which uses read-write try-locks, violates strong progressiveness.

Example 12.7 (Algorithm $\mathcal{A}_{IR}$) Let M_{IR} be any TM shared object implemented by algorithm $\mathcal{A}_{IR}$. Assume that all try-locks used by M_{IR} are strong. Consider any implementation history E of M_{IR}. We prove the following lemma:

Lemma 12.8 *Implementation history E of M_{IR} is a strong try-lock extension of E.*

Proof. We show in the following that E indeed ensures properties STLE1–3.

STLE1 Property STLE1 is trivially ensured because we assume that every try-lock $L[m]$ used by M is strong. Recall that $L[m]$, for $m = 1, 2, \ldots$, is the try-lock protecting t-variable x_m.

STLE2 Let p_i be any process that, at some time t, invokes operation *trylock* on some try-lock $L[m]$ in E. Since operation *trylock* can be executed only in line 11 of $\mathcal{A}_{IR}$, p_i must be executing operation $x_m.write$ within some transaction T_k at time t (and so $x_m \in WSet_E(T_k)$). When T_k aborts (function $abort(T_k)$ invoked in line 4, 12, 20, or 28) or commits (operation $tryC(T_k)$), T_k must release $L[m]$ (in line 32 or 24, respectively). Hence, $L[m]$ is not locked by p_i when p_i does not execute any transaction, or when p_i executes a transaction T_k that does not write to x_m. Therefore, property STLE2 is ensured.

STLE3 Let p_i be any process, and T_k in $E|p_i$ be any transaction that is forceably aborted. Transaction T_k must execute function $abort(T_k)$, invoked in line 4, 12, or 20. If T_k invokes $abort(T_k)$ in line 12, T_k must have been returned *false* from operation *trylock* executed in line 11 on some try-lock $L[m]$. Then, since T_k can invoke *trylock* on $L[m]$ at most once, property STLE3 is ensured.

Assume then that T_k calls $abort(T_k)$ in line 4 or 20. Hence, T_k has been returned *false* from function *validate*. This means that at some time t transaction T_k reads, in line 37, from some register $TVar[m]$, a value $(v, ts, locked)$ such that either (1) $locked = true$ and $m \notin wset$, or (2) $ts \neq readts[m]$.

Observe that register $TVar[m]$ can be modified only by a transaction that holds try-lock $L[m]$. Note also that $TVar[m]$ has a value $(-, -, true)$ only when some transaction holds $L[m]$. Therefore, in case (1) there must be some transaction that holds $L[m]$ at time t, and T_k cannot acquire $L[m]$ before t since $m \notin wset$ at T_k. In case (2), there must be some transaction T_i that holds $L[m]$ at some time t' after T_k reads $TVar[m]$ in line 2, because T_k reads at time t value $ts \neq readts[m]$. Moreover, if T_k ever acquires $L[m]$ then T_k must hold $L[m]$ until time t, and so, by mutual exclusion of $L[m]$, T_k cannot acquire $L[m]$ before time t'. Hence, in both cases (1) and (2) property STLE3 is ensured. □

From Lemma 12.8 and Theorem 12.5 we immediately obtain the following:

Theorem 12.9 *Algorithm $\mathcal{A}_{IR}$ implements a strongly progressive TM.*

Example 12.10   (TL2)   TL2 [Dice et al., 2006] is a lock-based TM that uses lazy acquisition. That is, acquiring and updating of t-variables is delayed until the commit time of transactions. TL2 uses a time-based heuristic to avoid incremental validation. The algorithm of TL2, which we denote by $\mathcal{A}_{\text{TL2}}$, is sketched in Figures 12.3 and 12.4. The most important phases of a transaction T_k are the following:

1. When T_k starts and invokes its first *read* operation, T_k gets its *read timestamp read-ver* from base fetch-and-increment object V (line 2).

2. When T_k reads a t-variable x_m, T_k checks whether x_m is not locked (flag *locked* in compare-and-swap object $C[m]$) and whether the version number of x is lower or equal to the read timestamp of T_k (lines 4–7). If any of those conditions is violated then T_k is aborted.

3. Once T_k invokes $tryC(T_k)$, it first tries to acquire (lock) all t-variables in its write set (lines 23–28). Locking of a t-variable x_m is done by executing a *compare-and-swap* operation on base object $C[m]$ in order to change the *locked* flag contained in $C[m]$ from *false* to *true* (line 26). If the compare-and-swap operation succeeds (i.e., returns *true*) then T_k becomes the exclusive owner of x_m; otherwise, T_k is aborted.

4. Once T_k acquires every t-variable in its write set, T_k obtains its *write timestamp write-ver* by executing a *fetch-and-increment* operation on object V (line 29).

5. Finally, T_k validates its read set (lines 30–33), and then updates and releases all t-variables in its write set (lines 34–36). When releasing a t-variable x_m, T_k writes to $C[m]$ its write timestamp, which then becomes the new version number of x_m.

Consider any TM shared object M_{TL2} implemented by $\mathcal{A}_{\text{TL2}}$. Let E be any implementation history of M_{TL2}. TL2 does not explicitly use try-locks. However, it is easy to see that operations *compare-and-swap* and *write* executed on each compare-and-swap object $C[m]$ are implementations of operations *trylock* and *unlock*, respectively, of a strong try-lock L_{x_m}. Let us then construct a strong try-lock extension E' of E by inserting, at each process p_i:

- an invocation event $inv_i(L_{x_m}.trylock)$ and a response event $ret_i(L_{x_m} \rightarrow locked)$, respectively before and after every *compare-and-swap* operation executed by p_i in line 26 on object $C[m]$, where *locked* is the return value of the operation; and

- an invocation event $inv_i(L_{x_m}.unlock)$ and a response event $ret_i(L_{x_m} \rightarrow ok)$, respectively before and after every *write* operation executed by p_i on $C[m]$ (in line 18 and in line 36).

Lemma 12.11   *Sequence E' is a strong try-lock extension of implementation history E of M_{TL2}.*

uses: V—fetch-and-increment object, $TVar[1, \ldots]$—array of registers, $C[1, \ldots]$—array
of compare-and-swap objects (other variables are process-local)
initially: $V = 0$, $TVar[1, \ldots] = 0$, $C[1, \ldots] = (0, false)$, $read\text{-}ver = \bot$,
$rset = wset = lset = \emptyset$ (at every process)

1 **operation** $x_m.read_k$
    ▶ In the first operation, get the read timestamp
2   **if** $read\text{-}ver = \bot$ **then** $read\text{-}ver \leftarrow V.read$;
3   **if** $m \in wset$ **then return** $wlog[m]$;
    ▶ Read consistent snapshot of $C[m]$ and $TVar[m]$
4      $(ver_1, locked_1) \leftarrow C[m].read$;
5      $v \leftarrow TVar[m].read$;
6      $(ver_2, locked_2) \leftarrow C[m].read$;
    ▶ Abort if validation fails
7   **if** $(ver_1 \neq ver_2)$ **or** $locked_2$ **or** $(ver_2 > read\text{-}ver)$ **then return** $abort(T_k)$;
8      $rset \leftarrow rset \cup \{m\}$;
9   **return** v;

10 **operation** $x_m.write(v)_k$
11      $wset \leftarrow wset \cup \{m\}$;
12      $wlog[m] \leftarrow v$;

13 **operation** $tryA(T_k)$
14   **return** $abort(T_k)$;

15 **function** $abort(T_k)$
    ▶ Release all locks
16   **foreach** $m \in lset$ **do**
17          $(ver, locked) \leftarrow C[m].read$;
18          $C[m].write\big((ver, false)\big)$;
19      $rset \leftarrow wset \leftarrow lset \leftarrow \emptyset$;
20      $read\text{-}ver \leftarrow \bot$;
21   **return** A_k;

Figure 12.3: A sketch of the TL2 algorithm $\mathcal{A}_{\text{TL2}}$ (continues in Figure 12.4)

```
22  operation tryC(T_k)
        ▶ Lock all t-variables in the write set
23      for m ∈ wset do
24          (ver, locked) ← C[m].read;
25          if locked then return abort(T_k);
26          locked ← C[m].compare-and-swap((ver, false), (ver, true));
27          if not locked then return abort(T_k);
28          lset ← lset ∪ {m};
        ▶ Get the write timestamp
29      write-ver ← V.fetch-and-increment;
        ▶ Validate the read set
30      if write-ver ≠ read-ver + 1 then
31          for m ∈ rset do
32              (ver, locked) ← C[m].read;
33              if (ver > read-ver) or locked then return abort(T_k);
        ▶ Write new values and release locks
34      for m ∈ wset do
35          TVar[m].write(wlog[m]);
36          C[m].write((write-ver, false));
37      wset ← rset ← lset ← ∅;
38      read-ver ← ⊥;
39      return C_k;
```

Figure 12.4: Algorithm $\mathcal{A}_{TL2}$—continuation of Figure 12.3

Proof. It is straightforward to see that E' ensures properties STLE1 and STLE2.

To prove that E' ensures property STLE3, consider any forceably aborted transaction T_k executed by some process p_i in E'. Transaction T_k can be forceably aborted only in lines 7, 27 and 33 of the algorithm, after accessing some object $C[m]$ (used to implement "logical" try-lock L_{x_m}). In the following paragraphs, we consider each of those three cases.

Case 1: T_k is aborted in line 7 Then, (a) $ver_1 \neq ver_2$, or (b) $locked_2$ equals *true*, or (c) $ver_2 > read$-ver. Note first that the state of $C[m]$ can be changed only by a transaction that is returned *true* from a compare-and-swap operation executed in line 26 on $C[m]$, i.e., a transaction that acquires try-lock L_{x_m} in E'. Note also that the state of $C[m]$ is changed to $(\ldots, true)$ by every transaction that acquires L_{x_m} and changed back to $(\ldots, false)$ only by a transaction that releases L_{x_m}. Hence, in cases (a) and (b) some transaction other than T_k must hold try-lock L_{x_m} while T_k executes operation

$x_m.read$. Because T_k can acquire try-lock L_{x_m} only at commit time (i.e., in operation $tryC(T_k)$), condition STLE3 is satisfied in cases (a) and (b).

In case (c), T_k reads from $C[m]$ a pair $(ver_2, \dots)$ such that ver_2 is higher than the read timestamp of T_k. But then, some transaction T_i other than T_k must have obtained its write timestamp in line 29, while holding try-lock L_{x_m}, after T_k obtained its read timestamp in line 2. Hence, condition STLE3 is also ensured in case (c).

Case 2: T_k is aborted in line 27   Then, a compare-and-swap operation on $C[m]$ must have returned *false*, and so the *trylock* operation on try-lock L_{x_m} must have also returned *false* in E'. Hence, because T_k can invoke a compare-and-swap operation on $C[m]$ only once, condition STLE3 is ensured.

Case 3: T_k is aborted in line 33   Then, either (a) $ver > read\text{-}ver$, or (b) *locked* equals *true*. Those cases are analogous to, respectively, cases (c) and (b) considered in case 1 above. Hence, condition STLE3 is satisfied.   □

From Lemma 12.11 and Theorem 12.5 we immediately obtain the following:

Theorem 12.12   *Algorithm $\mathcal{A}_{TL2}$ (of TL2) implements a strongly progressive TM.*

Example 12.13 (Algorithm $\mathcal{A}_{2PL}$)   Consider TM algorithm $\mathcal{A}_{2PL}$, which was presented in Section 5.1.2. Recall that $\mathcal{A}_{2PL}$ uses the 2-phase locking scheme, where accesses to t-variables are protected by read-write try-locks. Recall also that $\mathcal{A}_{2PL}$ uses visible reads: a transaction that wants to read a t-variable x_m has to acquire the corresponding read-write try-lock $L[m]$ in shared mode, which is an update operation on $L[m]$ since it changes the state of $L[m]$.

Algorithm $\mathcal{A}_{2PL}$ does not implement a strongly progressive TM. This is for the following reason. Consider an execution in which some transactions T_i and T_k invoke operation *read* on some t-variable x_m. Assume also there are no other transactions besides T_i and T_k. Then, both T_i and T_k acquire read-write try-lock $L[m]$ and successfully return the current value of x_m. Observe now what happens when both transactions invoke operation *write* on x_m afterwards. Since $L[m]$ is held by both transactions in shared mode, neither of them can acquire $L[m]$ in exclusive mode before the other one unlocks $L[m]$. Therefore, it can happen that both T_i and T_k are returned *false* from operation *trylock* on $L[m]$ (in line 9) and then both are forceably aborted. In this case, strong progressiveness would be violated; indeed, since T_i and T_k conflict only on a single t-variable, strong progressiveness allows at most one of them to be forceably aborted.

12.3   THE COMPUTATIONAL POWER OF A LOCK-BASED TM

In this section, we determine the computational power of those (lock-based) TM implementations that ensure strong progressiveness (in addition to opacity and wait-freedom of individual operations). We prove here that a strongly progressive TM can implement 2-process consensus, but it cannot necessarily implement 3-process consensus. (Refer to Section 2.1.8 for the definition of consensus, as well as for the discussion about the computational power of an object.) This means that, on the one hand, such a TM cannot be implemented using only registers, but, on the other hand, base objects such as compare-and-swap are not strictly necessary.

The proof goes through two steps: First, we show, in Section 12.3.1, that a strongly progressive TM is equivalent to a strong try-lock object (defined in Section 12.2.1). This result is interesting in its own right. Second, we determine, in Section 12.3.2, the computational power of a strong try-lock. That is, we prove that a strong try-lock can implement 2-process consensus, but cannot implement 3-process consensus.

12.3.1   EQUIVALENCE BETWEEN LOCK-BASED TMS AND TRY-LOCKS

To prove that a strongly progressive TM is (computationally) equivalent to a strong try-lock, we exhibit two algorithms: (1) an implementation of a strong try-lock from a (single) strongly progressive TM object and a register, and (2) an implementation of a strongly progressive TM from a number of strong try-locks and registers. In fact, implementation (2) has already been given in Section 5.2 (algorithm $\mathcal{A}_{IR}$), proved opaque in Section 8.4, and proved strongly progressive in Section 12.2.3. Hence, the following lemma holds:

Lemma 12.14   *There exists a strongly progressive TM implementation that uses only strong try-locks and registers.*

An algorithm $\mathcal{A}_{TM \to TLock}$ that implements a strong try-lock from a strongly progressive TM (and a register) is depicted in Figure 12.5. The algorithm uses an unbounded number of binary t-variables $x_1, x_2, \ldots$ (each initialized to *false*) and a single register V holding an integer (initialized to 1). The intuition behind $\mathcal{A}_{TM \to TLock}$ is the following. If the value of V is v, then the next operation (*trylock* or *unlock*) uses t-variable x_v. If x_v equals *true*, this means that the lock is held by some process. A process p_i acquires the try-lock when p_i manages to execute a transaction that changes the value of x_v from *false* to *true*. Then, p_i releases the try-lock by incrementing the value of register V, so that $x_{v'} = false$ where $v' = v + 1$ is the new value of V. (Note that incrementing V in two steps is safe here, as only one process—the one that holds the try-lock—may execute lines 10–11 at a time.) The implemented try-lock is strong because whenever several processes invoke *trylock*, at least one of those processes will commit its transaction (as the TM is strongly progressive) and acquire the try-lock.

Lemma 12.15   *Algorithm $\mathcal{A}_{TM \to TLock}$ implements a strong try-lock.*

Proof. Denote by L any shared object implemented by algorithm $\mathcal{A}_{TM \to TLock}$. We prove that the implementation of L is wait-free, and that L is indeed a strong try-lock.

First, because there is no loop in the implementation of L, and because both TM object M and register V are wait-free, the implementation of L is wait-free.

uses: M—strongly progressive TM object, $x_1, x_2, \ldots$—binary t-variables, V—register (v and *locked* are process-local variables)

initially: $x_1, x_2, \ldots = false$, $V = 1$

```
1  operation trylock
2      v ← V.read;
3      atomic using M
4          locked ← x_v.read;
5          if locked = true then abort ;
6          x_v.write(true);
7      on abort return false;
8      return true;

9  operation unlock
10     v ← V.read;
11     V.write(v + 1);
12     return ok;
```

Figure 12.5: Algorithm $\mathcal{A}_{\text{TM}\rightarrow\text{TLock}}$ that implements a strong try-lock from a strongly progressive TM object

To prove mutual exclusion, observe that if several processes invoke operation *trylock* on L and read the same value v in line 2, then, because TM object M ensures opacity, only one of those processes can commit a transaction that changes the value of t-variable x_v from *false* to *true*. (Note that once the value of x_v is changed to *true*, it is never changed back to *false*.) Hence, only one of those processes, say p_i, can return *true* from the operation, i.e., acquire L. Since we assume that only a process holding L can invoke *unlock* on L, only p_i can change (increment) the value of register V. Hence, until p_i releases L, no other process can acquire L, and so L ensures mutual exclusion.

Observe that the value of register V can never decrease, and all t-variables $x_1, x_2, \ldots$ are initially equal to *false*. Whenever a process p_i that holds L unlocks L, p_i increments the value of V (lines 10–11). Hence, when L is unlocked and there is no pending *trylock* operation on L, t-variable x_v has value *false*, where v is the current value of V.

Consider any time t at which L is unlocked, and denote by v the value of V at t. If $x_v = true$ at time t, this means that some process p_i executes operation *trylock* on L at t, has changed the value x_v from *false* to *true*, and thus will either will return *true* from its operation *trylock* or its operation will remain pending forever. Both cases are correct for a strong try-lock.

Assume then that $x_v = false$ at time t, and that some process p_i invokes operation *trylock* on L at t. Denote by Q the set of transactions (executed on M) that read from t-variable x_v. If Q is empty, then the operation of process p_i is pending forever (i.e., p_i crashes before accessing x_v). If Q is not empty, then, by strong progressiveness of M, some transaction in Q, say a transaction T_m executed by a process p_k, will not be forceably aborted and will read value *false* from t-variable x_v. Therefore, p_k cannot return *false* from its operation *trylock*, and so try-lock L is strong.   □

From Lemma 12.14 and Lemma 12.15, we immediately obtain the following result:

Theorem 12.16   *Every strongly progressive TM is equivalent to every strong try-lock.*

12.3.2   THE COMPUTATIONAL POWER OF A STRONG TRY-LOCK

We show here that every strong try-lock (and, a fortiori, by Theorem 12.16, every strongly progressive TM) can implement 2-process consensus but cannot implement 3-process consensus. Those results determine the computational power of a strong try-lock object, as well as of a strongly progressive TM (cf. Section 2.1.8).

An algorithm $\mathcal{A}_{\text{TLock}\to\text{Cons}}$ that implements 2-process consensus (for processes p_1 and p_2) using a single strong try-lock object (L) and two registers (V_1 and V_2) is depicted in Figure 12.6. The process p_i that acquires L is the winner: the value proposed by p_i, and written by p_i to register V_i, is decided by both p_1 and p_2. Because L is a strong try-lock, if the two processes concurrently execute operation *propose*, they cannot both acquire L and be the winners (because of mutual exclusion) or both fail to acquire L (in which case agreement of consensus could be violated).

> **uses**: L—strong try-lock, V_1, V_2—registers

```
1 operation propose(v)
2 │    Vᵢ.write(v);
3 │    locked ← L.trylock;
4 │    if locked then return v;
5 │    else return V₍₃₋ᵢ₎.read;
```

Figure 12.6: Algorithm $\mathcal{A}_{\text{TLock}\to\text{Cons}}$ implementing 2-process consensus from a strong try-lock (code for process p_i, $i = 1, 2$)

Theorem 12.17   *Every strong try-lock object can implement 2-process consensus.*

Proof. Consider algorithm $\mathcal{A}_{\text{TLock}\to\text{Cons}}$, and denote by C any shared object implemented by $\mathcal{A}_{\text{TLock}\to\text{Cons}}$. Observe that C is wait-free, because $\mathcal{A}_{\text{TLock}\to\text{Cons}}$ does not contain any loop or waiting statements, and the base objects used by C (L, V_1, and V_2) are themselves wait-free. We will prove now that C indeed implements 2-process consensus, i.e., that C ensures the validity and agreement properties of consensus.

First, a value returned by operation *propose* executed by a process p_i may be either the value proposed by p_i (in which case validity of consensus is trivially ensured) or the value of register $V_{(3-i)}$. The latter case is possible only if p_i is returned *false* from operation *trylock* on L, and this, in turn, is only possible if process $p_{(3-i)}$ holds L or is concurrently executing *trylock* on L. Then, however, $p_{(3-i)}$ must have already written its proposed value to $V_{(3-i)}$, and so also in this case validity is ensured at p_i.

Assume, by contradiction, that there is some implementation history E of C in which agreement of consensus is violated. That is, process p_1 decides value v_1 and p_2 decides value $v_2 \neq v_1$. But then both processes must have either returned *true* or *false* from operation *trylock* on L. If p_1 and p_2 both return *true* from *trylock*, then both processes hold L, which violates mutual exclusion of L. If p_1 and p_2 both return *false* from *trylock*, then, as there is no other invocation of *trylock* on L in E, this contradicts our assumption that L is a strong try-lock. Hence, agreement must be ensured. $\square$

Corollary 12.18   *There is no algorithm that implements a strong try-lock (or, by Theorem 12.16, a strongly progressive TM) using only registers.*

To prove that there is no algorithm that implements 3-process consensus using strong try-locks and registers, it is enough to give an algorithm that implements a strong try-lock using any other object that cannot implement 3-process consensus. In Section 12.2.1, we already gave an implementation of a strong try-lock from a single test-and-set object (Figure 12.2). Since no test-and-set object can implement 3-process consensus [Herlihy, 1991], we immediately obtain the following result:

Theorem 12.19   *There is a strong try-lock object that cannot implement 3-process consensus.*

12.4   WEAKENING STRONG PROGRESSIVENESS

We introduce here a progress property called *weak progressiveness*, which is weaker than strong progressiveness (but stronger than minimal progressiveness). We show then that it is possible to implement a weakly progressive TM using only registers. We do so by first proving that every such TM is equivalent to a *weak* try-lock, an object that we define in the following paragraphs.

Intuitively, a TM is weakly progressive if it can forceably abort a transaction T_i only if T_i conflicts with another transaction. More precisely:

Definition 12.20   (Weakly progressive TM).   A TM object M is *weakly progressive*, if in every history H of M the following property is satisfied: if a transaction T_i in H is forceably aborted, then T_i conflicts with some other transaction in H.

We correlate this notion with the concept of a *weak try-lock*: a try-lock which operation *trylock* executed by a process p_i may always return *false* if another process is concurrently executing *trylock* on the same try-lock object. That is, p_i is guaranteed to acquire a weak try-lock L only if L is not locked and no other process tries to acquire L at the same time. More precisely:

Definition 12.21   (Weak try-lock).   We say that a try-lock L is *weak* if L has the following property: if a process p_i invokes operation *trylock* on L at some time t, L is not locked at t, and no process other than p_i executes operation *trylock* on L at time t or later, then p_i is not returned *false* from its *trylock* operation.

An example algorithm $\mathcal{A}_{\text{Reg} \to \text{TLock}}$ that implements a weak try-lock using only registers is given in Figure 12.7. The intuition behind the algorithm is the following. If a process p_i invokes operation *trylock* on a try-lock L implemented by the algorithm, p_i first checks whether any other process holds L (lines 2–3). If not, p_i announces that it wants to acquire L by setting register $R[i]$ to 1 (line 4). Then, p_i checks whether it is the only process that wants to acquire L (lines 5–6). If yes, then p_i acquires L (returns *true*). Otherwise, p_i resets $R[i]$ back to 0 (so that future invocations of *trylock* may succeed) and returns *false*. Clearly, if two processes execute *trylock* in parallel, then both can reach line 6. However, then at least one of them must observe that more than one register in array R is set to 1, and return *false*.

> **uses:** $R[1, \ldots, n]$—array of registers
> **initially:** $R[k] = 0$ for $k = 1, \ldots, n$
>
> 1 **operation** *trylock*
> 2 $s \leftarrow getsum()$;
> 3   **if** $s > 0$ **then return** *false*;
> 4 $R[i].write(1)$;
> 5 $s \leftarrow getsum()$;
> 6   **if** $s = 1$ **then return** *true*;
> 7 $R[i].write(0)$;
> 8   **return** *false*;
>
> 9 **operation** *unlock*
> 10 $R[i].write(0)$;
> 11   **return** *ok*;
>
> 12 **function** *getsum()*
> 13 $s \leftarrow 0$;
> 14   **for** $k = 1$ **to** n **do** $s \leftarrow s + R[k].read$;
> 15   **return** s;

Figure 12.7: Algorithm $\mathcal{A}_{\text{Reg} \to \text{TLock}}$ that implements a weak try-lock using registers (code for process p_i)

Lemma 12.22   *Algorithm* $\mathcal{A}_{\text{Reg}\to\text{TLock}}$ *implements a weak try-lock.*

Proof. Denote by L any shared object implemented by $\mathcal{A}_{\text{Reg}\to\text{TLock}}$. First, it is straightforward to see that L is wait-free: algorithm $\mathcal{A}_{\text{Reg}\to\text{TLock}}$ does not have any unbounded loops or waiting statements, and all base objects used by $\mathcal{A}_{\text{Reg}\to\text{TLock}}$ are themselves wait-free.

Assume, by contradiction, that L does not ensure mutual exclusion. Hence, there is an implementation history E of L in which some two processes, say p_i and p_k, hold L at some time t. Consider only the latest *trylock* operations of p_i and p_k on L before t. Both of those operations must have returned *true*. Hence, process p_i observes in its *trylock* operation that $R[k] = 0$ in line 5, which means that p_i reads $R[k]$ before p_k writes 1 to $R[k]$ in line 4. Thus, p_k reads $R[i]$ (in line 5) after p_i writes 1 to $R[i]$. Therefore, p_k reads that $R[i]$ and $R[k]$ equal 1 and returns *false* in line 6—a contradiction.

Observe that, for every process p_i, if $R[i] = 1$ then either p_i holds L or p_i is executing operation *trylock* on L. Hence, if a process p_i returns *false* from *trylock*, then either L is held by another process or another process is executing *trylock* concurrently to p_i. This means that L is indeed a weak try-lock. $\qquad\square$

It is straightforward to see that using weak try-locks instead of strong ones in algorithm $\mathcal{A}_{\text{IR}}$ presented in Section 5.2 gives a TM that ensures weak progressiveness. Hence, by Lemma 12.22, we immediately obtain the following result:

Corollary 12.23   *There is an implementation of a weakly progressive TM from only registers.*

CHAPTER 13

Obstruction-Free TMs

In the previous chapter, we described the progress properties of lock-based TMs. The basic algorithms underlying those TMs are conceptually simple (as can be seen in the examples given in Chapter 5), and their implementations are rather lightweight. Still, lock-based TMs can give some reasonable liveness guarantees, for example wait-freedom of individual operations and strong progressiveness.

Lock-based TMs are however not resilient to crashes. (It is worth reminding here that crashes are just a modelling tool—they help express the property that processes could be swapped out, or otherwise delayed, for long periods. Tolerating crashes means that processes should make progress independently of each other.) Consider, for example, the following situation that could happen with a lock-based TM. Process p_1 executes a transaction T_1 that updates all t-variables. Just after T_1 acquires all the locks, p_1 stops any activity. Then, if any other process tries to execute any transaction, this transaction will be forceably aborted, since none of the locks is ever released. Hence, the progress of all transactions is blocked. If process p_1 does not stop completely but is instead delayed for a long time (e.g., after encountering a page fault), the situation is less severe. However, still no transaction can commit until p_1 resumes its execution and releases all the locks. In a sense, lock-based TMs are not live (in asynchronous systems), since one process can delay arbitrarily the progress of other processes.

Ideally, transactions should progress independently. For instance, in real-time systems, a high-priority transaction should not wait for a lower-priority one to release its locks. Similarly, a transaction that is executed by an interrupt or signal handler should not wait for any other transaction. In those situations, a transaction whose progress is vitally important should be able to immediately and unconditionally abort conflicting transactions in order to proceed with its own computation.

There indeed exist TM implementations in which a process that crashes while executing a transaction cannot prevent other processes from committing their transactions. An important class of those is *obstruction-free* TMs, or *OFTMs* for short. Intuitively, an OFTM guarantees progress for every transaction that executes *alone*, i.e., while concurrent transactions are suspended or crashed. Examples of existing OFTMs are: DSTM [Herlihy et al., 2003a], WSTM [Harris and Fraser, 2003], ASTM [Marathe et al., 2005], RSTM [Marathe et al., 2006], NZTM [Tabba et al., 2007], and MM-STM [Marathe and Moir, 2008].

It is important to understand the main difference between obstruction-freedom and strong progressiveness—the progress property of lock-based TMs. Strong progressiveness gives guarantees that depend on the number of conflicts between transactions. If a transaction T_k, executed by a process p_i, writes to some t-variable x, then T_k can cause conflicts on x until T_k commits or aborts. Hence, if process p_i crashes while executing T_k, then T_k can cause conflicts forever. On the contrary, obstruction-freedom gives guarantees that depend on the contention among *active* transactions, i.e., transactions that keep executing steps. Then, a crash of a process p_i removes one source of contention, thus potentially boosting the progress of other processes.

Obstruction-freedom may seem to be a very weak property since it does not give any guarantees if transactions execute steps concurrently. Therefore, it can happen that two concurrent transactions prevent each other from committing infinitely long—a situation called a *livelock*. However, in practice, contention tends to be low. Also, even very simple contention management schemes, like exponential back-off (used, e.g., in Ethernet networks to deal with collisions), can often effectively help deal with high-contention scenarios. Finally, typical OFTMs combine obstruction-freedom with some conflict-based guarantee such as weak or strong progressiveness.

In the following sections, we first define what it precisely means for a TM implementation to be an OFTM (Section 13.1). Then, we give a simple (and impractical) algorithm for an OFTM, which aims at highlighting the very basic idea used in existing OFTM implementations.

In Section 13.3, we determine the computational power of an OFTM. We do so in a similar way as we did for lock-based TMs: we prove first that every OFTM is equivalent to a very simple object that we call *fo-consensus*.[1] We show then that an fo-consensus object can implement 2-process consensus but cannot implement 3-process consensus. This means that it is impossible to implement an fo-consensus, or an OFTM, using only registers; however, this result also implies that strong objects, such as compare-and-swap, are not strictly necessary. Therefore, OFTMs have the same computational power as TMs that are strongly progressive. (For an introduction to the computational power of objects, refer to Section 2.1.8.)

In Section 13.4, we prove that OFTMs cannot ensure a property that we call *strict disjoint-access-parallelism*. This property requires, roughly speaking, that if some transactions access disjoint sets of t-objects, then the processes executing those transactions do not conflict on any base object. (Two processes conflict on a base object X if both access X and at least one of them updates X.) Strict disjoint-access-parallelism means, in particular, that transactions accessing disjoint sets of t-objects can be executed completely independently. This property is strictly weaker than strict data partitioning (cf. Section 9.1), and can be ensured by lock-based TMs—see, e.g., our TM algorithms $\mathcal{A}_{2PL}$ and $\mathcal{A}_{IR}$ described in Chapter 5.

Finally, we discuss, in Section 13.5, two alternative forms of obstruction-freedom. We prove that in an asynchronous system they are equivalent to our "basic" definition of an OFTM. We introduce them because they may be more convenient to use in certain models or applications.

13.1   OBSTRUCTION-FREEDOM

Before we define an OFTM, we first introduce the notion of *step contention*. Intuitively, we say that a transaction T_i encounters step contention when some other transaction executes a step concurrently to T_i. More formally, let E be any implementation history of any TM object M. We say that a

---

[1]This name is an abbreviation for *"fail-only"* *consensus*—an object introduced by Attiya et al. [2005]. The term "fail-only" is really meaningful only within the context of the original paper.

transaction T_k in E, executed by a process p_i, encounters *step contention* in E, if there is a step of a process other than p_i in E after the first event of T_k and, if T_k is completed in E, before the commit or abort event of T_k.

Intuitively, obstruction-freedom guarantees progress for every transaction that does *not* encounter step contention. That is:

Definition 13.1 (Obstruction-freedom).   An implementation history E of any TM ensures *obstruction-freedom* if, for every transaction T_k in E, if T_k is forceably aborted, then T_k encounters step contention.

Definition 13.2 (Obstruction-free TM).   A TM shared object M is *obstruction-free* if every implementation history of M ensures obstruction-freedom.

We call an *OFTM* every TM shared object that is obstruction-free, wait-free (cf. Section 2.1.7), and opaque (cf. Section 7.2).

Example 13.3   Consider an implementation history E of some TM, which corresponds to the execution depicted in Figure 13.1. In E, process p_1 executes one operation within transaction T_1 and then crashes. Then, process p_3 executes and completes transaction T_3. Process p_2 executes two operations within transaction T_2; however, p_2 is suspended for the entire duration of T_3, i.e., p_2 does not execute any step in E between the first and the last event of T_3. Hence, transaction T_3 does not encounter step contention, and so for implementation history E to ensure obstruction-freedom T_3 cannot be forceably aborted.

Note that all three transactions are pairwise concurrent and conflict on t-variable x. Hence, unlike obstruction-freedom, strong progressiveness requires that *some* transaction in E is not forceably aborted, but not necessarily T_3. In fact, the TM implementations that we presented in Chapter 5, as well as many existing lock-based TMs, would forceably abort both T_2 and T_3, as well as all further transactions that access t-variable x. (This does not violate strong progressiveness because then T_1 is not forceably aborted.)

Note 13.4   We assume that every OFTM is a wait-free shared object. That is, we require that a correct process p_i that executes a transaction T_k is never blocked inside any TM operation infinitely long, even if the TM is unable to ensure progress (i.e., commitment) of T_k. This means that, even if T_k is forceably aborted, the application using the TM is eventually returned control and can, for instance, choose a computation that is less likely to cause conflicts, or make processes cooperate in order to execute the computation of T_k.

An alternative view is to assume that the individual operations of an OFTM are obstruction-free [Attiya et al., 2005; Herlihy et al., 2003b]. Then, a correct process p_i that invokes an operation on a TM is guaranteed to return from this operation only if p_i eventually executes sufficiently many

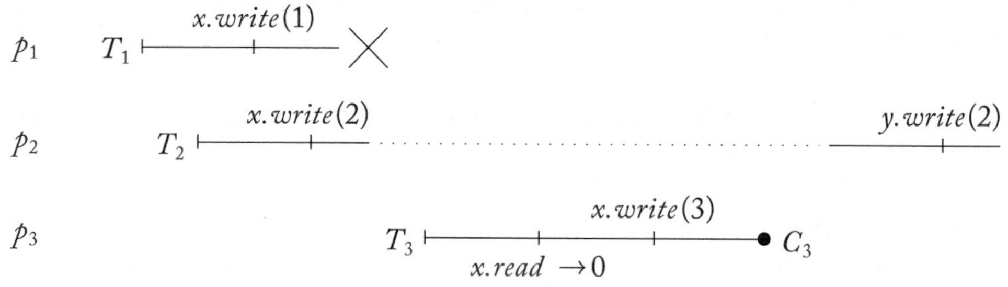

Figure 13.1: An example history of an OFTM (process p_1 crashes before transaction T_3 starts, and p_2 is suspended for the entire duration of T_3; the crash of p_1 is marked with a cross)

steps alone (i.e., with other processes suspended or crashed). Many existing OFTM implementations (e.g., DSTM and ASTM) ensure, by default, only obstruction-freedom of individual operations instead of wait-freedom. However, they support contention managers that can limit the number of steps executed by any process within a TM operation, thus providing operation wait-freedom. The simplest example of such a contention manager is one that immediately aborts every transaction T_k that needs to retry some code because T_k encountered step contention (e.g., when T_k is returned *false* from a step $X.compare\text{-}and\text{-}swap(v, v')$ after reading value v from X; indeed, in this case, there must have been another transaction that changed the value of X just before T_k executed *compare-and-swap*). Both OFTM algorithms that we present in this chapter use such a simplified contention management scheme.

Assuming wait-freedom of TM operations is important for some of the results that we present in this chapter. We explain this in more detail in the following sections.

13.2 IMPLEMENTING AN OFTM

We present here a simple algorithm $\mathcal{A}_{OF}$ that implements an OFTM. The sole purpose of this algorithm is to illustrate the basic idea underlying existing OFTM implementations such as DSTM. In Section 13.3.2, we give another OFTM algorithm that is used in the proof of equivalence between OFTMs and fo-consensus objects.

Algorithm $\mathcal{A}_{OF}$ is depicted in Figures 13.3 and 13.4. Unlike in the lock-based TMs we presented in previous chapters, array *TVar* consists in $\mathcal{A}_{OF}$ of compare-and-swap objects, and not registers, and contains *locators* of t-variable values, and not the values themselves. A locator of a t-variable x_m is a tuple of three pointers: to the current *owner* of x_m, to the *old* value of x_m, and to the *new* value of x_m. The values of t-variables are stored in array *Mem*, whose elements are dynamically allocated to transactions with the help of fetch-and-increment object C. The algorithm also uses array *State* of compare-and-swap objects, which stores the current state of every transaction.

The intuition behind algorithm $\mathcal{A}_{OF}$ is the following. If a transaction T_k wants to write to a t-variable x_m, or read from x_m, for the first time, T_k needs to acquire x_m (function *acquire* in Figure 13.4; see also Figure 13.2 for an illustration). To do so, T_k first reads the current locator (*owner, oldval, newval*) of x_m in line 16. Then, T_k determines the *current value* of x_m in the following way:

1. If $State[owner] = \texttt{aborted}$, then the current value of x_m is in register $Mem[oldval]$;

2. If $State[owner] = \texttt{committed}$, then the current value of x_m is in register $Mem[newval]$.

However, if $State[owner] = \texttt{live}$, then the current value of x_m is undecided. Hence, before checking the state of T_{owner} in line 19, T_k first attempts at aborting T_{owner} (in line 18) by atomically changing $State[owner]$ from value $\texttt{live}$ to $\texttt{aborted}$. Aborting T_{owner} may fail if T_{owner} manages to commit before, by changing $State[owner]$ from $\texttt{live}$ to $\texttt{committed}$ in line 11. However, no matter what the final state of T_{owner} is ($\texttt{aborted}$ or $\texttt{committed}$), the current value of x_m can be determined.

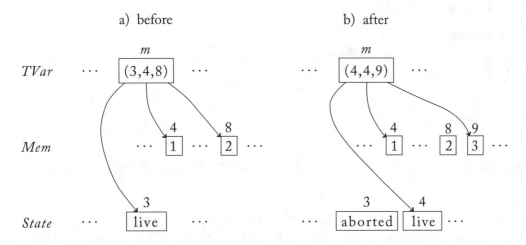

Figure 13.2: Illustration of an execution of algorithm $\mathcal{A}_{OF}$. Initially (the left part), transaction T_3 is the owner of t-variable x_m, and the *old* and *new* values of x_m are 1 and 2. Then (the right part), transaction T_4 aborts T_3 and changes the locator of x_m: value 1 remains the *old* value of x_m, and value 3, written in a newly allocated slot 9 of array *Mem*, becomes the *new* value of x_m. Transaction T_4 is now the current owner of x_m.

Once transaction T_k knows the current value of x_m, T_k allocates a new slot *myslot* in array *Mem* (in line 22), and copies to $Mem[myslot]$ the current value of x_m. Finally, T_k tries to replace the locator of x_m with a new one, which points to T_k (the new owner of x_m), the current value of x_m (which becomes the *old* value of x_m), and the *new* value of x_m in register $Mem[myslot]$ (cf. Figure 13.2b). Transaction T_k may fail to change the locator, when some other transaction acquires x_m after T_k

uses: $TVar[1,\ldots]$, $State[0,\ldots]$—arrays of compare-and-swap objects,
$Mem[0,\ldots]$—array of registers, C—fetch-and-increment object (all other variables
are transaction-local)

initially: $TVar[1,\ldots] = (0,0,0)$, $State[0] = \mathtt{committed}$, $State[1,\ldots] = \mathtt{live}$,
$Mem[0] = 0$, $C = 1$

1 **operation** $x_m.write(v)_k$
2    $addr \leftarrow acquire(T_k, m)$;
3   **if** $addr = A_k$ **then return** A_k;
4    $Mem[addr].write(v)$;
5   **return** ok;

6 **operation** $x_m.read_k$
7    $addr \leftarrow acquire(T_k, m)$;
8   **if** $addr = A_k$ **then return** A_k;
9   **return** $Mem[addr].read$;

10 **operation** $tryC(T_k)$
11   **if** $State[k].compare\text{-}and\text{-}swap(\mathtt{live}, \mathtt{committed})$ **then return** C_k;
12   **else return** A_k;

13 **operation** $tryA(T_k)$
14   **return** A_k;

Figure 13.3: Algorithm $\mathcal{A}_{\mathrm{OF}}$ that implements a simple OFTM (continues in Figure 13.4)

executes line 16, in which case T_k is forceably aborted. Also, T_k is forceably aborted as soon as T_k realizes that it has been aborted by some other transaction (in line 27). This is to prevent T_k from reading inconsistent values in subsequent *read* operations.

Once T_k acquires x_m, the value in $Mem[myslot]$ (i.e., the new value of x_m) may be subsequently read and modified by T_k many times. Until $State[k]$ changes to $\mathtt{committed}$, no transaction other than T_k can access register $Mem[myslot]$.

When T_k manages to change the state of $State[k]$ from $\mathtt{live}$ to $\mathtt{committed}$ (in line 11), all *new* values of t-variables written to by T_k become instantaneously the current values of those t-variables. If any transaction changes $State[k]$ to $\mathtt{aborted}$, then T_k can no longer commit. The important feature of the algorithm, which is in fact characteristic of many OFTMs, is that committing and aborting a transaction is done in a single step. Hence, T_k cannot crash in the middle of its commit or abort phase, leaving some t-variables with old values, and some with new ones.

It is worth highlighting why the TM implemented by algorithm $\mathcal{A}_{\mathrm{OF}}$ indeed ensures obstruction-freedom. Consider any transaction T_k that executes alone, i.e., without encountering

15 **function** *acquire*(T_k, m)
    ▶ Get the locator of x_m
16    $(owner, oldval, newval) \leftarrow TVar[m].read;$
17   **if** $owner \neq k$ **then**
       ▶ Abort the current owner of x_m
18       $State[owner].compare\text{-}and\text{-}swap(\texttt{live}, \texttt{aborted});$
19       $state \leftarrow State[owner].read;$
       ▶ Determine the current value of x_m
20   **if** $state = \texttt{committed}$ **then** $curr \leftarrow newval;$
21   **else** $curr \leftarrow oldval;$
       ▶ Allocate memory and initialize it with the current value of x_m
22       $myslot = C.fetch\text{-}and\text{-}increment;$
23       $Mem[myslot].write(Mem[curr].read);$
       ▶ Try to replace the locator of x_m
24       $s \leftarrow TVar[m].compare\text{-}and\text{-}swap((owner, oldval, newval), (k, curr, myslot));$
25   **if** $s = false$ **then return** $A_k;$
26   **else** $myslot \leftarrow newval;$
27   **if** $State[k].read \neq \texttt{live}$ **then return** $A_k;$
28   **return** $myslot;$

Figure 13.4: Algorithm $\mathcal{A}_{\mathrm{OF}}$ (continuation of Figure 13.3)

step contention. Transaction T_k will abort all conflicting transactions (crashed or suspended), and will not be aborted by any transaction. This is because the value of $State[k]$ can be changed to $\texttt{aborted}$ only after T_k acquires some t-variable, since only then the identifier of T_k is in some locator in array $TVar$. Hence, if T_k tries to commit, T_k will succeed. For T_k to be forceably aborted, T_k has to encounter step contention.

Many existing OFTMs, such as DSTM, use algorithms that are based on the same principle as $\mathcal{A}_{\mathrm{OF}}$. The main differences between $\mathcal{A}_{\mathrm{OF}}$ and, for example, DSTM, lie in the following. First, OFTMs handle *read* operations more efficiently, for instance using invisible reads and incremental validation in a manner similar to our lock-based TM algorithm $\mathcal{A}_{\mathrm{IR}}$ from Section 5.2. Second, since hardware compare-and-swap objects rarely can fit an entire locator of a t-variable (three pointers), OFTMs usually store only a pointer to a locator in each compare-and-swap object. This, clearly, creates an additional level of indirection that increases the cost of accessing a t-variable. Some OFTMs, such as ASTM, RSTM, and NZTM, reduce this indirection at least in certain cases. Third, instead of immediately aborting a conflicting transaction (line 18 in algorithm $\mathcal{A}_{\mathrm{OF}}$), OFTMs use contention managers that can, for instance, introduce bounded waiting to reduce contention, or prioritize some transactions (e.g., to limit process starvation). As we already mentioned in Section 13.1, for an OFTM to ensure wait-freedom, the contention manager has to limit the number of times that a transaction retries some steps (e.g., attempts to change a locator) within a single TM operation. The contention manager also cannot force transactions to wait for each other indefinitely. Finally, OFTMs do not use unbounded arrays *State* and *Mem*, but rather allocate the necessary storage on demand, and free the storage that is no longer needed.

Some OFTMs, such as WSTM and MM-STM, differ from algorithm $\mathcal{A}_{OF}$ in that they employ a helping mechanism: a transaction T_i helps each conflicting transaction T_k to commit instead of aborting T_k. The book of Harris et al. [2010] describes those TM implementations in detail.

13.3   THE COMPUTATIONAL POWER OF AN OFTM

We determine in this section the computational power of an OFTM. We prove that an OFTM can implement a consensus object in a system of 2 processes, but not in a system of 3 or more processes. This result implies that it is impossible to implement an OFTM using only read-write shared memory, i.e., registers, because a register cannot implement a 2-process consensus. On the other hand, however, it should be possible to implement an OFTM using objects weaker than compare-and-swap—an object that can implement consensus for any number of processes.

The proof goes through a result that is interesting on its own. We show that the abstraction of an OFTM is equivalent to that of an fo-consensus object, which we define in Section 13.3.1. That is, there exists an implementation of an OFTM using only fo-consensus objects and registers (which we give in Section 13.3.2), and there exists an implementation of a fo-consensus object using an OFTM and registers (given in Section 13.3.3). Then, we determine the computational power of an fo-consensus object (in Section 13.3.4).

Note 13.5   The results presented in this section rely on the assumption that an OFTM is a wait-free shared object. An OFTM that has obstruction-free operations can be implemented using only registers, because registers are sufficient to implement an obstruction-free compare-and-swap object [Attiya et al., 2005]. Hence, such an OFTM cannot implement a 2-process consensus.

13.3.1   DEFINITION OF AN FO-CONSENSUS OBJECT

A consensus object, which we defined in Section 2.1.8, solves an agreement problem. Every process can propose a value to the consensus object, via operation *propose*, and every (correct) process that invokes *propose* is eventually returned the same decision value, chosen from the values that have been proposed.

An *fo-consensus* shared object is very much like consensus: it also allows processes to agree on a single value chosen from the values those processes have proposed. However, operation *propose* of an fo-consensus object can *abort* when it cannot return a decision value because of contention from concurrent operations. When *propose* aborts, it means that the operation did not take place, and so the value proposed using this operation has not been "registered" by the fo-consensus object. Only a value that has been proposed, and "registered", can be decided. A process whose *propose* operation has been aborted may retry the operation many times (possibly with a different proposed value), until a decision value is returned.

More precisely, an fo-consensus shared object implements a single operation, called *propose*, that takes a value $v \neq \bot$ as an argument and returns a value v'. If a process p_i is returned a non-$\bot$ value v' from *propose*(v), we say that p_i *decides* value v'. When operation *propose* returns $\bot$, we say that the operation *aborts*.

Let X be any shared object, and E be any implementation history of X. Consider any operation e executed in E by any process p_i on X. We say that e is *step contention-free* if there is no step of a process other than p_i between the invocation and the response events of e.

Every fo-consensus shared object ensures the following properties in its every implementation history:

Fo-validity. If some process decides value v, then v is proposed by some *propose* operation that does not abort.

Agreement. No two processes decide different values, and no process decides two different values.

Fo-obstruction-freedom. If a *propose* operation is step contention-free, then the operation does not abort.

It is worth noting that, in our model, fo-obstruction-freedom is meaningless if we consider an fo-consensus *base* object. Since we assume that operations on base objects are executed in a single step, those operations are always step contention-free. Therefore, an fo-consensus base object is, in fact, a consensus base object—its *propose* operation can never abort. Hence, when determining the power of an fo-consensus object, we always assume an fo-consensus shared object. (The power of a consensus object is, clearly, infinite since such an object can trivially implement a consensus object for any number of processes.)

13.3.2 IMPLEMENTING AN OFTM FROM FO-CONSENSUS OBJECTS

An algorithm $\mathcal{A}_{\text{FCons} \rightarrow \text{TM}}$ that implements an OFTM using fo-consensus objects and registers is depicted in Figures 13.5 and 13.6. The sole purpose of this algorithm is to prove that such an implementation is indeed possible. We aimed here at simplicity of both the TM and its proof of correctness. The algorithm is not meant to be efficient or practical.

The idea behind the algorithm is the following: At a high level, every transaction T_k that wants to execute any operation (*read* or *write*) has to acquire, in an exclusive mode, a global logical lock that protects all t-variables. Then, T_k can execute all its operations and eventually release the lock. But T_k can at any time be aborted by another transaction, in which case T_k immediately loses the ownership of the global lock. Then, T_k can no longer commit.

When a transaction T_i wants to abort T_k, T_i proposes value `aborted` to fo-consensus object $State[k]$. When T_k wants to commit, T_k proposes value `committed` to $State[k]$. Once any transaction executes on $State[k]$ an operation *propose* that does not abort, T_k loses the ownership of the global lock. This way, if the process executing T_k crashes, any other transaction can abort T_k and acquire the global lock.

The basic problem that we have to deal with is that the logical global lock does not really provide any mutual exclusion. A transaction T_k that is aborted by another transaction does not know about it until T_k accesses fo-consensus object $State[k]$. Hence, T_k can execute many steps, possibly writing new values to several t-variables, after losing the global lock. Therefore, we need to ensure that transactions writing concurrently to t-variables do not overwrite each other's values. We do so by making every transaction T_k store and update values of t-variables only in its own register $TVar[k]$. Once T_k commits, $TVar[k]$ becomes the current snapshot of the values of all t-variables. Subsequent transactions will use $TVar[k]$ as the initial value for their registers in array $TVar$, until another transaction commits.

When a transaction T_k invokes its first operation, T_k first needs to get a new *version number*, which is larger then all previously given version numbers. To do so, T_k goes through subsequent elements of array $Owner$ of fo-consensus objects, proposing its own id to each of those objects (lines 24–36). When T_k is returned value k from some fo-consensus object $Owner[w]$ (in line 25), value w becomes the version number of T_k. We say then that T_k *acquired version w*.

Whenever transaction T_k is returned a value $i \neq k$ from a fo-consensus object $Owner[w]$, T_k tries to abort transaction T_i by proposing value `aborted` to fo-consensus object $State[i]$ (in line 32). If T_i has already proposed value `committed` to $State[i]$ (in line 14), then T_k might decide value `committed` in $State[i]$. In this case, T_k adopts the values of t-variables written by T_i in register $TVar[i]$ (line 34). Once T_k acquires a version, T_k writes the latest adopted snapshot in register $TVar[k]$ (line 28). Then, T_k executes all its *read* and *write* operations using register $TVar[k]$.

If a transaction T_k invokes operation *propose* on any fo-consensus object in array $Owner$ or $State$, this operation might abort if another transaction executes a concurrent operation on the same object. In this case, T_k is forceably aborted.

There is one remaining important detail of the algorithm. When traversing array $Owner$, every transaction T_k has to be sure that other transactions do not keep acquiring versions concurrently. Otherwise, if every time T_k is about to access an object $Owner[w]$ another transaction acquires version w, then T_k may remain in procedure *acquire* forever, which violates wait-freedom. Therefore, every time any transaction T_i acquires a version w, T_i writes value w to register V (line 29). Then, T_k can periodically check the value in V and get forceably aborted when it changes (line 35).

We prove now that algorithm $\mathcal{A}_{\text{FCons}\rightarrow\text{TM}}$, depicted in Figures 13.5 and 13.6, indeed implements an OFTM. Let $M_{\text{FCons}\rightarrow\text{TM}}$ be any shared object implemented by $\mathcal{A}_{\text{FCons}\rightarrow\text{TM}}$, and let E be any implementation history of $M_{\text{FCons}\rightarrow\text{TM}}$. In the following lemmas, we prove that E ensures wait-freedom (Lemma 13.6), (final-state) opacity (Lemma 13.11), and obstruction-freedom (Lemma 13.12), thus proving that $M_{\text{FCons}\rightarrow\text{TM}}$ ensures those properties (in its every implementation history).

Lemma 13.6 *Implementation history E of $M_{\text{FCons}\rightarrow\text{TM}}$ ensures wait-freedom.*

uses: $Owner[1, 2, \ldots]$, $State[1, 2, \ldots]$—arrays of fo-consensus objects;
  $TVar[1, 2, \ldots]$—array of registers, V—register (other variables are process-local)
initially: $V = 1$, $acquired[k] = false$ for $k = 1, 2, \ldots$ (at every process)

```
1  operation x_m.read_k
2  |  s ← acquire(T_k);
3  |  if s = A_k then return A_k;
4  |  values ← TVar[k].read;
5  |  return values[m];

6  operation x_m.write(v)_k
7  |  s ← acquire(T_k);
8  |  if s = A_k then return A_k;
9  |  values ← TVar[k].read;
10 |  values[m] ← v;
11 |  TVar[k].write(values);
12 |  return ok;

13 operation tryC(T_k)
14 |  state ← State[k].propose(committed);
15 |  if state = committed then return C_k;
16 |  else return A_k;

17 operation tryA(T_k)
18 |  return A_k;
```

Figure 13.5: Algorithm $\mathcal{A}_{\text{FCons}\rightarrow\text{TM}}$ that implements an OFTM from fo-consensus objects and registers (continues in Figure 13.6)

Proof. By contradiction, assume that some correct process p_i invokes an operation on $M_{\text{FCons}\rightarrow\text{TM}}$ in E but never returns from this operation. Since the objects used by the implementation of $M_{\text{FCons}\rightarrow\text{TM}}$ are assumed to be wait-free, p_i must at some time t enter the loop in lines 24–36 and never exit the loop thereafter. That is, after time t, p_i is always returned a value different than $\perp$ and k from operation *propose* executed in line 25, where T_k is the transaction executed by p_i at t. By fo-validity of fo-consensus objects in array $Owner$, if p_i is returned a value $q \notin \{\perp, k\}$ from some fo-consensus object $Owner[v]$, then transaction T_q must propose value q to $Owner[v]$. Unless the process executing T_q crashes, T_q eventually writes value v to register V in line 29. Therefore, since only finitely many processes can crash, and since p_i is returned a value different than $\perp$ and k in line 25 infinitely many times, the value of V changes infinitely often. Hence, since no two values

```
19  function acquire(T_k)
20      if acquired[k] then return ok;
21      curr-version ← V.read;
22      version ← 1;
        ▶ Initial values of t-variables
23      values ← (0, 0, . . .);
24      while true do
25          owner ← Owner[version].propose(k);
            ▶ Abort on step contention
26          if owner = ⊥ then return A_k;
27          if owner = k then
28              TVar[k].write(values);
29              V.write(version);
30              acquired[k] ← true;
31              return ok;

            ▶ Abort the current owner (if live)
32          state ← State[owner].propose(aborted);
            ▶ Abort on step contention
33          if state = ⊥ then return A_k;
            ▶ Adopt the committed values
34          if state = committed then values ← TVar[owner].read;
            ▶ Abort on step contention
35          if V.read ≠ curr-version then return A_k;
36          version ← version + 1;
```

Figure 13.6: The second part of algorithm $\mathcal{A}_{\text{FCons}\to\text{TM}}$ (in Figure 13.5)

written to V are the same, the value of V is eventually permanently different than the value read from V by p_i in line 21, and so p_i eventually exits the loop in line 35—a contradiction. □

Let H denote history $E|M_{\text{FCons}\to\text{TM}}$. Without loss in generality (cf. Chapter 8) we can assume that H has unique writes. We prove final-state opacity of H by using the framework introduced in Chapter 8. That is, we show that H is consistent (Lemma 13.9), and that there exists a version order function $V_{\ll}$ such that graph $OPG\left(H, V_{\ll}\right)$ is acyclic (Lemma 13.10).

Within the following proofs, we say that a transaction T_i reads (or writes) a value v from register $TVar[k][m]$, when T_i reads (respectively, writes) from $TVar[k]$ a value $values$ such that $values[m] = v$. We also say that a transaction T_i commits a version w, if T_i acquires version w and some transaction is returned value committed from operation $propose$ of fo-consensus object $State[i]$ (in line 32 or 14). (Note that, since only T_i can propose value `committed` to $State[i]$, and because $State[i]$ ensures agreement and fo-validity, if T_i commits a version, then T_i must have invoked operation *propose* on $State[i]$ in line 14 and can only be returned value `committed` from this operation.)

Before proving final-state opacity of history H, we prove two auxiliary lemmas.

Lemma 13.7   *For every transaction T_i in H, t-variable x_m, and value $v \neq 0$, if T_i writes value v to register $TVar[i][m]$ in line 28, then T_i acquires some version w_i, and there is a transaction T_k such that (a) T_k writes value v to $TVar[k][m]$ (in line 28 or line 11) before some time t, (b) T_k does not write to $TVar[k][m]$ after t, (c) T_k commits some version $w_k < w_i$, and (d) no transaction commits a version between w_k and w_i.*

Proof. Let T_i be any transaction in H that writes some value $v \neq 0$ to some register $TVar[i][m]$ in line 28. Since T_i reached line 28, T_i must have acquired some version w_i.

Transaction T_i writes to register $TVar[i]$, in line 28, the value of local variable *values*, with $values[m] = v$. Since *values* is initialized to $(0, 0, \ldots)$ (in line 23) and $v \neq 0$, T_i must read, in line 34, from some register in array $TVar$. Let $TVar[k]$ be the register from which T_i reads in line 34 for the last time, at some time t. Then, T_i must read from $TVar[k][m]$ value v.

Since T_i reads from $TVar[k]$ in line 34, T_i is returned value k from operation *propose* executed on $Owner[w_k]$ (line 25), for some value $w_k < w_i$, and then T_i is returned value `committed` from operation *propose* executed on $State[k]$ (line 32). Hence, since only T_k can propose value k to $Owner[w_k]$, and by the fo-validity and agreement properties of $Owner[w_k]$, T_k commits version w_k. Therefore, condition (c) is ensured.

Only transaction T_k can write to $TVar[k][m]$, and only before T_k accesses object $State[k]$ in line 14. Since T_i decides value `committed` in $State[k]$ before time t, by fo-validity of $State[k]$, and because only T_k can propose value `committed` to $State[k]$, T_k reaches line 14 before time t. Hence, since T_i reads value v from $TVar[k][m]$ at t, and only T_k can write to $TVar[k][m]$, T_k writes v to $TVar[k][m]$ in its last *write* operation on $TVar[k]$. Therefore, conditions (a) and (b) are ensured.

Recall that t is the last time when T_i reads a register in array $TVar$ in line 34. Hence, for every w between w_k and w_i, if T_i decides a value q in $Owner[q]$, then T_i decides value `aborted` in $State[q]$. Therefore, by the agreement property of $State[q]$, no transaction can commit version w, and so condition (d) is ensured.   □

Lemma 13.8   *For every transaction T_i in H, every t-variable x_m, and every value $v \neq 0$, if T_i reads v from x_m in history nonlocal(H), then T_i acquires some version w_i, and there exists exactly one transaction T_k, such that T_k commits some version $w_k < w_i$, T_k writes v to x_m in nonlocal(H), and no transaction that writes to x_m commits a version between w_k and w_i.*

Proof. Denote by e any operation $x_m.read \rightarrow v$ executed by T_i in *nonlocal*(H). Within e, transaction T_i reads value v from register $TVar[i][m]$ in line 4. Then, because only T_i can write to $TVar[i][m]$, and since e is a non-local operation, T_i writes to $TVar[i][m]$ value v in line 28. Therefore, by Lemma 13.7 applied recursively (a finite number of times), T_i acquires some version w_i, and there is a transaction T_k in H, such that (a) T_k writes v to register $TVar[k][m]$ in line 11 at some time t, (b) T_k does not write to $TVar[k][m]$ after t, (c) T_k commits some version $w_k < w_i$, and (d) there is no transaction T_q that commits a version between w_k and w_i, and that writes to $TVar[q][m]$ a value different than v. (Note that every transaction T_q can write to $TVar[q][m]$ in line 28 at most once, and this happens always before T_q executes any *write* operation in line 11.) By (a) and (b), T_k writes value v to t-variable x_m in *nonlocal*(H). Because history H has unique writes, only T_k writes v to x_m. Hence, by (d), there can be no transaction that writes to x_m and that commits a version between w_k and w_i. $\square$

Lemma 13.9   *History H of $M_{\text{FCons}\rightarrow\text{TM}}$ is consistent.*

Proof. Let e be any successful operation $x_m.read \rightarrow v$ in H, where x_m is any t-variable and v is any value. Let T_i be the transaction that executes e. We prove that e is consistent, thus proving that H is consistent.

Assume first that e is local. Then, T_i reads from register $TVar[i][m]$ value v in line 4. Hence, since e is local, and because only T_i can write to register $TVar[i]$, the latest *write* operation on x_m that precedes e in $H|T_i$ must be $x_m.write(v)$. Therefore, e is consistent.

Assume then that e is not local and that $v \neq 0$. Then, by Lemma 13.8, there is a transaction T_k that commits some version and writes value v to x_m. Hence, some transaction decides value committed in fo-consensus object $State[k]$. So, since only T_k can propose value committed to $State[k]$ and only in line 14, and because $State[k]$ ensures fo-validity and agreement, T_k must have invoked operation *propose* on $State[k]$ in line 14 and can only be returned value committed from this operation. Therefore, T_k is either committed or commit-pending. $\square$

Let $<_{\text{ver}}$ denote the partial order on the set of transactions in H, such that, for any two transactions T_i and T_k, if T_i acquires a version w_i, T_k acquires a version w_k, and $w_i < w_k$, then $T_i <_{\text{ver}} T_k$. Let T_i be any transaction that acquires some version w_i. To do so, T_i must have decided a non-$\perp$ value from every fo-consensus object $Owner[1], \ldots, Owner[w_i]$. Hence, if a transaction T_k starts after T_i commits or aborts, T_k cannot decide value k in any fo-consensus object $Owner[w]$ where $w \leq w_i$, because only T_k can propose value k to any fo-consensus object in array $Owner$. Therefore, since $<_{\text{ver}}$ is a total order on the set of transactions in H that acquire a version, the transitive closure of the union of $<_{\text{ver}}$ and $\prec_H$ (the real-time order of transactions in H) is also a partial order.

Let $\ll$ denote any total order on the set of transactions in H, such that both $<_{\text{ver}}$ and $\prec_H$ are subsets of $\ll$. Let $\ll_m$, for every $m = 1, 2, \ldots$, be the version order of t-variable x_m such that

$\ll_m \subseteq \ll$. That is, $\ll_m$ is the restriction of $\ll$ to those transactions that are committed or commit-pending and that write to t-variable x_m in H. Let $V_\ll$ be the version order function such that $V_\ll(x_m) = \ll_m$, for every t-variable x_m.

Lemma 13.10   *Graph* $OPG\left(H, V_\ll\right)$ *is acyclic.*

Proof. Denote graph $OPG\left(H, V_\ll\right)$ by G. Assume, by contradiction, that there is a cycle in G. Since $\ll$ is a total order on the set of transactions in H, there must be some two transactions T_i and T_k such that $T_i \ll T_k$ but there is an edge $T_k \longrightarrow T_i$ in G. We consider now four cases corresponding to the different types of edges in G, in each case showing a contradiction.

Case 1: $T_k \overset{rt}{\longrightarrow} T_i$ Then, $T_k \prec_H T_i$, contradicting the assumption that $T_i \ll T_k$.

Case 2: $T_k \overset{rf}{\longrightarrow} T_i$ Then, T_i reads from some t-variable x_m a value v that is written to x_m by T_k. Hence, by Lemma 13.8, T_k acquires (and commits) a version $w_k < w_i$—a contradiction with the assumption that $T_i \ll T_k$.

Case 3: $T_k \overset{ww}{\longrightarrow} T_i$ Then, $T_k \ll_{x_m} T_i$ for some t-variable x_m, contradicting the assumption that $T_i \ll T_k$.

Case 4: $T_k \overset{rw}{\longrightarrow} T_i$ Then, vertex T_i is labelled *vis* in G, and there exists a transaction T_q in H and a t-variable x_m such that: (a) $T_q \ll_m T_i$, and (b) T_k reads x_m from T_q. Since $T_q \ll_m T_i$, both T_q and T_i write to x_m, and both are either committed or commit-pending. Let v_q and v_i be the values written to x_m by, respectively, T_q and T_i in history *nonlocal*(H). Because H has unique writes, $v_q \neq v_i$ and $v_q \neq 0$.

Since T_k reads x_m from T_q, T_k reads value v_q from x_m in *nonlocal*(H). Therefore, by Lemma 13.8, and because only T_q writes v_q to x_m, T_q commits a version $w_q < w_k$ and no transaction commits a version between w_q and w_k.

Because vertex T_i of G is labelled *vis*, either T_i is committed or some transaction T_r reads some t-variable x_s from T_i. If T_i is committed, then, since T_i writes to x_m, T_i must commit some version w_i. If T_r reads x_s from T_i, then, by Lemma 13.8, and because H has unique writes, T_i must also commit some version w_i. Since $T_q \ll_m T_i \ll T_k$, $w_q < w_i < w_k$. Hence, we reach a contradiction with the fact that no transaction commits a version between w_q and w_k.   □

From Lemma 13.9 and Lemma 13.10, and by Theorem 8.2 (Section 8.2), we obtain the following result:

Lemma 13.11   *History H is final-state opaque.*

We prove now that TM object $M_{\text{FCons}\to\text{TM}}$ is indeed an OFTM.

Lemma 13.12   *Implementation history E of $M_{\text{FCons}\to\text{TM}}$ ensures obstruction-freedom.*

Proof. Consider any transaction T_k in E, executed by some process p_i, and assume that T_k does not encounter step contention. Hence, no process other than p_i executes any step between the first and the last event of T_k in E. Then, by fo-obstruction-freedom, T_k cannot be returned value $\perp$ from any *propose* operation executed on any of the fo-consensus objects in arrays *Owner* and *State*. Also, T_k cannot read from register V value v in line 21, and then value $v' \neq v$ in line 35. Hence, T_k acquires some version.

Because T_k does not encounter step contention, and only T_k can propose value k to any fo-consensus object in array *Owner*, no transaction can decide value k in any fo-consensus object in array *Owner* before T_k executes its last event. Hence, no transaction can propose value aborted to fo-consensus object *State*[k] before T_k proposes committed to *State*[k] in line 14 and decides a value in *State*[k]. Therefore, by fo-validity of *State*[k], T_k decides value committed in *State*[k], and so T_k cannot be forceably aborted.   □

By Lemmas 13.6, 13.11, and 13.12, and by Observation 7.4, shared object $M_{\text{FCons}\rightarrow\text{TM}}$ is indeed an OFTM. Since the implementation of $M_{\text{FCons}\rightarrow\text{TM}}$ uses only fo-consensus objects and registers, the following theorem is proved:

Theorem 13.13   *Every fo-consensus object can implement an OFTM.*

13.3.3 EQUIVALENCE BETWEEN OFTMS AND FO-CONSENSUS OBJECTS

To show that every OFTM is equivalent to every fo-consensus object one has to prove that: (1) every fo-consensus object can implement an OFTM, and (2) every OFTM can implement an fo-consensus object. We already proved (1) in the previous section. In this section, we prove (2).

An algorithm that implements an fo-consensus object using a single OFTM object is shown in Figure 13.7. The idea is very simple: a process p_i that executes operation *propose*(v) tries, within a transaction, to change the state of t-variable x from $\perp$ (the initial value of x) to v. Once the value of x becomes non-$\perp$, it does not change anymore. Then, every operation *propose* returns the value read from x. In the proof of the following lemma we only need to show that the algorithm is indeed correct.

Theorem 13.14   *Every OFTM can implement an fo-consensus object.*

Proof. Denote by C any object implemented by the algorithm shown in Figure 13.7. Let E be any implementation history of C. Note first that an operation *propose* executed by a process p_i can return a non-$\perp$ value only if the transaction executed by p_i between the invocation and response events of the operation is committed. By opacity of OFTM object M, if history $E|M$ contains at least one committed transaction, then (a) exactly one committed transaction, say T_k, reads value $\perp$ from t-variable x and writes a non-$\perp$ value v to x, and (b) every committed transaction different than T_k reads value v from x. (Transaction T_k is the first committed transaction in the witness

uses: M—OFTM, x—t-variable
initially: $x = \bot$

1 **operation** $propose(v)$
2   **atomic using** M
3          $v' \leftarrow x.read$;
4   **if** $v' = \bot$ **then** $x.write(v)$;
5   **else** $v \leftarrow v'$;
6   **on abort return** $\bot$;
7   **return** v;

Figure 13.7: Implementing fo-consensus from an OFTM

(sequential) history of $E|M$.) Hence, the process executing transaction T_k returns value v from operation $propose(v)$ (and not value $\bot$), while every other operation $propose$ returns either $\bot$ or v. Hence, fo-validity and agreement are ensured.

Consider now an operation $propose$, executed by a process p_i, that aborts (i.e., returns $\bot$). Then, the transaction T_m that is executed by p_i inside this operation also aborts. But, by obstruction-freedom of M, T_m encounters step contention, and so the $propose$ operation is not step contention-free. Hence, fo-obstruction-freedom is ensured. $\qquad\square$

From Theorem 13.13 and Theorem 13.14 we immediately obtain the following result:

Theorem 13.15   *Every OFTM is equivalent to every fo-consensus object.*

13.3.4 THE POWER OF AN FO-CONSENSUS OBJECT

We determine in this section the power of an fo-consensus shared object. First, we show that every fo-consensus object can implement 2-process consensus. Second, we prove that fo-consensus objects cannot, in general, implement 3-process consensus. (We say "in general" because there are fo-consensus objects that can implement k-process consensus, for every k. For instance, every consensus object is also an fo-consensus object, although its $propose$ operation never aborts.)

An algorithm that implements a 2-process consensus object using a single fo-consensus object and a register is depicted in Figure 13.8.[2] We assume here that only values different than $\bot$ can be proposed. In the following theorem, we prove that the algorithm is correct.

Theorem 13.16   *Every fo-consensus object can implement 2-process consensus.*

---

[2]The algorithm was first proposed by Attiya et al. [2005].

uses: F—fo-consensus, X—register
initially: $X = \perp$

Process p_1:

```
1  operation propose(v)
2      d ← F.propose(v);
3      if d = ⊥ then
4          d ← X.read;
5      return d;
```

Process p_2:

```
1  operation propose(v)
2      X.write(v);
3      repeat
4          d ← F.propose(v);
5      until d ≠ ⊥;
6      return d;
```

Figure 13.8: An implementation of 2-process consensus using an fo-consensus object and a register (adapted from Attiya et al. [2005])

Proof. Let C be any object implemented by the algorithm depicted in Figure 13.8. Consider any implementation history E of C. We prove that C ensures validity, agreement, and wait-freedom in E.

First, both p_1 and p_2 can propose to fo-consensus object F only a value proposed to C. Hence, by fo-validity of F, process p_2 can decide in C only a value proposed to C. If operation *propose* executed by p_1 does not abort, then p_1 also decides in C the value proposed in F. Otherwise, p_1 decides in C the value read from register X. Operation *propose* on F executed by p_1 can abort only if p_2 concurrently executes *propose* on F. But then, p_2 must have written to X the value that p_2 proposed to C. Therefore, C ensures validity.

Assume that p_1 decides value v in C. If p_1 decided v in F, then, by the agreement property of F, p_2 must also decide v. If operation *propose* executed by p_1 on F aborts, then p_1 decides the value written to register X by p_2. But then, by fo-validity of F, p_2 must decide value v in F, and so p_2 must also decide v in C. Hence, C ensures agreement.

Since p_1 executes only one *propose* operation on F, eventually some *propose* operation executed by p_2 on F is step contention-free and so, by fo-obstruction-freedom of F, p_2 eventually decides a value in F. Also, both F and register X are wait-free. Hence, C is also wait-free. □

Corollary 13.17 *There is no algorithm that implements an fo-consensus object (or, by Theorem 13.15, an OFTM) using only registers.*

We prove now that there is no algorithm that implements 3-process consensus using arbitrary fo-consensus objects and registers. The intuition behind the proof is the following: We assume, by contradiction, that there exists an implementation of a 3-process consensus shared object C using only fo-consensus objects and registers. We then derive a contradiction by using a classical "valency argument" [Fischer et al., 1985]. Basically, we show that if C ensures the validity and agreement properties of consensus, then C may violate wait-freedom in some executions, i.e., it may happen that some correct process proposes a value and is never returned a decision value. We do so by proving that any finite implementation history E of C, after which more than one value can be decided, can be extended into an implementation history E' in such a way that still more than one value can be decided after E'. Note that a process p_i may decide value v after an implementation history E of C only if p_i is sure that no value other than v can be decided by other processes after E (otherwise, agreement could be violated).

To simplify the proof, we introduce some additional terms and notation, which are used within this section. Let E be any implementation history of C. Every implementation history E' of C of which E is a prefix is called an *extension* of E. If an extension E' of E is of a form $E \cdot E_i$, where E_i consists of only steps and events of process p_i, then E' is an extension of E *by* p_i. An extension of E by a process p_i corresponds, e.g., to a situation in which all processes except for p_i crash just after executing their last step or event in E.

In the following, we consider only those implementation histories of C in which at most two operations on any fo-consensus object are concurrent. That is, we restrict the power of the scheduler that acts as an adversary against the implementation of C. Clearly, our impossibility result holds also when there is no such restriction.

When we say that a process p_i proposes or decides a value v we mean that p_i proposes v to C or decides v in C. (We do not use this shorthand notation for fo-consensus objects used by the implementation of C.)

Consider the following implementation history E_0 of C:

$$E_0 = \langle inv_1(C.propose(0)), \ inv_2(C.propose(1)), \ inv_3(C.propose(1)) \rangle.$$

Let E be any extension of E_0. We say that E is *0-valent* (or *1-valent*) if, in every extension E' of E, no process decides a value different than 0 (respectively, 1). If E is neither 0-valent nor 1-valent, then E is called *bivalent*.

Recall from Section 2.1.6 that two implementation histories E and E' are indistinguishable for a process p_i if $E|p_i = E'|p_i$. We prove first the following lemma:

Lemma 13.18   *Implementation history E_0 of C is bivalent.*

Proof. By contradiction, assume that E_0 is 0-valent (the 1-valent case is symmetrical). Consider an extension E of E_0 by process p_2 in which p_2 decides a value. In E_0, processes only invoke operations on C and do not execute any steps, i.e., they do not communicate. Hence, sequence $E|p_2$, which is indistinguishable for process p_2 from E, must also be an implementation history of C. By validity of C, p_2 decides value 1 in $E|p_2$ since this is the only proposed value. Because E and $E|p_2$ are indistinguishable for p_2, p_2 also decides 1 in E—a contradiction with the assumption that E_0 is 0-valent.   □

Let E and E' be any implementation histories of C. We say that E and E' are *strongly indistinguishable* for a process p_i, if (a) E and E' are indistinguishable for p_i, and (b) for every extension $E \cdot E_i$ of E by p_i, sequence $E' \cdot E_i$ is an extension of E'. That is, if processes execute all steps and events in E or E', and then only process p_i continues executing steps and events (i.e., other processes crash just after their last action in E or E'), then p_i cannot determine whether the execution began with E or E'.

Before we prove the key lemma of this proof, we prove the following auxiliary result:

Lemma 13.19 *If E and E' are any implementation histories of C, E is 0-valent, and E' is 1-valent, then, for every process p_i, E and E' are not strongly indistinguishable for p_i.*

Proof. By contradiction, assume that there exist implementation histories E and E' of C, such that E is 0-valent and E' is 1-valent, but E and E' are strongly indistinguishable for some process p_i. Consider any extension $E \cdot E_i$ of E by process p_i, in which p_i decides a value. Since E is 0-valent, p_i decides value 0. Because implementation histories E and E' are strongly indistinguishable for p_i, sequence $E' \cdot E_i$ is also an implementation history of C. Then, since in $E' \cdot E_i$ process p_i decides value 0, E' cannot be 1-valent. □

Let E be any implementation history of C. We say that E is *complete* if E has no pending operation on any fo-consensus object. In particular, E_0 is complete. We prove now the main lemma of the proof:

Lemma 13.20 *For every complete bivalent implementation history E of C that is an extension of E_0, there exists an extension E' of E, $E' \neq E$, such that E' is also complete and bivalent.*

Proof. By contradiction, assume that there exists a bivalent complete implementation history E of C, such that every complete extension E' of E is 0-valent or 1-valent. Clearly, no process decides in E, as otherwise E would not be bivalent.

Every process p_i after executing all its steps and events of E is about to invoke some operation op_i on some object X_i that can be either a register (base object) or an fo-consensus shared object. More specifically, there exists a sequence E_i of steps and events, such that $E_i | X_i = \langle X_i.op_i \to v_i \rangle$, $E_i | X_k = \langle \rangle$ for every object X_k other than X_i, and $E \cdot E_i$ is a (complete) extension of E. If X_i is a register then E_i consists of a single step of p_i. If X_i is an fo-consensus object then E_i consists of an execution of a single *propose* operation on X_i by p_i. Observe that if X_i is an fo-consensus object, then $v_i \neq \bot$ because p_i executes operation *propose* in E_i alone and because X_i ensures fo-obstruction-freedom.

Let p_i and p_k, $i \neq k$, be any processes. If X_i or X_k is an fo-consensus object, then we also consider extensions of implementation history E in which processes p_i and p_k execute operations $X_i.op_i$ and $X_k.op_k$ concurrently. Each such extension of E is of the form $E \cdot E_{ik}(v_i', v_k')$, where v_i' and v_k' are some values, $E_{ik}(v_i', v_k') | X_i = \langle X_i.op_i \to v_i' \rangle$, $E_{ik}(v_i', v_k') | X_k = \langle X_k.op_k \to v_k' \rangle$,

$E_{ik}(v'_i, v'_k)|X_m = \langle\rangle$ for every object X_m other than X_i and X_k, and the two operations in $E_{ik}(v'_i, v'_k)$ are concurrent. If $X_i = X_k$, i.e., X_i and X_k is the same (fo-consensus) object, then the following pairs of values v'_i and v'_k are allowed by the agreement, fo-validity, and fo-obstruction-freedom properties of X_i: (v_i, v_i), (v_k, v_k), $(v_i, \bot)$, $(\bot, v_k)$, and $(\bot, \bot)$. If, however, $X_i \neq X_k$, then $v'_i = v_i$ and $v'_k = v_k$. (Recall that v_i and v_k are the values returned to p_i and p_k in implementation histories $E \cdot E_i$ and $E \cdot E_k$, respectively.)

Assume first that extensions $E \cdot E_1$, $E \cdot E_2$, and $E \cdot E_3$ are all 0-valent (the 1-valent case is symmetrical). Then, since E is bivalent, there must be some processes p_i and p_k, $i \neq k$, such that X_i and X_k is the same fo-consensus object, and $E \cdot E_{ik}(v_i, v_i)$, $E \cdot E_{ik}(v_i, \bot)$ or $E \cdot E_{ik}(\bot, \bot)$ is 1-valent. Assume that $E \cdot E_{ik}(v_i, v_i)$ or $E \cdot E_{ik}(v_i, \bot)$ is 1-valent. Since $v_i \neq \bot$ (i.e., p_i decides a value in X_i), implementation history $E \cdot E_{ik}(v_i, v_i)$ or $E \cdot E_{ik}(v_i, \bot)$ is strongly indistinguishable for p_i from $E \cdot E_i$, contradicting Lemma 13.19. Therefore, implementation history $E \cdot E_{ik}(\bot, \bot)$ of C is 1-valent. But $E \cdot E_{ik}(\bot, \bot)$ is strongly indistinguishable for process $p_m, m \neq i, m \neq k$, from implementation history E. Thus, since $E \cdot E_m$ is an extension of E by p_m, $E \cdot E_{ik}(\bot, \bot) \cdot E_m$ is also an extension of E. But the 0-valent implementation history $E \cdot E_m$ is strongly indistinguishable for p_m from the 1-valent implementation history $E \cdot E_{ik}(\bot, \bot) \cdot E_m$; so again we reach a contradiction with Lemma 13.19.

Assume then that $E \cdot E_1$ is 0-valent, and both $E \cdot E_2$ and $E \cdot E_3$ are 1-valent (the other cases are symmetrical). Consider the case when X_1 and X_2 are two different objects. Then, there is a 0-valent extension $E \cdot E_1 \cdot E_2$ of E, and a 1-valent extension $E \cdot E_2 \cdot E_1$ of E. But those implementation histories are strongly indistinguishable for process p_3, and so we contradict Lemma 13.19. Analogously, we can prove that X_1 and X_3 must be the same. Therefore, X_1, X_2, and X_3 must be the same object, which we denote by X.

Consider now a case when X is a register. If both op_1 and op_2 are *read* operations, or both are *write* operations, or op_1 is a *read* operation and op_2 is a *write* operation, then 0-valent extension $E \cdot E_1 \cdot E_2$ of E is strongly indistinguishable for process p_3 from 1-valent extension $E \cdot E_2$ of E; hence, we contradict Lemma 13.19. If op_1 is a *write* operation and op_2 is a *read* operation, then 0-valent extension $E \cdot E_1$ of E is strongly indistinguishable for process p_3 from 1-valent extension $E \cdot E_2 \cdot E_1$; hence, we again contradict Lemma 13.19. Therefore, X must be an fo-consensus object.

Consider extension $E' = E \cdot E_{12}(\bot, \bot)$ of E. Implementation history E' is strongly indistinguishable for process p_3 from implementation history E. Hence, since $E \cdot E_3$ is a 1-valent implementation history of C, and by Lemma 13.19, sequence $E' \cdot E_3$ is also a 1-valent implementation history of C. Therefore, since E' cannot be bivalent, E' must be 1-valent.

Consider extension $E'' = E \cdot E_{23}(\bot, \bot)$ of E. Implementation history E'' is strongly indistinguishable for process p_2 from E'. Hence, by Lemma 13.19, E'' must be 1-valent. But E'' is strongly indistinguishable for process p_1 from E. Therefore, since $E \cdot E_1$ is an extension of E by p_1, $E'' \cdot E_1$ is also an extension of E. But the 0-valent implementation history $E \cdot E_1$ is strongly indistinguishable for p_1 from the 1-valent implementation history $E'' \cdot E_1$, which contradicts Lemma 13.19. $\square$

By Lemma 13.18 and Lemma 13.20, we can construct an implementation history of C that has an arbitrary length and is bivalent. Hence, there is an infinite implementation history of C in which all three processes invoke operation *propose* on C, some processes execute infinitely many steps (i.e., they are correct), but none of those processes ever return from their operation. This contradicts the assumption that C is a wait-free shared object. Therefore, the following theorem is proved:

Theorem 13.21   *There is an fo-consensus object that cannot implement 3-process consensus.*

13.4   IMPOSSIBILITY OF STRICT DISJOINT-ACCESS-PARALLELISM

In this section, we prove that no OFTM can be strictly disjoint-access-parallel. Intuitively, strict disjoint-access-parallelism requires that if some two transactions access disjoint sets of t-objects, then the processes executing those transactions do not conflict on any base object. More precisely:

Definition 13.22   (Strict disjoint-access-parallelism).   A TM shared object M is *strictly disjoint-access-parallel* if, for every implementation history E of M, and for all transactions T_i and T_k in E, the following is true: if T_i accesses some base object that is updated by T_k, then T_i and T_k access some common t-object.

Theorem 13.23   *No OFTM is strictly disjoint-access-parallel.*

Proof.   Assume, by contradiction, that there exists an OFTM shared object M that is strictly disjoint-access-parallel. In the following, we consider implementation histories of M involving three transactions, T_1, T_2, and T_3, executed by processes p_1, p_2, and p_3, respectively, accessing t-variables x, y, w, and z initialized to 0.

Let E be any implementation history of M and H be any TM history. We say that E can be *extended with H by a process p_i*, if there exists an implementation history E' of M, such that E' is of the form $E \cdot E_i$, where $E_i | p_i = E_i$ (i.e., E_i consists of only events and steps of process p_i), and $E_i | M = H$.

Consider the following TM histories, each involving a single committed transaction:

1. H_1 in which transaction T_1 reads value 0 from w and z, and then writes value 1 to x and y;

2. H_2 in which T_2 reads 0 from x, and then writes 1 to w;

3. H_2' in which T_2 reads 1 from x, and then writes 1 to w;

4. H_3 in which T_3 reads 0 from y, and then writes 1 to z; and

5. H_3' in which T_3 reads 1 from y, and then writes 1 to z.

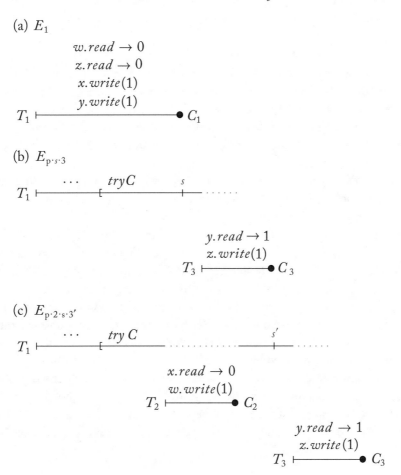

(a) E_1

$w.read \to 0$
$z.read \to 0$
$x.write(1)$
$y.write(1)$

$T_1 \vdash \longrightarrow \bullet\ C_1$

(b) $E_{p \cdot s \cdot 3}$

$\cdots \quad tryC \qquad s$
$T_1 \vdash \longrightarrow$

$y.read \to 1$
$z.write(1)$
$T_3 \vdash \longrightarrow \bullet\ C_3$

(c) $E_{p \cdot 2 \cdot s \cdot 3'}$

$\cdots \quad try\ C \qquad\qquad s'$
$T_1 \vdash \longrightarrow$

$x.read \to 0$
$w.write(1)$
$T_2 \vdash \longrightarrow \bullet\ C_2$

$y.read \to 1$
$z.write(1)$
$T_3 \vdash \longrightarrow \bullet\ C_3$

Figure 13.9: Illustration of the proof of Theorem 13.23

By opacity and obstruction-freedom of M, and since M is a wait-free shared object, there exists an implementation history E_1 of M, such that $E_1|M = H_1$ and $E_1|p_1 = E_1$ (cf. Figure 13.9a). Let E_p be the longest prefix of E_1, such that E_p can be extended with neither H'_2 by process p_2, nor with H'_3 by p_3. That is, intuitively, a transaction executed after E_p can read from x and y only value 0, i.e., the initial value of those t-variables. Note that, since opacity of M requires that no transaction reads value 1 from x or y in E until T_1 invokes operation $tryC$ and since events are local to processes, T_1 is commit-pending in E_p.

By obstruction-freedom of M, and since M is a wait-free shared object, we can extend E_p with H_2 by process p_2, obtaining an implementation history $E_{p \cdot 2}$ of M of the form $E_p \cdot E_2$, where $E_2|M = H_2$ and $E_2|p_2 = E_2$. Indeed, since E_p cannot be extended with H'_2 by p_2, transaction T_2

can only read value 0 from x, and, since only p_2 executes steps after prefix E_p, T_2 cannot be forceably aborted in $E_{p \cdot 2}$.

Let $E_{p \cdot s}$ be the prefix of E_1 that contains exactly one step of p_1 (step s) more than E_p, i.e., $E_{p \cdot s} = E_p \cdot \langle s \rangle$, where $s = X.op \to v$ (for some base object X, operation op of X, and return value v of op). By the definition of E_p, implementation history $E_{p \cdot s}$ can be extended with H_2' by p_2, or with H_3' by p_3. Assume that $E_{p \cdot s}$ can be extended with H_3' by p_3 (the case when $E_{p \cdot s}$ can be extended with H_2' but not with H_3' is symmetrical). Denote by $E_{p \cdot s \cdot 3}$ the resulting implementation history of M (cf. Figure 13.9b), i.e., an implementation history of M of the form $E_{p \cdot s} \cdot E_3'$, where $E_3'|M = H_3'$ and $E_3'|p_3 = E_3'$.

Consider implementation history $E_{p \cdot 2 \cdot s} = E_{p \cdot 2} \cdot \langle s' \rangle$ of M obtained by extending $E_{p \cdot 2}$ with a single step s' of process p_1. Since processes are deterministic, $s' = X.op \to v'$, i.e., s' can differ from s (in $E_{p \cdot s}$) only by its return value.

Assume first that $E_{p \cdot 2 \cdot s}$ can be extended with H_3' by process p_3, giving an implementation history $E_{p \cdot 2 \cdot s \cdot 3'}$ of M, in which T_3 reads value 1 from y (cf. Figure 13.9c). Consider any sequential TM history S that is equivalent to any completion of $E_{p \cdot 2 \cdot s \cdot 3'}|M$. If transaction T_1 is aborted in S, then T_3 is not legal in S. However, if T_1 is committed in S, then either T_1 or T_2 is not legal in S. Hence, $E_{p \cdot 2 \cdot s \cdot 3'}$ violates opacity—a contradiction with the assumption that M is opaque.

Therefore, $E_{p \cdot 2 \cdot s}$ can be extended with H_3 by process p_3, giving an implementation history $E_{p \cdot 2 \cdot s \cdot 3}$ of M, in which T_3 reads value 0 from y. Since M is strictly disjoint-access-parallel, and because the sets of t-objects accessed by T_2 and T_3 in $E_{p \cdot 2 \cdot s \cdot 3}$ are disjoint, process p_3, while executing T_3 in $E_{p \cdot 2 \cdot s \cdot 3}$, cannot access any base object whose state is changed by process p_2 executing T_2. Hence, because p_1 accesses only a single base object X between the end of T_2 and the beginning of T_3, implementation history $E_{p \cdot 2 \cdot s \cdot 3}$ is indistinguishable for p_3 from $E_{p \cdot s \cdot 3}$. But then, it is not possible that T_3 is returned value 0 from its *read* operation on y in $E_{p \cdot 2 \cdot s \cdot 3}$, but value 1 in $E_{p \cdot s \cdot 3}$—a contradiction. $\qquad \square$

Note 13.24   The proof of Theorem 13.23 relies on the assumption that an OFTM is a wait-free shared object. However, the same result can also be proved for OFTMs whose operations are obstruction-free (in the sense that we explained in Section 13.1).

13.5   ALTERNATIVE FORMS OF OBSTRUCTION-FREEDOM

In an OFTM, a transaction that runs *alone* is never forceably aborted. So far, we defined "alone" as "not encountering step contention". That is, a transaction T_i can be forceably aborted only if there is another transaction that executes a step concurrently to T_i. One could, however, argue that a transaction T_i is really alone only if all processes that execute transactions concurrent to T_i crash before T_i starts, or if those processes crash well in advance before T_i starts. In this section, we formalize those alternative definitions of an OFTM; we show, however, that in an asynchronous system they are equivalent to our initial definition.

We consider two alternative definitions. In the simpler case, which we call *ic-obstruction-freedom*,[3] we assume that a process that crashes cannot cause any further transaction to be forceably aborted. A weaker variant of this definition (*eventual ic-obstruction-freedom*) allows a crashed process to obstruct other processes (and their transactions) for arbitrary, but finite time. More specifically:

Definition 13.25 (Ic-obstruction-free TM). We say that a TM shared object M is *ic-obstruction-free* (i.e., M is an *ic-OFTM*), if in every implementation history E of M, and for every transaction T_k in E, if T_k is forceably aborted, then there exists a transaction T_q, executed by some process p_i, such that T_q is concurrent to T_k, and p_i does not crash before the first event of T_k.

Definition 13.26 (Eventually ic-obstruction-free TM). We say that a TM shared object M is *eventually ic-obstruction-free* (i.e., is an *eventual ic-OFTM*), if, for every implementation history E of M, there exists a finite period of time d, such that, for every transaction T_k in E that is forceably aborted, there exists a transaction T_q, executed by some process p_i, such that T_q is concurrent to T_k and p_i does not crash earlier than d before the first event of T_k.

Clearly, every TM that is obstruction-free is also ic-obstruction-free: a process that has crashed can no longer perform any steps. In an asynchronous system, the opposite is also true: because slow processes cannot be distinguished from crashed ones, the only way for a process p_i to ensure that other processes are alive is for p_i to observe steps of other processes. Thus:

Theorem 13.27 *Every OFTM is an ic-OFTM, and every ic-OFTM is an OFTM.*

Clearly, every TM that is (ic-)obstruction-free is also eventually ic-obstruction-free. However, the opposite is not true: a history of an eventual ic-OFTM may contain finite sequences of forceably aborted transactions that are concurrent only to some transaction whose executing process crashed a long time ago.

Nevertheless, we show that every eventual ic-OFTM can implement an OFTM. We do so by giving an algorithm that implements an fo-consensus object using a single eventual ic-OFTM object and a number of registers. Since every fo-consensus object can implement an OFTM, every eventual ic-OFTM can also do so.

Theorem 13.28 *Every eventual ic-OFTM can implement an OFTM. Every OFTM is an eventual ic-OFTM.*

Proof. Let F be a shared object implemented by the algorithm depicted in Figure 13.10. We prove the theorem by proving that F is indeed an fo-consensus object. That is, F ensures agreement, fo-validity, fo-obstruction-freedom, and wait-freedom.

[3]The prefix "ic-" stands for "interval contention" [Aguilera et al., 2007].

uses: $R[1, \ldots, n]$—registers, M—eventual ic-OFTM, x—t-variable (array r is process-local)
initially: $R[1, \ldots, n] = 0, x = \bot$

```
1  operation propose(v)
2      for k = 1, ..., n do r[k] ← R[k].read;
3      while true do
4          r[i] ← r[i] + 1;
5          R[i].write(r[i]);
6          atomic using M
7              if x.read = ⊥ then x.write(v);
8              return x.read;
           ▶ Transaction aborted, check for step contention
9          if ∃_{m≠i} : R[m].read ≠ r[m] then return ⊥;
```

Figure 13.10: An implementation of an fo-consensus object from an eventual ic-OFTM object and registers (code for process p_i)

Agreement and fo-validity Since M ensures opacity, there can be at most one committed transaction T_k that reads value $\bot$ from t-variable x and then writes some value v to x. All the other committed transactions must read v from x. Hence, since operation *propose* can return only $\bot$ or a value read from x by a committed transaction, agreement is ensured. Moreover, because value v written by T_k to x is a proposed value, and, since T_k commits, the *propose* operation within which T_k is executed cannot abort, fo-validity is also ensured.

Fo-obstruction-freedom Assume that a *propose* operation at some process p_i aborts. This can happen only if p_i observes that $r[m] \neq R[m]$ for some $m \neq i$. But then, process p_m must have changed the value of $R[m]$ since p_i invoked its *propose* operation. Hence, the *propose* operation of p_i is not step contention-free.

Wait-freedom Assume, by contradiction, that a correct process p_i invokes operation *propose* and never returns from this operation. This means that (1) every transaction executed by p_i aborts, and (2) eventually no process p_m other than p_i changes the value of register $R[m]$. But then, eventually no correct process except for p_i executes any transaction. Hence, since M is an eventual ic-OFTM, p_i must eventually commit some transaction and return from operation *propose*—a contradiction. □

CHAPTER 14

General Liveness of TMs

So far we assumed that individual TM operations are wait-free, and then we focused on progress properties that a TM can provide. We presented four such properties: strong progressiveness (Section 12.1), characterizing lock-based TMs; obstruction-freedom (Section 13.1), ensured by OFTMs; weak progressiveness (Section 12.4); and minimal progressiveness (Section 9.1), which is what could be considered a bare minimum that a practical TM should guarantee. Those four properties stipulate when a particular transaction can be forceably aborted by a TM. They do so by taking into account either conflicts or step contention encountered by the transaction.

In this chapter, we focus on *high-level* liveness properties of TMs. That is, we do not consider separately the liveness of individual TM operations and the progress of each transaction, but instead we ask when a process that starts a transaction and keeps executing steps (i.e., does not crash) is guaranteed to (eventually) commit this (or any other) transaction.

The motivation behind considering this kind of liveness properties is the following. Processes execute transactions to perform some computations. When a transaction T_k at some process p_i is forceably aborted, it often happens that p_i immediately retries the computation of T_k using another transaction, and does so until p_i manages to commit a transaction, thus executing the corresponding computation. Retrying forceably aborted transactions (i.e., their computations) is often the default behavior of programming language constructs such as **atomic** blocks. It is thus important to ask when a process that keeps executing transactions is guaranteed to eventually commit some transaction or when a process that enters an **atomic** block is guaranteed to leave this block.

We focus on those high-level liveness properties that are, when possible, unconditional. That is, we want to guarantee certain liveness for transactions regardless of what computations they perform, what conflicts they encounter, and how the steps of concurrent transactions are interleaved. We say "when possible" because, clearly, we cannot ensure liveness for transactions executed by processes that crash or for transactions that keep executing operations but never invoke operation *tryC*—which we call *parasite* transactions.

Ideally, a TM would ensure that every process that keeps executing transactions eventually commits a transaction—a property that we call *local progress* and that is similar in spirit to wait-freedom or starvation-freedom. It could seem that a TM that protects all t-objects using a single global (and fair) lock, and thus executes transactions one by one, ensures local progress. Indeed, such a TM does not have to forceably abort any transaction. Yet, this TM does not guarantee any liveness when some processes crash, or when some transactions are parasites. Namely, a process that crashes, or executes a parasite transaction, while holding the global lock will never release the lock, thus preventing any transaction from making progress. It is thus interesting to ask what is the strongest high-level liveness property that a TM can ensure in an asynchronous system (in which processes can crash), with or without parasite transactions.

It is worth recalling here that the crashes of processes serve as a modeling tool that helps capture the requirement that processes make progress independently of each other. That is, an implementation of a shared object (e.g., a TM) should not force any process to wait indefinitely for another process.

Being able to tolerate parasite transactions increases the robustness of a TM. Such transactions should never appear in a correct application. However, in big software projects involving large groups of programmers, there is always a chance that some component misbehaves due to a mistake, or even malicious behavior, of some programmer. Then, it is often desirable to isolate the failure of such components, thus preventing them from hampering progress of the entire application.

In the following sections, we first define a simple framework for reasoning about high-level liveness properties of TMs (Section 14.1), which we call simply *TM liveness properties*. We also give there several examples of such properties. Then, in Section 14.2, we identify a class of TM liveness properties that are impossible to implement in an asynchronous system. This class includes local progress. Finally, in Section 14.3, we identify a TM liveness property that is, in a precise sense, the strongest one that is implementable when processes can crash and/or when transactions can be parasite. We summarize and discuss our results in Section 14.4.

14.1   HIGH-LEVEL LIVENESS OF A TM

14.1.1   PRELIMINARIES

Super transactions   Let H be any TM history. A *super transaction* in H is any maximal sequence of transactions in $H|p_i$, for any process p_i, in which all transactions, except possibly the last one, are forceably aborted. Intuitively, a super transaction gathers all transactions (of a given process) that correspond to subsequent restarts of some computation. Every transaction in a TM history is part of some super transaction.

We say that a super transaction performs some action (e.g., issues an event or executes a step) in a TM history H, if one of its transactions performs this action in H. (Recall from Chapter 3 that when we say that a transaction T_i executes an event or a step, we mean that some process executes this event or step, within some TM operation, while executing T_i.)

We refer to each super transaction in a TM history H using an identifier from infinite set $STrans = \{T_1^*, T_2^*, \dots\}$. In order to avoid introducing additional notation, we assume that the first operation of the first transaction of any super transaction can take, as an optional argument, an identifier from set $STrans$, which then becomes the identifier of this super transaction. When this argument is not given, the TM assigns an arbitrary id to the super transaction.

Therefore, a process p_i starts its first super transaction T_k^* by starting any transaction T_m. Then, once p_i commits some transaction (possibly T_m), super transaction T_k^* becomes *completed*. Process p_i can explicitly finish (complete) super transaction T_k^* by invoking operation *tryA*, i.e., by aborting its current transaction. When T_k^* is completed and p_i starts any transaction, p_i also starts a new super transaction, and so forth.

More precisely, a super transaction T_k^* in a TM history H is *completed* if the last transaction of T_k^* is either committed, or aborted but not forceably aborted. A super transaction that is not completed is called *live*. If t is some point in time, we say that a super transaction T_k^* is *live at time t* (in H) if T_k^* is live in the prefix of H containing all events executed at latest at time t.

Note that every transaction of a super transaction T_k^* can perform different operations on different t-objects. Indeed, every transaction of T_k^* can observe different states of t-objects, and thus follow a different code path. Also, a process that encounters some number of subsequent forceable aborts may decide to switch to an alternative computation (e.g., one that is less likely to cause conflicts) for the next transaction.

Note also that in our definition of a super transaction we aim at simplicity. We could, e.g., introduce explicit TM operations to start and finish a super transaction, but this would not add any insight to the problems we discuss in this chapter.

Let H be any TM history, and T_i^*, T_k^* be any super transactions in H. We say that T_i^* *precedes T_k^** (in H) if T_i^* is completed and the last event of T_i^* precedes the first event of T_k^*. We say that T_i^* and T_k^* are *(directly) concurrent* if neither T_i^* precedes T_k^*, nor T_k^* precedes T_i^*. We say that T_i^* and T_k^* are *transitively concurrent*, if there exist super transactions $T_{\sigma_1}^*, \ldots, T_{\sigma_m}^*$ in H, such that T_i^* and $T_{\sigma_1}^*$ are concurrent, $T_{\sigma_m}^*$ and T_k^* are concurrent, and, for every $l = 1, \ldots, m-1$, $T_{\sigma_l}^*$ and $T_{\sigma_{l+1}}^*$ are concurrent.

All the above terms concerning super transactions in TM histories can be defined analogously for implementation histories of arbitrary TMs.

Parasite super transactions   Let E be any implementation history of any TM. We say that a transaction T_k in E, or a super transaction T_k^* in E, is *infinite*, if T_k (respectively, T_k^*) executes infinitely many steps or events in E. Clearly, there can be at most n infinite (super) transactions in E since we have n processes in the system and every process can execute at most one (super) transaction at a time.

Intuitively, a *parasite* super transaction is a super transaction that keeps executing operations but, from some point in time, never attempts to complete (by invoking operation *tryC* or *tryA*). Consider any implementation history E of any TM, and any infinite super transaction T_k^* in E. If the last transaction of T_k^* executes infinitely many operations, then T_k^* is clearly parasite. Indeed, T_k^* gets to execute infinitely many operations without being forceably aborted, but, from some point in time, T_k^* does not attempt to complete. On the contrary, if T_k^* invokes operation *tryC* infinitely many times, then T_k^* is clearly *not* parasite. Consider, however, a situation in which T_k^* is infinite and does not invoke *tryC* infinitely many times, but T_k^* is either blocked inside some TM operation infinitely long or T_k^* is forceably aborted infinitely many times. Then, looking just at implementation history E, we cannot say whether T_k^* is parasite, or T_k^* is simply starving. Indeed, since the TM did not allow any transaction of T_k^* to execute infinitely many operations and since the maximum number of operations of a given transaction is not known, we do not know whether T_k^*, if given a chance, would eventually attempt to complete.

Therefore, when considering any implementation history E of any TM, we say explicitly which super transactions in E are parasite. We observe, however, the following restrictions for every super transaction T_k^* in E:

- If the last transaction of T_k^* executes infinitely many operations (i.e., issues infinitely many events), then T_k^* must be parasite.

- If T_k^* is finite (e.g., completed) or if T_k^* invokes operation *tryC* infinitely many times, then T_k^* cannot be parasite.

Correct super transactions   Let E be any implementation history of any TM. We say that a super transaction T_k^* in E is *correct* if either (1) T_k^* is completed, or (2) T_k^* is infinite but T_k^* is not parasite.

Systems   An asynchronous system allows arbitrary schedules. That is, any number of processes can crash. Also, in an asynchronous system, any number of super transactions can be parasite.

In the following, we define two restrictions of an asynchronous system. We say that an asynchronous system $\mathcal{S}$ is *crash-free* if no process ever crashes in $\mathcal{S}$. That is, $\mathcal{S}$ allows only those infinite schedules in which every process identifier appears infinitely many times. We say that an asynchronous system $\mathcal{S}$ is *parasite-free* if no super transaction is ever parasite in $\mathcal{S}$. A *fault-prone* system is any of the following: (1) an asynchronous system (without any restrictions), (2) a crash-free system, or (3) a parasite-free system. That is, in a fault-prone system, any number of processes can crash, or any number of super transactions can be parasite.

To make our impossibility result (Theorem 14.11) stronger, we assume that, intuitively, in a crash-free system, every process that starts some super transaction T_k^* keeps executing transactions until T_k^* is completed. More precisely, for every execution ε in a crash-free system, every TM shared object M, every process p_i, and every super transaction T_k^* in $E|p_i$, where E is the implementation history of M in ε, either T_k^* is completed in E, or T_k^* is infinite in E.

Note that a system in which only some processes can crash (e.g., a majority of processes is correct in every execution), or in which only some super transactions can be parasite, is not fault-prone according to the above definition.

14.1.2   DEFINITION OF (HIGH-LEVEL) TM LIVENESS

Let H be any (implementation) history of some TM, and t be any time. The *concurrent group* in H at time t, denoted by *Concurr*$_H(t)$, is the set of those super transactions in H that are either (1) live at time t or (2) live after time t and directly or transitively concurrent to some super transactions that are live at t.

Roughly speaking, a TM liveness property specifies which *correct* super transactions from any concurrent group Q in an implementation history of a TM must be completed. We define a TM liveness property in the following way:

Definition 14.1   A *TM liveness* property L is any function $L : 2^{STrans} \mapsto 2^{2^{STrans}}$ such that, for every set $C \subseteq STrans$, we have: (1) $L(C) \neq \emptyset$, and (2) $S \subseteq C$ for every set $S \in L(C)$.

Since a TM liveness property is a function of a set of super transaction identifiers, those identifiers can be used to encode priorities of super transactions. For instance, if L is a TM liveness property such that $L(\{T_1^*, T_2^*\}) = \{\{T_1^*\}\}$, then L gives a higher priority to T_1^* than to T_2^*. That is, if T_1^* and T_2^* are the only correct transactions in some concurrent group, then T_1^* must be completed (T_2^* can be completed, but does not have to). Note that a TM is free to commit T_2^* before T_1^*—L only requires that T_1^* eventually becomes completed.

Intuitively, if Q is the set of correct super transactions in the concurrent group at some time t in an implementation history E of some TM, and L is a TM liveness property, then $L(Q)$ is a set of subsets $Q_1, Q_2, \ldots$ of Q. In order to ensure L, all super transactions from *some* set $Q_m \in L(Q)$ must be completed in E. (Super transactions that are not in Q_m may be either completed or live.)

More formally, let E be any implementation history of any TM, and Q be any subset of the set of super transactions in E. We denote by $Correct_E(Q)$ the set of those super transactions in Q that are correct in E. We denote by $Completed_E(Q)$ the set of those super transactions in set Q that are completed in E.

Definition 14.2   An implementation history E of a TM *ensures* a TM liveness property L if, for every time t, if $Q = Correct_E(Concurr_E(t))$ then $Completed_E(Q) \supseteq C$ for some set $C \in L(Q)$.

Definition 14.3   A TM shared object M ensures a TM liveness property L if every implementation history of M ensures L.

In order to compare any two TM liveness properties L and L', we define when L is *weaker* than L'. The "weaker than" relation is a partial order on the set of all TM liveness properties. If L is weaker than L', then every TM that ensures L' also ensures L. More formally:

Definition 14.4   Let L and L' be any two TM liveness properties. We say that L is *weaker* than L' (and L' is *stronger* than L) if, for every implementation history E of every TM, if E ensures L' then E also ensures L.

14.1.3   EXAMPLES OF TM LIVENESS PROPERTIES

We give here examples of common TM liveness properties. We prove that our definitions of those properties, expressed within our formal framework, do indeed capture the common intuition behind those properties (Theorems 14.5, 14.6, and 14.7). We also give examples of TM implementations that ensure those properties.

Local progress   Intuitively, a TM implementation M ensures *local progress* (analogous to *wait-freedom* [Herlihy, 1991] or *starvation-freedom* for shared object implementations), if it guarantees that every correct super transaction will be eventually completed. More formally, local progress is the function

$$L_1(C) = \{C\}.$$

Every TM liveness property is weaker than L_1. (Recall that the "weaker than" relation, as we defined it in Section 14.1.2, is reflexive; that is, every TM liveness property is weaker than, and also stronger than, itself.)

As we discussed in the introduction of this chapter, and as we prove in Section 14.2, implementing a TM that guarantees local progress in any fault-prone system is impossible. That is, local progress inherently requires some form of indefinite blocking of transactions.

Ensuring local progress in a system that is both crash-free and parasite-free is possible, e.g., with a simple TM that synchronizes all transactions using a single global lock, and thus never forceably aborts any transaction. However, none of the major existing TM implementations ensures local progress.

Theorem 14.5   *An implementation history E of any TM ensures L_1 if, and only if, every correct super transaction in E is completed.*

Proof. Let M be any TM shared object, and E be any implementation history of M.

($\Rightarrow$) Assume that E ensures L_1. Consider any correct super transaction T_k^* in E. Let t be any time at which T_k^* is live in E. Then, since $T_k^* \in Correct_E(Concurr_E(t))$, and since $L_1(C) = \{C\}$, T_k^* must be completed in E.

($\Leftarrow$) Assume that every correct super transaction in E is completed. Let t be any time, and let $C = Correct_E(Concurr_E(t))$. Because every super transaction in C is completed, $Completed_E(C) = C \in L_1(C)$.   □

Global progress   Intuitively, a TM implementation M ensures *global progress* (analogous to *lock-freedom*, or *livelock-freedom* for shared object implementations), if it guarantees that, if some correct super transaction is live at some time t, then *some* super transaction will be eventually completed after t. More formally, global progress is the function

$$L_g(C) = \left\{ \left\{ T_{i_1}^* \right\}, \left\{ T_{i_2}^* \right\}, \dots \right\},$$

where $T_{i_1}^*, T_{i_2}^*, \dots$ are all elements of set C.

Global progress is ensured by so-called *lock-free* TM implementations such as OSTM [Fraser, 2003], WSTM [Harris and Fraser, 2003], and MM-STM [Marathe and Moir, 2008]. We give a simple TM implementation that guarantees global progress in Section 14.3. In a crash-free system, global-progress is ensured by TM implementations such as RingSTM [Spear et al., 2008b], NOrec [Dalessandro et al., 2010], and TML [Spear et al., 2009]. (However, lock-based TM implementations such as TL2, TinySTM, or SwissTM do not ensure global progress since they allow livelock situations—scenarios in which two concurrent correct super transactions are live forever.)

Theorem 14.6   *An implementation history E of any TM ensures L_g if, and only if, either there is no live correct super transaction in E, or infinitely many super transactions are completed in E.*

Proof. Let M be any TM shared object, and E be any implementation history of M.

($\Rightarrow$) Assume that E ensures L_g, and that there is a live correct super transaction T_k^* in E. By contradiction, assume that after some time t no super transaction becomes completed in E. Because T_k^* is live, set $Q = Correct_E(Concurr_E(t'))$, where $t' > t$, contains at least super transaction T_k^*. Hence, by L_g, some transaction from set Q must be completed in E—a contradiction.

($\Leftarrow$) If E has no live correct super transactions, then E trivially ensures L_g. Assume then that there are infinitely many completed super transactions in E. Hence, for every time t, set $Q = Correct_E(Concurr_E(t))$ contains either (1) only completed transactions or (2) some live transactions and infinitely many completed transactions. In both cases, E ensures L_g. $\square$

Solo progress   Intuitively, a TM shared object M ensures *solo progress* (analogous to *obstruction-freedom* [Herlihy et al., 2003b] for shared object implementations), if M guarantees that every correct super transaction that eventually runs *alone* for sufficiently long time becomes completed. The classical meaning of the term "alone" refers to the absence of step contention [Attiya et al., 2005] (cf. also Chapter 13). Parasite super transactions, however, have never been considered before in this context. In the following definition, we assume that a super transaction T_i^* is alone if T_i^* is eventually concurrent only to incorrect transactions. In a parasite-free system, this is equivalent to saying that T_i^* is alone if T_i^* eventually does not encounter step contention (as we prove below). More formally, solo progress is the following function:

$$L_s(C) = \begin{cases} \{C\} & \text{if } |C| = 1 \\ \{\emptyset\} & \text{otherwise.} \end{cases}$$

Obstruction-free TM implementations (cf. Chapter 13) ensure solo progress in parasite-free systems. Lock-based TMs (cf. Chapter 12) ensure solo progress in systems that are both parasite-free and crash-free. Those lock-based TMs that use deferred updates, however, such as TL2 (cf. Section 12.2.3), ensure solo progress in crash-free systems.

Theorem 14.7   *Let E be any implementation history of any TM, such that there are no parasite super transactions in E. Then, E ensures property L_s if, and only if, for every process p_i, and every correct super* *transaction T_k^* executed by p_i in E, if only p_i executes steps and events in some suffix of E, then T_k^* is completed in E.*

Proof. Let M be any TM shared object, and E be any implementation history of M. Assume that there are no parasite super transactions in E.

($\Rightarrow$) Assume that E ensures property L_s. By contradiction, assume that there is a process p_i, such that in some suffix E' of E only p_i executes steps and events, but some correct super transaction T_k^* in $E|p_i$ is live. Since no process other than p_i can execute infinitely many steps or events in E, only T_k^* is correct and live in E. Hence, there exists time t, such that $Correct_E(Concurr_E(t)) = \{T_k^*\}$. But then, since $L_s(\{T_k^*\}) = \{\{T_k^*\}\}$, T_k^* must be completed in E—a contradiction.

($\Leftarrow$) Assume that E violates property L_s. That is, for some time t, $Correct_E(Concurr_E(t)) = \{T_k^*\}$, where T_k^* is some super transaction that is live in E. Let p_i be the process executing T_k^* in E. Then, since no correct super transaction is live at any time after t, and since only T_k^* is correct and live in E, there is a time t' after which only p_i executes steps and events.   □

Priority-based properties   Local progress, global progress, and solo progress give the same guarantees to all super transactions, regardless their identifiers. We can, however, encode some priority scheme into those identifiers, thus giving preference to some super transactions. For instance, let $\ll$ be any total order on set *STrans*, such that there is a minimal element in set *STrans* ordered by $\ll$, and let k be any natural number. We define the following TM liveness property:

$$L_{\ll,k}(C) = \begin{cases} \{C\} & \text{if } |C| \leq k \\ \{\{T_{\sigma_1}^*\}, \dots, \{T_{\sigma_k}^*\}\} & \text{otherwise,} \end{cases}$$

where $T_{\sigma_1}^*, \dots, T_{\sigma_k}^*$ are the k least super transactions in set C according to total order $\ll$. Intuitively, $L_{\ll,k}$ guarantees progress for *one* of the k correct transactions with the lowest id from a given concurrent group.

14.1.4 CLASSES OF TM LIVENESS PROPERTIES

Intuitively, we say that a TM liveness property L is *nonblocking* if L guarantees progress for every correct super transaction that eventually runs alone, i.e., with no concurrent correct and live super transactions. More formally:

Definition 14.8   We say that a TM liveness property L is *nonblocking* if, for every super transaction $T_i^* \in STrans$, $L(\{T_i^*\}) = \{\{T_i^*\}\}$. Properties that are not nonblocking are called *blocking*. Local

progress, global progress, an solo progress, as well as properties $L_{\ll,1}, L_{\ll,2}, \dots$, for every total order $\ll$ on set *STrans*, are all nonblocking. Note that solo progress is weaker than every nonblocking TM liveness property.

Intuitively, a TM liveness property L is $(n-1)$-*prioritizing* if L specifies a set P of at most $n-1$ super transactions, and it guarantees progress for some super transaction in P in some (at least one) concurrent group containing infinitely many correct super transactions. In a sense, P can be thought of as a set of super transactions with higher priority—L guarantees that one of those super transactions has to be completed in one specific execution. More formally:

Definition 14.9 We say that a TM liveness property L is $(n - 1)$-*prioritizing*, if there exists an infinite subset C of set *STrans*, and a subset P of C of size at most $n - 1$, such that, for every set S in $L(C)$, $P \cap S \neq \emptyset$. Local progress is $(n - 1)$-prioritizing (take, e.g., $C = STrans$ and $P = \left\{T_k^*\right\}$

for any $T_k^* \in STrans$). Also, every property $L_{\ll,m}$ (for any $\ll$), where $m < n$, is $(n - 1)$-prioritizing (take, e.g., $C = STrans$ and P to be the set of the m least elements in set *STrans* ordered by $\ll$). Global progress, solo progress, and every property $L_{\ll,m}$, where $m \geq n$, are, however, not $(n - 1)$-prioritizing. Therefore, $(n - 1)$-prioritization is all about choice—how constrained a TM is when it must choose which of the concurrent transactions to forceably abort.

14.2 IMPOSSIBILITY RESULT

In this section, we prove that all TM liveness properties that are nonblocking and $(n - 1)$-prioritizing are impossible to implement in any fault-prone system. Before we do so, however, we explain intuitively why local progress, which is a nonblocking and $(n - 1)$-prioritizing TM liveness property, cannot be ensured when processes can crash or when super transactions can be parasite.

Consider a TM history depicted in Figure 14.1. Consider two processes, p_1 and p_2, that execute transactions T_1 and T_2, respectively. Transaction T_1 reads value 0 from a t-variable x and then gets suspended for a long time. Then, transaction T_2 also reads value 0 from x, and attempts to write value 1 to x and commit. Because of asynchrony, processes (and their transactions) can be arbitrarily delayed. Hence, process p_2 does not know whether p_1 has crashed or is just very slow, and so, in order to ensure progress of transaction T_2, p_2 might eventually commit T_2. But then, if transaction T_1 attempts to write value 1 to x, T_1 cannot commit, as this would violate opacity. A similar situation can arise if T_1 keeps repeatedly reading variable x instead of being suspended—then p_2 cannot say whether the super transaction containing T_1 is parasite or not without waiting for T_1 indefinitely. This situation, in which a transaction executed by process p_1 is forceably aborted, can repeat any number of times, suggesting that ensuring progress for every super transaction is impossible.

We prove now that TM liveness properties that are nonblocking and $(n - 1)$-prioritizing, such as local progress, are impossible to implement in any fault-prone system (Theorem 14.11). We start by proving the following lemma, which says, intuitively, that a process executing infinitely many super transactions can block progress of all other processes, if the TM ensures any nonblocking TM liveness property.

Lemma 14.10 *For every fault-prone system $\mathcal{S}$, every TM shared object M that ensures any nonblocking TM liveness property in $\mathcal{S}$, and for every pair of sets P and C, where $P \subset C \subseteq STrans$, $|C| = \infty$, and*

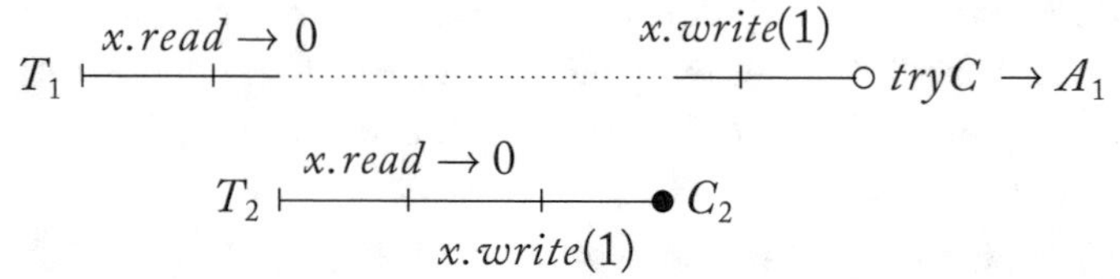

Figure 14.1: An illustration of why ensuring local progress is impossible in an asynchronous system. The depicted scenario can repeat infinitely many times, and so the super transaction of T_1 might never be able to commit.

$|P| = n - 1$, *there exists an infinite implementation history E of M in S and a time t, such that the concurrent group at time t in E is C, all super transactions from set C are correct in E, and all super transactions from set P are live in E.*

Proof. Let M be any TM shared object that ensures some nonblocking TM liveness property L in some fault-prone system S. Let P and C be any sets such that $P \subset C \subseteq STrans$, $|C| = \infty$, and $|P| = n - 1$. Denote by σ any one-to-one function from the set of natural numbers to set C. For simplicity of notation, but without loss in generality, we assume in the following that $\sigma(k) = k$ for $k = 1, \ldots, n - 1$, and that $P = \{T_1^*, \ldots, T_{n-1}^*\}$.

We consider two cases: when system S is *not* crash-free, and when S is *not* parasite-free. In each case, we show an infinite implementation history E of M in S, in which every super transaction from set P is correct, live, and concurrent to every super transaction from set C.

Case 1: S is not crash-free   Consider an implementation history E of M that corresponds to an execution of the following algorithm (initially, $k = n$; x is some t-variable initialized to 0):

1. Super transactions $T_1^*, \ldots, T_{n-1}^*$ read x one by one, i.e., each super transaction T_i^*, $i = 2, \ldots, n - 1$, invokes operation $x.read$ after T_{i-1}^* returns from its operation $x.read$.

2. Super transaction $T_{\sigma(k)}^*$ reads some value v from t-variable x and writes value $1 - v$ to x. Then, $T_{\sigma(k)}^*$ attempts to commit, i.e., executes operation $tryC$. Whenever $T_{\sigma(k)}^*$ is forceably aborted, $T_{\sigma(k)}^*$ retries the same operations until $T_{\sigma(k)}^*$ becomes completed. No super transaction executes steps concurrently to $T_{\sigma(k)}^*$.

3. Those super transactions from set $\{T_1^*, \ldots, T_{n-1}^*\}$ that were not forceably aborted in step 1 write value $1 - v$ to x and attempt to commit one by one. If all of them get forceably aborted, go back to step 1 with $k \leftarrow k + 1$.

Assume that, in E, each super transaction T_i^*, $i \in \{1, \ldots, n - 1\}$, is executed by process p_i, and all super transactions $T_{\sigma(n)}^*, T_{\sigma(n+1)}^*, \ldots$, are executed by process p_n.

We prove first that the above algorithm cannot be blocked in step 1 or 3, i.e., that no super transaction T_i^*, $i = 1, \ldots, n - 1$, can be blocked by M inside its operation $x.read$, $x.write$, or $tryC$, infinitely long. Assume otherwise—that some super transaction T_i^*, $1 \leq i \leq n - 1$, invokes an operation op, executes infinitely many steps, but never receives a response event from op. Then, by the above algorithm, only super transaction T_i^* executes infinitely many steps and events in E, and so T_i^* is the only correct and live super transaction in E. Hence, there is some time t such that $Correct_E(Concurr_E(t)) = \{T_i^*\}$. But then, since M ensures L and $L(\{T_i^*\}) = \{\{T_i^*\}\}$, T_i^* must be completed in E—a contradiction.

We prove now that every super transaction $T_{\sigma(k)}^*$, $k = n, n + 1, \ldots$, is completed in E. Assume otherwise: that, for some value $k \geq n$, super transaction $T_{\sigma(k)}$ is live and correct in E. Then, no super transaction T_i^*, $i = 1, \ldots, n - 1$, issues any event or step after the first event of $T_{\sigma(k)}^*$ in E. Hence, $T_{\sigma(k)}^*$ is the only correct and live super transaction in E, and so, since E ensures L, $T_{\sigma(k)}^*$ is completed in E—a contradiction.

Finally, we prove that super transactions $T_1^*, \ldots, T_{n-1}^*$ are live in E. Assume otherwise: that some super transaction T_m^*, $m \in \{1, \ldots, n - 1\}$, is completed in E. Let T_q be the last (committed) transaction of super transaction T_m^*. Let T_w be the committed transaction that is executed by process p_n and that is concurrent to T_q. (T_w belongs to some super transaction $T_{\sigma(k)}^*$, $k \geq n$.) Finally, let T_r be the latest committed transaction in E that is executed by p_n and that precedes T_q. Note that T_r also precedes T_w. Let v be the value written to t-variable x by T_r.

Consider the prefix H of TM history $E|M$, such that the last element of H is the response event of operation $read$ on x executed by T_w. Since H is opaque, and since T_r writes value v to x and commits before both T_q and T_w start, both T_q and T_w read value v from x. Consider then the prefix H' of $E|M$, such that the last element of H' is the commit event of T_q. In H', transactions T_q and T_w are concurrent and committed, and each of those transactions reads value v from x and then writes value $1 - v$ to x. But then, since, in H', there is no transaction that writes value v to x and is concurrent to either T_q or T_w, TM history H' violates opacity—a contradiction with the assumption that M is opaque.

Case 2: S is not parasite-free   Consider an implementation history E of M that corresponds to an execution of the following algorithm: Processes $p_1, \ldots, p_{n-1}$ execute, concurrently, super transactions $T_1^*, \ldots, T_{n-1}^*$, respectively. Process p_n executes super transactions $T_{\sigma(n)}^*, T_{\sigma(n+1)}^*, \ldots$. The algorithm proceeds in rounds $0, 1, \ldots$. Round 0 starts at time 0, and every round r, $r > 0$, starts immediately after round $r - 1$ ends. In round r, process p_n executes super transaction $T_{\sigma(n+r)}^*$. Round r ends when (a) $T_{\sigma(n+r)}^*$ becomes completed, and (b) some transaction of super transaction T_m, where $m = r$ mod $(n - 1) + 1$, is forceably aborted in round r. The following operations are executed by super transactions in each round r:

- Super transaction T_m^*, where $m = r$ mod $(n - 1) + 1$, repeatedly executes operation $read$ on x until super transaction $T_{\sigma(n+r)}^*$ becomes completed. Then, if T_m^* has not been forceably aborted in the current round, T_m^* writes value $v + 1$ to x, where v is the value returned by the latest operation $x.read$ of T_m^*. If the $write$ operation of T_m^* is successful, then T_m^* executes operation *tryC*. If, at any time, T_m^* is forceably aborted, T_m^* repeatedly executes operation $x.read$ until the end of the current round.

- Super transaction $T_{\sigma(n+r)}^*$ starts when super transaction T_m^* returns from some $x.read$ operation in the current round. (The operation $x.read$ of T_m^* does not have to start in the current round, and it can return A_m.) Then, $T_{\sigma(n+r)}^*$ tries to execute, within each of its transactions, operations: $x.read \to v', x.write(v' + 1)$, and *tryC*, and does so until $T_{\sigma(n+r)}^*$ becomes completed.

- Every super transaction $T_i^*, i \in \{1, ..., n - 1\}, i \neq m$, repeatedly executes operation *read* on x.

In the following, we prove that the above execution goes through infinitely many rounds. Then, in E, every super transaction $T_k^*, k = 1, ..., n - 1$, is live and forceably aborted infinitely many times, while all super transactions $T_{\sigma(n)}^*, T_{\sigma(n+1)}^*, ...$, are completed and concurrent to all super transactions T_1^*, ..., T_{n-1}^*. Hence, assuming that $T_1^*, ..., T_{n-1}^*$ are not parasite, the claim of the lemma is proved.

By contradiction, assume that some round r of the above execution does not end. Let $m = r$ mod $(n - 1) + 1$. Hence, in E, either super transaction T_m^* does not get forceably aborted after round r starts, or super transaction $T_{\sigma(n+r)}^*$ does not start, or $T_{\sigma(n+r)}^*$ is live.

Assume first that $T_{\sigma(n+r)}^*$ does not start. Then, super transaction T_m^* does not receive any response event after round r starts. Hence, T_m^* executes infinitely many steps within some operation of M. Assume that T_m^* is correct (i.e., not parasite). Every super transaction $T_i^*, i = 1, ..., n - 1$, $i \neq m$, keeps executing operation *read* on x and, after the beginning of round r, does not invoke operation *tryC*. Therefore, every such super transaction T_i^* can be parasite, in which case T_m^* is the only correct and live super transaction in E. But then, since M ensures TM liveness property L that is nonblocking, T_m^* must be completed in E—a contradiction.

Assume then that super transaction $T_{\sigma(n+r)}^*$ is correct and live in E. Then, all super transactions $T_1^*, ..., T_{n-1}^*$ keep reading t-variable x, and do not invoke operation *tryC* in round r. Hence, assuming that super transactions $T_1^*, ..., T_{n-1}^*$ are all parasite, $T_{\sigma(n+r)}^*$ is the only correct and live super transaction in E—a contradiction with the assumption that M ensures a nonblocking TM liveness property L.

Finally, assume that T_m^* is not forceably aborted after the beginning of round r. Hence, T_m^* is either live or completed in E. The case when T_m^* is live in E is analogous to the case when T_m^* does not receive any response event in round r, which we consider above. Assume then that T_m^* is completed in E. Let T_q be the last (committed) transaction of T_m^*. Hence, T_q reads some value v from t-variable x, writes value $v + 1$ to x, and commits.

Observe that all committed transactions in E, except for T_q, are executed by process p_n. In each round $r' \leq r$, p_n executes and commits exactly one transaction that effectively increments the value of x. Let $T_{s_1}, ..., T_{s_r}$ denote the committed transactions executed by p_n in rounds $1, ..., r$, respectively. Consider any transaction $T_{s_k}, k \in \{1, ..., r\}$. Transaction T_{s_k} reads from x some value v_k, and writes to x value $v_k + 1$. All transactions that are concurrent to T_{s_k} in E, except possibly T_q, are either aborted, or live but not commit-pending. Transaction T_q executes its (first) *write* operation on x after the last event of T_{s_k}. Hence, by opacity of E, $v_k = v_{k-1} + 1$ if $k > 1$, or $v_k = 0$ if $k = 1$. Therefore, T_{s_k} reads from x value $k - 1$ and writes to x value k.

Since transaction T_q executes its first *read* operation on x before transaction T_{s_r} starts, and since E is opaque, the value v that T_q reads from x must be lower than $v_r + 1$. Therefore, there are two committed transactions in E that read value v from x and write value $v + 1$ to x. But then, since at most one committed transaction writes value v to x in E, implementation history E of M violates opacity—a contradiction with the assumption that M is opaque. $\square$

Theorem 14.11   *For every TM liveness property L and every fault-prone system $\mathcal{S}$, if L is nonblocking and $(n - 1)$-prioritizing, then there is no TM that ensures L in $\mathcal{S}$.*

Proof. Let L be any nonblocking, $(n - 1)$-prioritizing TM liveness property. Because L is $(n - 1)$-prioritizing, there exists an infinite set $C \subseteq STrans$ and a set $P \subset C$ of size at most $n - 1$ such that $P \cap S \neq \emptyset$ for every $S \in L(C)$. Let P' be any subset of C of size $n - 1$ that contains all elements of set P. Clearly, $P' \cap S \neq \emptyset$ for every $S \in L(C)$.

By contradiction, assume that there is a TM shared object M that ensures L in some fault-prone system $\mathcal{S}$. By Lemma 14.10, and because L is nonblocking, there exists an implementation history E of M and a time t, such that $Correct_E(Concurr_E(t)) = C$ and all transactions from set P' are correct and live in E. But then, for every $S \in L(C)$, since $P' \cap S \neq \emptyset$ then $Completed_H(C) \not\supseteq S$. Hence, implementation history E of M violates L—a contradiction with the assumption that M ensures L. $\square$

14.3   ENSURING NON-(N−1)-PRIORITIZING TM LIVENESS PROPERTIES

In the previous section, we showed that TM liveness properties that are nonblocking and $(n - 1)$-prioritizing are impossible to implement in any fault-prone system. In this section, we prove that every TM liveness property L that is *not* $(n - 1)$-prioritizing, regardless of whether L is blocking or nonblocking, can be implemented in every fault-prone system. In fact, we prove that every such property L is weaker than global progress. We show then a TM implementation that implements global progress, and so also any weaker property, in an asynchronous system.

Note that OSTM [Fraser, 2003], WSTM [Harris and Fraser, 2003], and MM-STM [Marathe and Moir, 2008] also ensure global progress in every fault-prone system. However, we do not know if this has been formally proved. Hence, for completeness, we give here our own TM algorithm and prove that it indeed ensures opacity and global progress in presence of crashed and parasite transactions. The purpose of the TM we show in this section is only to prove our result—the TM is not meant to be practical or efficient.

Theorem 14.12   *Every TM liveness property that is not $(n - 1)$-prioritizing is weaker than L_g.*

Proof. Let L be any TM liveness property that is not $(n-1)$-prioritizing. Consider any implementation history E of any TM, such that E ensures L_g. By contradiction, assume that E does not ensure L. That is, there is a time t, such that, if $C = Correct_E(Concurr_E(t))$, then $Completed_E(C) \not\supseteq S$ for every $S \in L(C)$.

Assume first that set C is finite. By global progress, some super transaction, say T_i^*, from set C is completed in E. Take any time $t' > t$, such that some super transaction from set C is live at t', but T_i^* is not live at t'. Since set $C' = Correct_E(Concurr_E(t'))$ is a proper subset of C, by global progress, some super transaction from C' is completed in E. By continuing the same line of reasoning, we can prove that every super transaction in set C is completed in E, contradicting the assumption that $Completed_E(C) \not\supseteq S$ for every $S \in L(C)$.

Therefore, set C is infinite. Denote by P the set of super transactions in C that are live in E, i.e., $P = C - Completed_E(C)$. Because set C is infinite, and since at most n super transactions can be concurrent at any time in E, the size of set P is at most $n - 1$.

Let P' be any set such that $P \subseteq P' \subseteq C$ and $|P'| = n - 1$. Because L is not $(n-1)$-prioritizing, there exists an element $S \in L(C)$ such that $P' \cap S = \emptyset$. But then, since P' contains all super transactions from set C that are live in E, and because $S \subseteq C$, all super transactions in set S are completed in E—a contradiction with the assumption that $Completed_E(C) \not\supseteq S$ for every $S \in L(C)$. $\square$

An algorithm $\mathcal{A}_{GP}$ implementing a TM that ensures global progress is shown in Figure 14.2. The idea behind the algorithm is very simple: the snapshot of the states of all t-variables is stored in a single compare-and-swap object C, together with a version number of the snapshot. Every transaction T_k first copies the value of C into its local variables *version*, *values*, and *oldval*. Then, T_k performs all its *read* and *write* operations only on array *values*. In order to commit, T_k atomically changes the value of C to the new snapshot from variable *values*, with a new version number.

Lemma 14.13   *Algorithm $\mathcal{A}_{GP}$ implements a TM that ensures opacity and global progress in every fault-prone system.*

Proof. Consider any shared object M implemented by $\mathcal{A}_{GP}$, and any implementation history E of M. Denote history $E|M$ by H. Within this proof, we say that a transaction T_k *reads version* w if T_k is returned in line 20 a tuple (*version*, *oldval*), where *version* $= w$. We say that T_k *commits version* w if T_k reads version $w - 1$ and is returned value *true* from operation *compare-and-swap* on C in line 12.

Opacity   Observe that the version number stored in object C can only increase with time. Hence, if a transaction T_i precedes a transaction T_k in H, then T_i cannot read a version higher than the version read by T_k. Note also that from any set of transactions that read the same version w at most one transaction can commit version $w + 1$. Therefore, there exists a total order $\ll$ on the set of transactions in H, such that, for all transactions T_i and T_k in H, $T_i \ll T_k$ if:

uses: C—compare-and-swap object (other variables are process-local)
initially: $C = (1, (0, 0, \ldots))$, *version* $= \perp$ (at every process p_i)

1 **operation** $x_m.read_k$
2 | *acquire*();
3 | **return** *values*[m];

4 **operation** $x_m.write(v)_k$
5 | *acquire*();
6 | *values*[m] $\leftarrow v$;
7 | **return** *ok*;

8 **operation** $tryA(T_k)$
9 | *version* $\leftarrow \perp$;
10 | **return** A_k;

11 **operation** $tryC(T_k)$
12 | **if** $C.compare\text{-}and\text{-}swap((version, oldval), (version + 1, values))$ **then**
13 | *version* $\leftarrow \perp$;
14 | **return** C_k;
15 | **else**
16 | *version* $\leftarrow \perp$;
17 | **return** A_k;

18 **function** *acquire*()
19 | **if** *version* $\neq \perp$ **then return**;
20 | (*version*, *oldval*) $\leftarrow C.read$;
21 | *values* $\leftarrow$ *oldval*;

Figure 14.2: Algorithm $\mathcal{A}_{\text{GP}}$ implementing a TM that ensures global progress

- $T_i \prec_H T_k$; or

- T_i reads a version w_i, T_k reads a version w_k, and $w_i < w_k$; or

- T_i reads a version w_i and T_k commits version $w_i + 1$.

Let H' be the completion of history H such that a transaction T_k in H' is committed in H' if, and only if, T_k commits some version in E. Let S be the following sequential TM history:

$$S = H'|T_{\sigma_1} \cdot H'|T_{\sigma_2} \cdots,$$

where $T_{\sigma_1} \ll T_{\sigma_2} \ll \ldots$. Clearly, S is equivalent to H' and S preserves the real-time order of H. Every transaction T_k that is aborted in S does not commit any version, and so T_k does not change the state of object C. Hence, aborted transactions are effectively invisible to other transactions. Every transaction T_k that is committed in S reads some version w and commits version $w + 1$. Since the version number stored in C never decreases, no other transaction commits version $w + 1$ in E. Transaction T_k thus reads the current snapshot of t-variable values from C, modifies the snapshot locally within operations *read* and *write*, and then atomically changes the state of C from the old snapshot, with version number w, to the new snapshot, with version number $w + 1$. Therefore, all transactions that follow T_k in S observe all the values written to t-variables by T_k, and by all preceding transactions that are committed in S. Therefore, every transaction in S is legal in S, and so history H is final-state opaque. This means that, by Observation 7.4, TM implementation M is opaque.

Global progress   Consider any correct and live super transaction T_k^* in implementation history E of M. Since every operation of M is wait-free, and since T_k^* is not parasite, T_k^* consists of infinitely many forceably aborted transactions. A transaction T_i can be forceably aborted by M only if T_i reads some version w and then fails to commit version $w + 1$; this can happen only if some other transaction commits version $w + 1$. Since a transaction that commits any version cannot be forceably aborted, there are infinitely many transactions in E that are not forceably aborted. Hence, T_k^* is concurrent to infinitely many completed super transactions, and so, by Theorem 14.6, implementation history E, and thus also TM implementation M, ensures global progress. $\square$

From Theorem 14.11, Theorem 14.12, and Lemma 14.13, we obtain the following result:

Corollary 14.14   *Global progress is the strongest nonblocking TM liveness property that can be ensured by any TM in any fault-prone system.*

14.4   SUMMARY AND DISCUSSION

We proved in this chapter the following results, summarized in Figure 14.3, which hold in every fault-prone system:

1. There is no TM shared object that ensures a TM liveness property that is nonblocking and $(n - 1)$-prioritizing, e.g., local progress.

2. Every TM liveness property that is not $(n - 1)$-prioritizing is weaker than global progress.

3. There exists a TM shared object that ensures global progress.

Those results imply that global progress is the strongest nonblocking TM liveness property that can be ensured by a TM implementation (in any fault-prone system). Hence, TM algorithms such as OSTM, WSTM, MM-STM, and $\mathcal{A}_{GP}$ can be thought of as optimal with respect to liveness, at least within our framework for expressing TM liveness properties.

In the following, we discuss our results, and present some open questions.

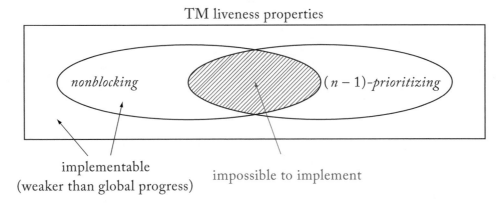

Figure 14.3: Summary of the results

Practical perspective   Local progress is an important property—it guarantees freedom from starvation of every process in the system. Other practically relevant nonblocking and $(n-1)$-prioritizing properties, besides local progress, may, e.g., guarantee progress for all transactions with certain priority. Our results imply that ensuring any such TM liveness property inherently requires processes to wait for each other. This means, for instance, that ensuring worst-case liveness, such as local progress, may hamper the average-case performance of a TM.

Ensuring local progress without making transactions wait for each other is possible if transactions are static and predefined. That is, if, upon the first event of every transaction T_i, the TM implementation knows exactly which operations, on which t-variables T_i will execute, our impossibility result does not hold. However, assuming static transactions may be often too limiting for an application.

Dissecting the "grey area"   The class of TM liveness properties that are $(n-1)$-prioritizing and blocking is a "grey area". It contains properties that are implementable and properties that are impossible to implement (by a TM) in a fault-prone system.

Within this "grey area", there are many TM liveness properties that become $(n-1)$-prioritizing and nonblocking if the set of super transactions is restricted to some infinite subset of set *STrans*. It is straightforward to see that Theorem 14.11 holds also for such properties. There are also certain TM liveness properties that give some guarantees only for those concurrent groups that contain finite numbers of super transactions. Such properties can be shown to be weaker than global progress, which means that they are ensured by TM algorithm $\mathcal{A}_{GP}$. Those two groups of TM liveness properties probably include all properties from the "grey area" that can potentially be of any practical relevance. Hence, we believe that dissecting the class of $(n-1)$-prioritizing and blocking properties further makes little sense.

CHAPTER 15

Further Reading

Conflict-based progress semantics Scott [2006] proposed to define the semantics of a TM (both correctness and progress) by first assuming that individual TM operations are linearizable [Herlihy and Wing, 1990], and then reasoning only about TM histories in which no two TM operations are concurrent. For correctness, he proposes a condition that, as he argues, is equivalent to strict serializability [Papadimitriou, 1979]. To define the progress semantics of a TM, he characterizes each TM implementation M by two functions: a *conflict* function and an *arbitration* function. The conflict function says which transactions in a given history of M have a conflict. That is, the notion of a conflict depends on the TM. Scott then requires that M never aborts any transaction that does not have any conflict. The arbitration function specifies, for every pair of conflicting transactions, which of those transactions (if any) cannot be forceably aborted by M. This function thus models contention management.

The framework of Scott [2006] enables to define properties that are similar to our minimal progressiveness (Section 9.1) and weak progressiveness (Section 12.4). Strong progressiveness (Section 12.1) cannot be specified in this framework because it requires that, from any group of concurrent transactions that conflict only on a single t-object, *some* transaction cannot be forceably aborted. An arbitration function, however, would have to specify *which* transaction in this group cannot be forceably aborted. Indeed, the example progress properties proposed by Scott are either rather weak (similar to our weak progressiveness) or specific to particular TM protocols (i.e., not as general as strong progressiveness). Obstruction-freedom (Section 13.1) also cannot be expressed in the framework of Scott because there is no notion of a step of a TM implementation in this framework.

There is also one subtlety of the framework of Scott that makes it impossible to express (in that framework) a property strictly equivalent to our minimal or weak progressiveness. Consider the following TM history H:

$$H = \langle inv_1(x.write(1)), \ x.write(2)_2, \ C_2, \ ret_1(x \to ok) \rangle.$$

In H, transactions T_1 and T_2 conflict on t-variable x because the *read* operation of T_1 is concurrent to both operations of T_2. Hence, weak progressiveness allows both of those transactions to be forceably aborted. However, in the framework of Scott, one only considers TM histories in which individual TM operations are never concurrent. Hence, a conflict function would take as an argument, e.g., the following TM history, which is equivalent to H:

$$H' = \langle x.write(2)_2, \ C_2, \ x.write(1)_1 \rangle.$$

However, in H', transactions T_1 and T_2 are no longer concurrent, and so the conflict function would say that they do not have any conflict. Thus, the TM would not be able to forceably abort any of those transactions.

Weak try-locks   Algorithm $A_{\text{Reg} \rightarrow \text{TLock}}$ (Section 12.4), which implements a weak try-lock using only registers, was inspired by the Lamport's Bakery algorithm [Lamport, 1974], which implements a (blocking) mutual exclusion mechanism.

Obstruction-freedom   Obstruction-freedom was first proposed by Herlihy et al. [2003b] as a liveness property for shared object implementations. Subsequently, Attiya et al. [2005] provided a formal definition of obstruction-freedom. The first obstruction-free TM implementation was DSTM [Herlihy et al., 2003a]; however, there was so far no precise definition of an obstruction-free TM. Our definition uses the notion of step contention, also used by Attiya et al. [2005], and it tries to capture the progress semantics of existing OFTMs such as DSTM, ASTM [Marathe et al., 2005], and NZTM [Tabba et al., 2007].

Computability results   Afek et al. [1996] and Ruppert [1998, 1999] proved several bounds on the computational power of operations (or transactions) that span multiple base objects. The transactions considered there are, however, predefined, i.e., given as a function (or code) that is executed entirely by the shared object that handles transactions. In contrast, transactions in a TM are executed interactively; in particular, the TM cannot predict what operations a given transaction will perform. Those papers also do not talk about aborted transactions, i.e., they assume that every transaction is executed as a single wait-free operation.

Strict disjoint-access-parallelism   Our strict disjoint-access-parallelism property is inspired by the notion of disjoint-access-parallelism as defined by Israeli and Rappoport [1994]. Those two properties are, however, incomparable. In particular, disjoint-access-parallelism takes into account transactions that conflict *indirectly* with other transactions, e.g., transactions that are related by the transitive closure of the "conflicts with" relation.

An impossibility result and a complexity lower bound for disjoint-access-parallel TMs were proved by Attiya et al. [2009].

Attiya et al. [2006] established space and time complexity lower bounds for obstruction-free implementations of so-called *perturbable shared objects*. Since an OFTM can be used to implement any perturbable shared object, these lower bounds naturally hold also for OFTMs. The last result of Attiya et al. [2006], which is a lower bound on the number of memory stalls a process may incur in some executions, is similar in scope to our strict disjoint-access-parallelism proof. However, this particular result of Attiya et al. holds only when there are no aborts, which is not the case for OFTMs.

The strongest liveness in an asynchronous system   Our results in Chapter 14 imply that there is no TM that ensures local progress in a (parasite-free) asynchronous system, or in a crash-free system in which transactions can be parasite. Fetzer [2009] showed recently that such a TM exists in a stronger model where processes can simulate transactions executed by the other processes, and thus, for instance, predict what operations those transactions will execute.

The proof of Lemma 14.10 (in Section 14.2) uses a similar technique as the proof of Lemma 1 in a recent paper by Keidar and Perelman [2009]. Those two results were, however, developed independently.

A liveness property similar to local progress has already been considered in the database context by Pedone and Guerraoui [1997].

CHAPTER 16

Conclusions

This book establishes a formal framework for reasoning about transactional memory (TM). We gave a model of a TM and defined *opacity*—a correctness condition for TM implementations. We also defined properties that capture the progress semantics of two major classes of TMs: lock-based and obstruction-free TM implementations. We finally presented a framework that helps expressing and reasoning about (high-level) liveness properties of TMs.

To aid in proving the correctness of TM algorithms, we presented two reduction theorems. The former one relates the opacity of a given TM history H to the acyclicity of the graph that represents the dependencies between transactions in H. The second theorem reduces the problem of proving strong progressiveness of a TM to the problem of proving a simple property of each try-lock (or a similar mutual exclusion object) that this TM uses. Those two theorems helped us establish the correctness of the TM algorithms that we present in this manuscript.

Within our theoretical framework, we proved several results. First, we showed that there is a fundamental difference between opacity and database atomicity. Namely, we proved a complexity lower bound that holds for TMs ensuring opacity, but not for TMs ensuring only atomicity. From a practical standpoint, the lower bound shows that there is an inherent cost of guaranteeing that transactions always observe consistent states of the system.

Second, we determined the computational power of lock-based and obstruction-free TMs by proving that they can implement consensus for at most 2 processes. This means, in particular, that such TMs cannot be implemented from only read/write registers, and that such TMs are not universal objects, i.e., they cannot be used alone to provide implementations of arbitrary wait-free shared objects. However, strong base objects, such as compare-and-swap, are not strictly necessary to implement those TMs.

To determine the computational power of lock-based and obstruction-free TMs, we first proved that those TMs are computationally equivalent to, respectively, strong try-locks and fo-consensus objects. This result is interesting in its own right since it might aid in proving further theorems.

Third, we proved that obstruction-free TM implementations cannot be strictly disjoint-access-parallel. This means that even if some transactions access disjoint sets of t-objects, the processes executing those transactions might conflict on some base objects, thus possibly encountering cache contention.

Finally, we determined a boundary between those TM liveness properties that can be implemented in an asynchronous system, and those that cannot. Some of the properties that cannot be ensured by any TM implementation are of great practical relevance. Our result shows that in order to guarantee such properties, a TM must sometimes force transactions to wait for each other indefinitely. This might be a problem in some systems, especially those in which formal liveness guarantees are indeed crucial (e.g., real-time systems).

Even though the work we present in this manuscript is fairly extensive, it is only the first step towards a complete theory of TMs. There are many possible directions in which our theoretical framework can be extended, and many open fundamental problems of great interest. Some of those directions have already been partially explored (cf. Chapter 10): defining opacity in systems with possible non-transactional accesses to t-objects, computer-aided verification of opacity and liveness properties, or relaxing opacity without violating the intuitive semantics of memory transactions. We discuss some other research directions in the following paragraphs.

Nested transactions   For simplicity, we did not consider transaction nesting (although flat nesting trivially maps to our model). Defining opacity and our progress properties in models with various forms of nested transactions is an interesting problem. What is more interesting, however, is exploring the inherent complexities involved in handling closed, parallel, or even open nesting. For instance, the common intuition is that parallel nesting involves costly mechanisms for conflict detection [Agrawal et al., 2008; Barreto et al., 2010]; however, there is no formal proof that this is indeed inherent to parallel nesting.

Programming language-level semantics   As pointed in Chapter 10, there have been several proposals to describe the correctness of a TM by defining formally the semantics of a programming language with built-in support for memory transactions (e.g., in the form of **atomic** blocks). It would be interesting to see whether one could define in this way a correctness condition equivalent (from the application's perspective) to opacity, or progress/liveness properties characterizing major classes of TM implementations.

In principle, defining TM semantics at this level could help overcome some of our impossibility or complexity results. Indeed, if a TM can see the code executed by every process, it can predict, to some extent, what operations will be performed by transactions. The TM can also undo some non-transactional operations of processes, and track information flow between transactions and non-transactional code. Then, the TM could allow some inconsistencies, which are disallowed by opacity, to occur while ensuring that those are never visible to the application. Whether this could lead to TM algorithms that are more efficient or that provide stronger guarantees is, however, an open question.

Complexity   Most of the results in this manuscript are related to *computability*. We ask, for instance, what kinds of objects are necessary and sufficient to implement a TM with given properties, or what liveness properties can be ensured by a TM in a given system. Many open questions that are worth exploring are related to *complexity*. For example, it is interesting to know what are the (space or time) complexity lower bounds for TM implementations that ensure given properties. We proved one such result in Chapter 9, but many more related questions are still open.

Hardware TM The TM API that we model corresponds to those TMs that are implemented as software libraries. Such TMs may internally use only simple base objects, such as registers or compare-and-swap objects, or they can offload some tasks to a hardware TM. Both scenarios can be expressed in our model. Hardware TMs, however, which are typically not meant to be used directly by a user's application, have interfaces that are lower-level than what we assume, and provide weaker properties that the ones we define. It would be interesting to develop a theoretical framework, possibly similar to the one described in this manuscript, for purely hardware TM implementations.

Average-case performance The complexity lower bound that we proved in Chapter 9 concerns the *worst* case. Indeed, we show a particular execution in which some operation takes a given number of steps to complete. It would be worthwhile to consider also the *average* case—determine the average space or time complexity of a TM with given properties. (The average can be taken, for instance, over all possible executions, or over executions that are most relevant in practice, such as those in which all processes are correct.)

Bibliography

Martín Abadi, Andrew Birrell, Tim Harris, and Michael Isard. Semantics of transactional memory and automatic mutual exclusion. In *Proceedings of the 35th ACM SIGPLAN-SIGACT Symposium on Principles of Programming Languages (POPL)*, 2008. DOI: 10.1145/1328438.1328449 95

Ali-Reza Adl-Tabatabai, Brian T. Lewis, Vijay Menon, Brian R. Murphy, Bratin Saha, and Tatiana Shpeisman. Compiler and runtime support for efficient software transactional memory. In *Proceedings of the ACM SIGPLAN 2006 Conference on Programming Language Design and Implementation (PLDI)*, 2006. DOI: 10.1145/1133981.1133985 54

Yehuda Afek, Michael Merritt, and Gadi Taubenfeld. The power of multi-objects. In *Proceedings of the 15th Annual ACM Symposium on Principles of Distributed Computing (PODC)*, 1996. DOI: 10.1145/248052.248096 164

Kunal Agrawal, Jeremy T. Fineman, and Jim Sukha. Nested parallelism in transactional memory. In *Proceedings of the 13th ACM SIGPLAN Symposium on Principles and Practice of Parallel Programming (PPoPP)*, 2008. DOI: 10.1145/1345206.1345232 168

Marcos K. Aguilera, Svend Frolund, Vassos Hadzilacos, Stephanie L. Horn, and Sam Toueg. Abortable and query-abortable objects and their efficient implementation. In *Proceedings of the 26th Annual ACM Symposium on Principles of Distributed Computing (PODC)*, 2007. DOI: 10.1145/1281100.1281107 143

Bowen Alpern and Fred B. Schneider. Defining liveness. *Inf. Process. Lett.*, 21(4):181–185, 1985. DOI: 10.1016/0020-0190(85)90056-0 99

Hagit Attiya and Jennifer L. Welch. *Distributed Computing: Fundamentals, Simulations and Advanced Topics (2nd edition)*. Wiley, 2004. 53

Hagit Attiya, Rachid Guerraoui, and Petr Kouznetsov. Computing with reads and writes in the absence of step contention. In *Proceedings of the 19th International Symposium on Distributed Computing (DISC)*, 2005. DOI: 10.1007/11561927_11 120, 121, 126, 135, 136, 151, 164

Hagit Attiya, Rachid Guerraoui, Danny Hendler, and Petr Kouznetsov. Synchronizing without locks is inherently expensive. In *Proceedings of the 25th Annual ACM Symposium on Principles of Distributed Computing (PODC)*, 2006. DOI: 10.1145/1146381.1146427 164

Hagit Attiya, Eshcar Hillel, and Alessia Milani. Inherent limitations on disjoint-access parallel implementations of transactional memory. In *Proceedings of the 21st Annual Symposium on Parallelism in Algorithms and Architectures (SPAA)*, 2009. DOI: 10.1145/1583991.1584015 164

João Barreto, Aleksandar Dragojević, Paulo Ferreira, Rachid Guerraoui, and Michał Kapałka. Leveraging parallel nesting in transactional memory. In *Proceedings of the 15th ACM SIGPLAN Symposium on Principles and Practice of Parallel Programming (PPoPP)*, 2010. DOI: 10.1145/1693453.1693466 168

Philip A. Bernstein and Nathan Goodman. Multiversion concurrency control—theory and algorithms. *ACM Transactions on Database Systems*, 8(4):465–483, 1983. DOI: 10.1145/319996.319998 93

Colin Blundell, E Christopher Lewis, and Milo M. K. Martin. Deconstructing transactions: The subtleties of atomicity. In *Fourth Annual Workshop on Duplicating, Deconstructing, and Debunking*, 2005. 95

Colin Blundell, E Christopher Lewis, and Milo M. K. Martin. Subtleties of transactional memory atomicity semantics. *IEEE Computer Architecture Letters*, 5(2), 2006. DOI: 10.1109/L-CA.2006.18 95

Yuri Breitbart, Dimitrios Georgakopoulos, Marek Rusinkiewicz, and Abraham Silberschatz. On rigorous transaction scheduling. *IEEE Transactions on Software Engineering*, 17(9):954–960, 1991. DOI: 10.1109/32.92915 93

Joao Cachopo and Antonio Rito-Silva. Versioned boxes as the basis for memory transactions. In *Proceedings of the Workshop on Synchronization and Concurrency in Object-Oriented Languages (SCOOL)*, 2005. DOI: 10.1016/j.scico.2006.05.009 51, 54

Luke Dalessandro and Michael Scott. Strong isolation is a weak idea. In *4th ACM SIGPLAN Workshop on Transactional Computing (TRANSACT)*, 2009. 95

Luke Dalessandro, Michael F. Spear, and Michael L. Scott. NOrec: Streamlining STM by abolishing ownership records. In *Proceedings of the 15th ACM SIGPLAN Symposium on Principles and Practice of Parallel Programming (PPoPP)*, 2010. DOI: 10.1145/1693453.1693464 151

Dave Dice, Ori Shalev, and Nir Shavit. Transactional locking II. In *Proceedings of the 20th International Symposium on Distributed Computing (DISC)*, 2006. DOI: 10.1007/11864219_14 50, 52, 54, 91, 93, 95, 101, 108

Edsger Dijkstra. Solution of a problem in concurrent programming control. *Communications of the ACM*, 8(9):569, 1965. DOI: 10.1145/365559.365617 53

Simon Doherty, Lindsay Groves, Victor Luchangco, and Mark Moir. Towards formally specifying and verifying transactional memory. In *Proceedings of the 14th BCS-FACS Refinement Workshop (REFINE)*, 2009. DOI: 10.1016/j.entcs.2010.01.001 94

Aleksandar Dragojević, Rachid Guerraoui, and Michał Kapałka. Stretching transactional memory. In *Proceedings of the ACM SIGPLAN 2009 Conference on Programming Language Design and Implementation (PLDI)*, 2009. DOI: 10.1145/1542476.1542494 50, 54, 101

Robert Ennals. Software transactional memory should not be obstruction-free. Technical Report IRC-TR-06-052, Intel Research Cambridge Tech Report, January 2006. 54

Kapali P. Eswaran, Jim N. Gray, Raymond A. Lorie, and Irving L. Traiger. The notions of consistency and predicate locks in a database system. *Communications of the ACM*, 19(11):624–633, 1976. DOI: 10.1145/360363.360369 54, 93

Pascal Felber, Torvald Riegel, and Christof Fetzer. Dynamic performance tuning of word-based software transactional memory. In *Proceedings of the 13th ACM SIGPLAN Symposium on Principles and Practice of Parallel Programming (PPoPP)*, 2008. DOI: 10.1145/1345206.1345241 50, 54, 101

Christof Fetzer. Robust transactional memory and the multicore system model. Presentation at the DISC'09 workshop *What Theory for Transactional Memory? (WTTM)*, 2009. 164

Michael J. Fischer, Nancy A. Lynch, and Michael S. Paterson. Impossibility of distributed consensus with one faulty process. *Journal of the ACM*, 32(3):374–382, 1985. DOI: 10.1145/3149.214121 53, 137

Keir Fraser. *Practical Lock-Freedom*. PhD thesis, University of Cambridge, 2003. 151, 157

Jim Gray and Andreas Reuter. *Transaction Processing: Concepts and Techniques*. Morgan Kaufmann, 1992. 54

Dan Grossman, Jeremy Manson, and William Pugh. What do high-level memory models mean for transactions? In *Proceedings of the ACM SIGPLAN Workshop on Memory Systems Performance and Correctness*, 2006. DOI: 10.1145/1178597.1178609 95

Rachid Guerraoui and Michał Kapałka. On the correctness of transactional memory. In *Proceedings of the 13th ACM SIGPLAN Symposium on Principles and Practice of Parallel Programming (PPoPP)*, 2008a. DOI: 10.1145/1345206.1345233 6

Rachid Guerraoui and Michał Kapałka. On obstruction-free transactions. In *Proceedings of the 20th Annual Symposium on Parallelism in Algorithms and Architectures (SPAA)*, 2008b. DOI: 10.1145/1378533.1378587 6

Rachid Guerraoui and Michał Kapałka. The semantics of progress in lock-based transactional memory. In *Proceedings of the 36th ACM SIGPLAN-SIGACT Symposium on Principles of Programming Languages (POPL)*, 2009a. DOI: 10.1145/1480881.1480931 6

Rachid Guerraoui and Michał Kapałka. How live can a transactional memory be? Technical Report LPD-REPORT-2009-001, EPFL, February 2009b. 6

Rachid Guerraoui, Maurice Herlihy, Michał Kapałka, and Bastian Pochon. Robust contention management in software transactional memory. In *OOPSLA'05 Workshop on Synchronization and Concurrency in Object-Oriented Languages (SCOOL)*, 2005a. 54

Rachid Guerraoui, Maurice Herlihy, and Bastian Pochon. Toward a theory of transactional contention managers. In *Proceedings of the 24th Annual ACM Symposium on Principles of Distributed Computing (PODC)*, 2005b. DOI: 10.1145/1073814.1073863 51, 54

Rachid Guerraoui, Maurice Herlihy, and Bastian Pochon. Polymorphic contention management. In *Proceedings of the 19th International Symposium on Distributed Computing (DISC)*, 2005c. DOI: 10.1007/11561927_23 54

Rachid Guerraoui, Thomas Henzinger, Barbara Jobstmann, and Vasu Singh. Model checking transactional memories. In *Proceedings of the ACM SIGPLAN 2008 Conference on Programming Language Design and Implementation (PLDI)*, 2008a. DOI: 10.1145/1379022.1375626 95

Rachid Guerraoui, Thomas A. Henzinger, and Vasu Singh. Completeness and nondeterminism in model checking transactional memories. In *Proceedings of the 19th International Conference on Concurrency Theory (Concur)*, 2008b. DOI: 10.1007/978-3-540-85361-9_6 95

Rachid Guerraoui, Thomas A. Henzinger, Michał Kapałka, and Vasu Singh. Generalizing the correctness of transactional memory. In *CAV'09 Workshop on Exploiting Concurrency Efficiently and Correctly (EC2)*, 2009. 95

Vassos Hadzilacos. A theory of reliability in database systems. *Journal of the ACM*, 35(1):121–145, 1988. DOI: 10.1145/42267.42272 93

Tim Harris and Keir Fraser. Language support for lightweight transactions. In *Proceedings of the ACM SIGPLAN International Conference on Object-Oriented Programming, Systems, Languages, and Applications (OOPSLA)*, 2003. DOI: 10.1145/949305.949340 53, 119, 151, 157

Tim Harris, Mark Plesko, Avraham Shinnar, and David Tarditi. Optimizing memory transactions. In *Proceedings of the ACM SIGPLAN 2006 Conference on Programming Language Design and Implementation (PLDI)*, 2006. DOI: 10.1145/1133981.1133984 54

Tim Harris, James R. Larus, and Ravi Rajwar. *Transactional Memory, 2nd edition*. Morgan&Claypool, 2010. DOI: 10.2200/S00272ED1V01Y201006CAC011 54, 126

Maurice Herlihy. Wait-free synchronization. *ACM Transactions on Programming Languages and Systems*, 13(1):124–149, 1991. DOI: 10.1145/114005.102808 18, 19, 53, 115, 150

Maurice Herlihy and Eric Koskinen. Transactional boosting: A methodology for highly-concurrent transactional objects. In *Proceedings of the 13th ACM SIGPLAN Symposium on Principles and Practice of Parallel Programming (PPoPP)*, 2008. DOI: 10.1145/1345206.1345237 3

Maurice Herlihy and J. Eliot B. Moss. Transactional memory: Architectural support for lock-free data structures. In *Proceedings of the 20th Annual International Symposium on Computer Architecture (ISCA)*, 1993. DOI: 10.1109/ISCA.1993.698569 3, 53

Maurice Herlihy and Jeannette M. Wing. Linearizability: a correctness condition for concurrent objects. *ACM Transactions on Programming Languages and Systems*, 12(3):463–492, 1990. DOI: 10.1145/78969.78972 15, 53, 94, 163

Maurice Herlihy, Victor Luchangco, Mark Moir, and William N. Scherer. Software transactional memory for dynamic-sized data structures. In *Proceedings of the 22nd Annual ACM Symposium on Principles of Distributed Computing (PODC)*, 2003a. DOI: 10.1145/872035.872048 49, 53, 54, 93, 95, 119, 164

Maurice Herlihy, Victor Luchango, and Mark Moir. Obstruction-free synchronization: Double-ended queues as an example. In *Proceedings of the 23rd IEEE International Conference on Distributed Computing Systems (ICDCS)*, 2003b. DOI: 10.1109/ICDCS.2003.1203503 2, 49, 121, 151, 164

Damien Imbs, José Ramon de Mendivil, and Michel Raynal. Brief announcement: virtual world consistency: a new condition for STM systems. In *Proceedings of the 28th Annual ACM Symposium on Principles of Distributed Computing (PODC)*, 2009. DOI: 10.1145/1582716.1582764 94

Amos Israeli and Lihu Rappoport. Disjoint-access-parallel implementations of strong shared memory primitives. In *Proceedings of the 13th Annual ACM Symposium on Principles of Distributed Computing (PODC)*, 1994. DOI: 10.1145/197917.198079 164

Suresh Jagannathan, Jan Vitek, Adam Welc, and Antony Hosking. A transactional object calculus. *Science of Computer Programming*, 57(2):164–186, 2005. DOI: 10.1016/j.scico.2005.03.001 95

Idit Keidar and Dmitri Perelman. On avoiding spare aborts in transactional memory. In *Proceedings of the 21st Annual Symposium on Parallelism in Algorithms and Architectures (SPAA)*, 2009. DOI: 10.1145/1583991.1584013 165

Leslie Lamport. A new solution of Dijkstra's concurrent programming problem. *Communications of the ACM*, 17(8):453–455, 1974. DOI: 10.1145/361082.361093 164

Leslie Lamport. On interprocess communication—part II: Algorithms. *Distributed Computing*, 1(2), 1986. 53

Leslie Lamport, Marshall Pease, and Robert Shostak. Reaching agreement in the presence of faults. *Journal of the ACM*, 27(3):228–234, 1980. 53

Michael C. Loui and Hosame H. Abu-Amara. Memory requirements for agreement among unreliable asynchronous processes. *Advances in computing research*, 4:163–183, 1987. 53

Nancy A. Lynch. *Distributed Algorithms*. Morgan Kaufmann, 1996. 53

Nancy A. Lynch, Michael Merritt, William E. Weihl, and Alan Fekete. *Atomic Transactions*. Morgan Kaufmann, 1994. 54, 93

Jeremy Manson, William Pugh, and Sarita V. Adve. The Java memory model. In *Proceedings of the 32nd ACM SIGPLAN-SIGACT Symposium on Principles of Programming Languages (POPL)*, 2005. DOI: 10.1145/1040305.1040336 95

Virendra J. Marathe and Mark Moir. Toward high performance nonblocking software transactional memory. In *Proceedings of the 13th ACM SIGPLAN Symposium on Principles and Practice of Parallel Programming (PPoPP)*, 2008. DOI: 10.1145/1345206.1345240 119, 151, 157

Virendra J. Marathe, William N. Scherer, and Michael L. Scott. Adaptive software transactional memory. In *Proceedings of the 19th International Symposium on Distributed Computing (DISC)*, 2005. DOI: 10.1007/11561927_26 119, 164

Virendra J. Marathe, Michael F. Spear, Christopher Heriot, Athul Acharya, David Eisenstat, William N. Scherer, and Michael L. Scott. Lowering the overhead of software transactional memory. In *1st ACM SIGPLAN Workshop on Transactional Computing (TRANSACT)*, 2006. 49, 119

Vijay Menon, Steven Balensiefer, Tatiana Shpeisman, Ali-Reza Adl-Tabatabai, Richard L. Hudson, Bratin Saha, and Adam Welc. Practical weak-atomicity semantics for Java STM. In *Proceedings of the 20th Annual Symposium on Parallelism in Algorithms and Architectures (SPAA)*, 2008. DOI: 10.1145/1378533.1378588 95

Maged M. Michael and Michael L. Scott. Simple, fast, and practical non-blocking and blocking concurrent queue algorithms. In *Proceedings of the 15th Annual ACM Symposium on Principles of Distributed Computing (PODC)*, 1996. DOI: 10.1145/248052.248106 2

Katherine F. Moore and Dan Grossman. High-level small-step operational semantics for transactions. In *Proceedings of the 35th ACM SIGPLAN-SIGACT Symposium on Principles of Programming Languages (POPL)*, 2008. DOI: 10.1145/1328438.1328448 95

Christos H. Papadimitriou. The serializability of concurrent database updates. *Journal of the ACM*, 26(4):631–653, 1979. DOI: 10.1145/322154.322158 85, 93, 163

Fernando Pedone and Rachid Guerraoui. On transaction liveness in replicated databases. In *IEEE Pacific Rim International Symposium on Fault-Tolerant Systems (PRFTS)*, 1997. DOI: 10.1109/PRFTS.1997.640133 165

Michel Raynal. *Algorithms for Mutual Exclusion*. The MIT Press, 1986. 53

Torvald Riegel, Pascal Felber, and Christof Fetzer. A lazy snapshot algorithm with eager valida-tion. In *Proceedings of the 20th International Symposium on Distributed Computing (DISC)*, 2006. DOI: 10.1007/11864219_20 51

Eric Ruppert. Consensus numbers of multi-objects. In *Proceedings of the 17th Annual ACM Sympo-sium on Principles of Distributed Computing (PODC)*, 1998. DOI: 10.1145/277697.277736 164

Eric Ruppert. Consensus numbers of transactional objects. In *Proceedings of the International Symposium on Distributed Computing (DISC)*, 1999. DOI: 10.1007/3-540-48169-9_22 164

William N. Scherer and Michael L. Scott. Contention management in dynamic software transac-tional memory. In *Proceedings of the PODC Workshop on Concurrency and Synchronization in Java Programs (CSJP)*, July 2004. DOI: 10.1145/1073814.1073861 54

William N. Scherer and Michael L. Scott. Advanced contention management for dynamic software transactional memory. In *Proceedings of the 24th Annual ACM Symposium on Principles of Distributed Computing (PODC)*, 2005. DOI: 10.1145/1073814.1073861 54

Michael L. Scott. Sequential specification of transactional memory semantics. In *1st ACM SIGPLAN Workshop on Transactional Computing (TRANSACT)*, 2006. 94, 163

Michael L. Scott and William N. Scherer. Scalable queue-based spin locks with timeout. In *Proceedings of the 8th ACM SIGPLAN Symposium on Principles and Practice of Parallel Programming (PPoPP)*, 2001. DOI: 10.1145/379539.379566 53

Nir Shavit and Dan Touitou. Software transactional memory. In *Proceedings of the 14th Annual ACM Symposium on Principles of Distributed Computing (PODC)*, 1995. DOI: 10.1145/224964.224987 3, 53

Michael F. Spear, Virendra J. Marathe, William N. Scherer, and Michael L. Scott. Conflict detection and validation strategies for software transactional memory. In *Proceedings of the 20th International Symposium on Distributed Computing (DISC)*, 2006. DOI: 10.1007/11864219_13 54, 101

Michael F. Spear, Luke Dalessandro, Virendra J. Marathe, and Michael L. Scott. Ordering-based semantics for software transactional memory. In *12th International Conference On Principles Of Distributed Systems (OPODIS)*, 2008a. DOI: 10.1007/978-3-540-92221-6_19 95

Michael F. Spear, Maged M. Michael, and Christoph von Praun. RingSTM: scalable transactions with a single atomic instruction. In *Proceedings of the 20th Annual Symposium on Parallelism in Algorithms and Architectures (SPAA)*, 2008b. DOI: 10.1145/1378533.1378583 151

Michael F. Spear, Arrvindh Shriraman, Luke Dalessandro, and Michael Scott. Transactional mutex locks. In *4th ACM SIGPLAN Workshop on Transactional Computing (TRANSACT)*, 2009. 151

Fuad Tabba, Cong Wang, James R. Goodman, and Mark Moir.   NZTM: nonblocking zero-indirection transactional memory. In *2nd ACM SIGPLAN Workshop on Transactional Computing (TRANSACT)*, 2007. DOI: 10.1145/1583991.1584048 119, 164

William E. Weihl. Local atomicity properties: Modular concurrency control for abstract data types. *ACM Transactions on Programming Languages and Systems*, 11(2):249–282, 1989. DOI: 10.1145/63264.63518 85, 93

Gerhard Weikum and Gottfried Vossen. *Transactional Information Systems: Theory, Algorithms, and the Practice of Concurrency Control and Recovery*. Morgan Kaufmann, 2001. 54

Authors' Biographies

RACHID GUERRAOUI

Rachid Guerraoui is professor of computer science at EPFL, the Swiss Federal Institute of Technology in Lausanne. He graduated from the University of Orsay and has also been affiliated with MIT and HP. He chaired the program committees of ACM PODC, ACM Middleware, ECOOP and DISC, and is associate editor of JACM.

MICHAŁ KAPAŁKA

Michał Kapałka got his PhD from EPFL, the Swiss Federal Institute of Technology in Lausanne, and his MSc degree from the AGH University of Science and Technology in Kraków, Poland. He currently works for the Swissquote Bank SA.

Printed in the United States
by Baker & Taylor Publisher Services